C0-AUZ-744

A Comparative Anthology of Baseball Around the World

A COMPARATIVE ANTHOLOGY
OF BASEBALL AROUND THE WORLD
The Many Different Meanings of the Game

Robert B. Edgerton

The Edwin Mellen Press
Lewiston•Queenston•Lampeter

796.357
E Z 3 C

Library of Congress Cataloging-in-Publication Data

Edgerton, Robert B.
  A comparative anthology of baseball around the world : the many different meanings of
the game / Robert B. Edgerton.
     p. cm.
  Includes bibliographical references and index.
  ISBN 0-7734-5914-6
  I. Title.

hors série.

A CIP catalog record for this book is available from the British Library.

Copyright © 2006   Robert B. Edgerton

All rights reserved. For information contact

The Edwin Mellen Press
Box 450
Lewiston, New York
USA 14092-0450

The Edwin Mellen Press
Box 67
Queenston, Ontario
CANADA L0S 1L0

The Edwin Mellen Press, Ltd.
Lampeter, Ceredigion, Wales
UNITED KINGDOM SA48 8LT

Printed in the United States of America

For Karen

University Libraries
Carnegie Mellon University
Pittsburgh, PA 15213-3890

Table of Contents

Preface

Baseball is a game, sport, and source of entertainment for countless people in the Americas, Asia, Australia, Europe, the Middle East, and across many other familiar and unfamiliar lands. But, as Robert Edgerton points out in this fascinating book, to see baseball only through a narrow set of lens restricts us from fully appreciating its multiple and layered dimensions. Even the story of baseball's origins is given a rich and nuanced twist. Some genealogies of baseball begin with the notion that Abner Doubleday created the game; other accounts set out to debunk the myth. Edgerton uses his anthropological insights to tell a more complex and interesting story that describes how elements of baseball are represented in disparate cultures. For example, while the English game of "rounders" is often seen as the precursor to the American form of baseball, rubber ball games on masonry courts were common in Meso-America for over 2000 years. Accordingly, baseball was not founded by one person or another, but shaped and reshaped by cultural influences over decades and centuries. Against this historical backdrop, one can appreciate the timeless quality of baseball.

In many respects, Edgerton is the perfect person to author this book on baseball, especially in presenting a perceptive and textured examination of its past and presence around the globe. Edgerton is a scholar of distinction, renowned for his outstanding accomplishments in the social sciences, and he is a prolific writer who has published over forty books during his distinguished career. Edgerton is also a former baseball player, and, while he did not achieve his childhood wish of becoming a major league baseball player, he still accomplished more on the diamond than many of us could ever dream. He threw several no-hitters for his American Legion team and pitched for his high school and junior college teams. Edgerton drew the attention of several major league baseball scouts and made it for one season in the professional class-D league. Edgerton remains a fan of baseball, especially following his beloved Angels. The combination that Edgerton brings to this book—the scholarship, the perspective of a former player, and the passion of a fan—makes for a wonderful read.

Six chapters are devoted to how countries play and watch baseball. Despite the fairly uniform guidelines and rules of baseball, countries have incorporated the game to fit their unique cultural frames. In Japan, baseball is not seen as a pastime but rather as their national religion. Unlike the American focus on individual statistics, such as batting averages and homeruns, Japanese players consider *Wa*, team spirit, as the essential element of baseball. A Japanese player who fails in the game is expected to apologize for his mistake. In the Dominican Republic, baseball is seen as a way of life. Fans often watch the game with a passion that seems to border on verbal or physical confrontation, but little violence ensues. The intent of fan enthusiasm is to bruise the ego, not to cause bodily harm. Taken together, the chapters provide insights about how a cultural product like baseball can be thrust upon another culture through colonialism, military interventions, or migration; resisted and then adopted; and adapted.

The story of baseball is one of contradictions. Baseball has reinforced the inequities in societies, especially the racial stratification in the United States. Professional baseball barred African American players from playing in the major leagues until the Dodgers signed Jackie Robinson to a contract in 1946. Prior to the signing, unless they were able to pass as whites, African Americans often resigned themselves to play in Latin America or the black professional leagues, a separate and unequal alternative. On the other hand, baseball has been a source of income and mobility for men from poor families and immigrants. In fact, American baseball has changed dramatically over the past twenty years with a large increase in Latino baseball players. The book provides an even-handed examination of baseball across the globe that shows the polish and the blemish of the game.

Opinion polls over the past decade suggest that football is America's favorite spectator sport with baseball second. This reminds me of an excerpt from a George Carlin routine comparing football and baseball:

> And finally, the objectives of the two games are completely different: In football, the object is for the quarterback, also known as the field general, to be on target with his aerial assault, riddling the defense by hitting his receivers with deadly accuracy in spite of the blitz, even if he has to use shotgun. With short bullet passes and long bombs, he marches his troops into enemy territory, balancing this aerial assault with a sustained ground attack that punches holes in the forward wall of the enemy's defensive line.
>
> In baseball, the object is to go home! And to be safe!

Given the times we live in—the shadows of terrorism, an unpopular war in the Middle East, and the looming threat of nuclear devastation—it may be opportune to establish baseball as America's pastime once again. Edgerton's work provides ample reasons to make it so.

David T. Takeuchi, Ph.D.
University of Washington
August, 2005

Acknowledgements

I want to thank all those who taught me the game, from my father, who got me started, to former big-league manager Fred Haney, who encouraged me, and his brother Carl, who provided the uniforms, equipment and coaching for my American Legion team. I was a successful pitcher on that team with several no-hitters and was encouraged by several major league scouts. But I stopped growing at age 13, and, aside from Bobby Shantz, there were no five foot, eight inch tall pitchers in the majors. I went on to play in high school, junior college and the military but after one partial season of professional play in a class-D league, I was gently told by management that my future in baseball was in the front office, not on the pitcher's mound.

Taking the hint, I returned to college, went to graduate school, and became an anthropologist. My research travels as a university professor have taken me to several parts of Africa, Asia, Europe, and Latin America, where I have been able to see baseball played in vastly different cultural settings. It was slow in coming, but this book is a product of those travels and my lifelong fascination with the game.

Thanks to all those wonderful people who have helped put this book together. I am grateful to UCLA athletic director and former professional baseball player in Italy, Dan Guerrero; Igor Veselinovic from Slovenia; Simon Vasileva from Bulgaria; Dennis M. Zermeno from Guam; Rasmus Nørgard from Denmark; Dedan Kariuki from Kenya; Harry Trisnadi from Indonesia; FANG Ka-wor from Hong Kong; Suryo Adi Prasetyo from Indonesia; Violet Soko from Zimbabwe; and Robert Coulter from American Samoa for their information. I am also grateful to members of the UCLA Semel Institute Center for Culture and Health, particularly Jean Cadigan, Edward D. Lowe, and Warren Thompson. Finally, I can't thank my wonderful assistant, Kristen Hatch, enough.

Introduction

Library shelves are packed with books about baseball. Many of them describe the history of "America's game." Others focus on particular teams, like the New York Yankees or the Brooklyn Dodgers, or particular players like Jackie Robinson, Babe Ruth, Lou Gehrig, Ty Cobb, Sandy Koufax or Satchel Paige. Still others contain reminiscences about particular games or players off-the-field activities. Many of these volumes are thoughtful and very well written. Some, such as those written by Roger Angell, Roger Kahn, and Jim Bouton, have become bestsellers. A recent book by Michael Lewis about the career of Oakland Athletics general manager Billie Beane is also very popular. With so much material already in print, why on earth should there be another book about baseball?

This book tries to do what the others have not—look carefully at baseball as it is played all around the world. And it is played in more than 100 countries as different as Finland, Iran, Nigeria, Pakistan, and the United Arab Emirates. This book looks at how players practice and play the game, as well as fan behavior, and the role of the game in the culture of the country where it is played. Is baseball akin to a religious experience as it has been in Japan? Does it mean everything to those who play it, as it does in Cuba? Or is it merely one more sport among many, as is the case in many countries? And why do people in different parts of the world look at the game in different ways?

Consider the Indians of Cochiti pueblo in New Mexico. Long tormented by their fear of witchcraft, the people of Cochiti insisted upon social harmony and cooperation above all else. Baseball was sometimes played in the pueblo before World War II, but soon after the war two Cochiti teams were formed. During their first game, the players were well behaved, but their mothers began to revile each other. Then, an actual brawl broke out among these women. Women who had formerly lacked any means of expressing their dislike for other women used baseball as a vehicle for attacking their enemies without risking accusations of witchcraft. Baseball, it seems, was welcomed by these women as a safe means of expressing their hostility toward one another.[1] As we will see, people in many parts of the world adopted baseball for reasons that would never have occurred to the founders of the game.

In 1901, American army officer Frederick Funston was awarded the Congressional Medal of Honor when he helped to end the anti-U.S. uprising in the Philippines by capturing the Filipino rebel leader Emilio Aguinaldo. By the eve of World War I, Funson had become a major general. But in 1894 he was a government botanist who left an unforgettable description of Eskimos, or Inuit, as they are now usually known, playing baseball. The game had been taken to the Arctic by an American whaling fleet that had been stranded there for the winter by an ice floe. The Eskimos gleefully watched the whalers play, then, borrowing their bats, baseballs, and gloves, took up the game themselves. Funston recalled that their games rarely went beyond the first inning because play usually wound up in "a general mêlée and hair pulling. One of their umpires, who insisted on allowing a nine to bat after it had three men out in order to even up the score, was dragged off the diamond by his heels."[2] The Eskimos played baseball on an icy field, using a frozen ball while dressed entirely in fur, sometimes in temperatures of 38 degrees below zero. Funston went on to comment:

A fact that impressed me very much at one of the games that I saw was that the crowd of several hundred people watching our national sport at this faraway corner of the earth, only twenty degrees from the pole, and thousands of miles from railroads or steamship lines, was more widely cosmopolitan than could have been found at any other place on the globe. From the ships were Americans, a hundred or more, men from every seafaring nationality of Europe—Chinese, Japanese and Malays from Tahiti and Hawaii. The colored brother, too, was there, a dozen of him, and several of the players were negroes. Esquimaux of all ages were everywhere, while the red men were represented by the eleven wiry fellows who had snowshoed with me from their home in the valley of the Yukon. One day I noticed that in a little group of eleven, sitting on an overturned sled watching a game, there were representatives of all the five great divisions of the human race.[3]

How people like these over much of the world took up baseball is what this book is about.

Most baseball fans are aware that baseball is played outside the United States, in Canada, Latin America, Japan, Korea, and Australia. But baseball is not limited to these places. Today, the game is quite literally played all over the world. Founded in 1938, the International Baseball Federation (IBAF) now consists of 112 countries whose baseball and softball teams compete not only within each country, but also in various IBAF tournaments. It is also played in dozens of countries that don't belong to the IBAF.

Consider the following alphabetical list of the world's baseball-playing countries and territories: Afghanistan, Algeria, American Samoa, Argentina, Armenia, Aruba, Australia, Austria, Bahamas, Bahrain, Bangladesh, Barussalama, Belarus, Belgium, Belize, Bolivia, Botswana, Brazil, British Virgin Islands, Brunei, Bulgaria, Cameroon, Canada, Chile, China, Colombia, Congo Republic, Cook Islands, Costa Rica, Croatia, Cuba, Curaçao, Cyprus, Czech Republic, Denmark, Djibouti, Dominican Republic, Ecuador, Egypt, El Salvador, Estonia, Fiji, Finland, France, Georgia, Germany, Ghana, Great Britain, Greece, Guam, Guatemala, Honduras, Hong Kong, Hungary, India, Indonesia, Iran, Ireland, Israel, Italy, Ivory Coast, Jamaica, Japan, Jordan, Kazakhstan, Kenya, Laos, Lesotho, Liberia, Libya, Lithuania, Luxembourg, Madagascar, Malaysia, Mali,

Malta, Marshall Islands, Mexico, Micronesia, Moldova, Mongolia, Morocco, Namibia, Netherland Antilles, Netherlands, New Zealand, Nicaragua, Nigeria, North Korea, Norway, Pakistan, Palau, Panama, Papua New Guinea, Peru, Philippines, Poland, Ponape, Portugal, Puerto Rico, Romania, Russia, Saipan, Samoa, San Marino, Singapore, Slovakia, Slovenia, South Africa, South Korea, Spain, Sri Lanka, St. Vincent and the Grenadines, Sudan, Sweden, Switzerland, Taiwan, Tanzania, Thailand, Togo, Trinidad and Tobago, Truk, Tunisia, Turkey, Uganda, Ukraine, United Arab Emirates, United States of America, U.S Virgin Islands, Uzbekistan, Venezuela, Vietnam, Western Samoa, Yemen, Yugoslavia, Zaire, Zambia, and Zimbabwe. Seventeen of these countries have players in the U.S. major leagues.

In some of these countries only a few boys teams exist, but in others there are surprisingly large numbers of teams for juniors and adults alike. For example, Bulgaria has 30 teams and 501 players. Cameroon has 18 teams and 283 players. The Czech Republic has 56 teams and 2,527 players. Great Britain has 140 teams and 2,000 players. Hong Kong has 28 teams and 408 players. Hungary has 28 teams and 860 players. Indonesia has 20 teams and 500 players. Israel has 84 teams and 1,024 players. Kenya has 34 teams and 1,125 players. Pakistan has 24 teams and 480 players. Poland has 44 teams and 720 players. And, amazingly, South Africa has 6,000 teams and some 370,000 players.

Unfortunately, little information is available about baseball in many countries. Nevertheless, what follows is a reasonably comprehensive overview of baseball around the world. After an introductory chapter that sketches the origins of baseball, Chapter Two describes the history of baseball in North America. Chapter Three examines the experiences of players and fans in Asia, especially China, Japan, Taiwan, and Korea. Chapter Four looks at the game in the Caribbean and Latin America. Chapter Five explores baseball in Australia, New Zealand, and Oceania while Chapter Six looks at baseball in Europe. Chapter Seven examines the game in Africa, the Middle East, and elsewhere around the world. The final chapter asks what we have learned by this multisocietal look at baseball's players and its fans. Why do so many different kinds of people in so many diverse countries play baseball?

6

---

[1] Fox (1961).

[2] Spalding (1911: 373-374).

[3] <u>Ibid</u>., p.374.

Chapter One: "Baseball's" Beginnings

As several previous students of baseball have noted, Columbia University's famous French-born professor of history, Jacques Barzun, spoke for many when he wrote, "Whoever wants to know the heart and mind of America had better learn baseball, the rules, the realities of the game."[1] Not everyone would agree with Barzun that baseball represents the "heart and mind" of America, but if we are interested in understanding why people in so many different kinds of countries play baseball, we do need to look into its origins. The source of the American baseball game has long been hotly contested. Was it a British game, such as rounders, that came to America, as many insist? Was it invented in New York, as many others believe? Did it come from somewhere else?

It is well known by archaeologists and historians that games calling for a small ball to be struck with a stick or part of one's body were widespread in many parts of the world for several centuries. Although the earliest known human societies--those that lived a foraging existence by hunting animals and gathering what edibles they could--did not play bat-and-ball games, some simple horticultural societies, such as the Pueblo Indians, the Cherokee, the Crow, and numerous South American peoples, did. In one of these South American societies, the Otomac Indians, women enthusiastically played a game in which a rubber ball was batted with a straight, thick-ended club.[2] However, in most societies it was typically men and boys who played such games, not women. Some parts of the world had no bat-and-ball games of any kind. Until recently, most African societies lacked such games, even though the rubber commonly used to make balls was readily available in Africa. Today, baseball is played over much of the African continent. And neither the Inca, nor most Mediterranean states such as the Romans or Greeks played bat-and-ball games. Nor did the imperial Chinese or Japanese.[3] But, as Egyptologist Peter Piccione has pointed out, the Egyptians did. As early as 2400 B.C., Egyptian kings played bat-and-ball games using a ball very much like a modern baseball. Later, hieroglyphs actually pictured King Thutmose III playing the game circa 1500 B.C. Egyptian women are known to have played the game as well, and Egyptian children who died were often buried with baseball-sized clay, leather, or wooden balls.[4]

Rubber ball games on masonry courts were so common in Meso-America that they were played over an area of one million square miles for at least 2,000 years. At the peak of its growth, the Aztec city of Tenochtitlan imported 16,000 rubber balls each year from the rubber-rich lowlands. Most of their masonry court ball games involved players attempting to strike a rubber ball the size of a human head through a hoop secured high on the wall of a court. The ball could only be struck by players' hips, buttocks or knees, never their hands or feet, and no bats were used. Some groups apparently played the game for entertainment, but for others it was nothing less than a potentially deadly form of combat.[5] In some of these societies, the games were fought by rival chiefs, as huge crowds looked on and priests served as referees. Quite often, the loser was killed.[6] This so-called "ball-court game" eventually diffused all the way to the Hohokam Indians in southern Arizona, where the earliest Spanish explorers reported watching the game. In addition to these ball-court games, in some parts of Meso-America, such as Michoacan on Mexico's west coast, Vera Cruz on the east, and Central Mexico, rubber balls were struck with various kinds of sticks, clubs or bats.[7]

A game that was actually called "baseball" was played in England in the 1600s, and this game, as well as "rounders," usually played by boys and girls, is a partial ancestor of American baseball, So was an English game called "trapball" that was played even earlier and may have been ancestral to cricket. And "stool ball" was played by English milkmaids, as the batter tried to protect her upturned milking stool against a pitched ball. And even earlier bat-and-ball games might have been ancestors to baseball.[8] A bat-and-ball game known as "cat" was played by the Norse, Dutch, Danes, French, Belgians, Germans, and other Europeans. "Cat" was a diminutive form of the Greek word "catapult." The old French ball game called *tcheque*, which is still played by French schoolboys, was imported to America by French Huguenots who settled in New Amsterdam. In the 1700s, the Germans played a similar ball game that spread widely across Europe. It was called *das Deutsche Ballspiel* (the German ballgame) and involved bats, bases, and a pitcher.[9]

A comparable game was played throughout Scandinavia and spread to Poland and even Russia, where it was called *lapta*.[10] In fact, this very old game matches almost exactly the so-called "Massachusetts" or "New England" game, which had become so popular in the United States by 1787 that the Presbyterian College of New Jersey (later Princeton) tried to ban it because it interfered with studies and because these ball games, known as "baste ball," were said to be neither honorable nor useful.[11] Daniel Webster played this early form of baseball at Dartmouth from 1797 to 1801, and Oliver Wendell Holmes, the father of the Supreme Court Justice, played it at Harvard a few years later.[12] Even earlier, in 1778, George Washington's soldiers also played the game during their leisure moments.[13] Baseball was played so often and avidly in Massachusetts that in 1791 the town of Pittsfield in the Berkshires passed a bylaw prohibiting anyone from playing the game within 80 yards of their new meeting house, a building with valuable and vulnerable glass windows.[14] And in 1824, Henry Wadsworth Longfellow, then a student at Bowdoin College, enthusiastically wrote, "there is nothing now heard of, in our leisure hours, but ball, ball, ball."[15]

Bat-and-ball games were particularly popular in England. Contrary to modern conceptions of upper-class Englishmen as quiet, calm and dignified, in earlier times they loved crowds, noise and violent games.[16] Boxing was very popular, and so were sword fights. There were cockfights, too, and even scratching matches. The popular sports of football, as well as rugby, were extremely violent. Despite this aura of violence, and despite the fact that people of all classes, often including children, got drunk every night that they possibly could, the peaceful game of cricket grew in popularity with people of all classes, although it was most popular with upper-class men who did not have to work.[17] In southern England, the bat-and-ball game was called "baseball," but it was known as "rounders" in the west and "feeder" in London.[18] And another game, called "bittle-battle," which was played in Kent, closely resembled baseball, with four bases, a pitcher and a catcher. It came to America when the English did. When cricket came to America, it was initially played widely, but as the bat-and-ball "Massachusetts game" or "townball" grew in popularity, cricket's popularity waned. When baseball was taken up fervently by New Yorkers as the "New York game," cricket faded even more from public view although it was still played in a number of private gentlemen's clubs, especially in Philadelphia where the sport had its greatest popularity in America.

"Townball" was originally played in a square, but in 1835 bankteller, surveyer, and volunteer firefighter Alexander Jay "Alick" Cartwright, who was not a ball player himself, gave the "New York game" a diamond-shaped infield like the one used in rounders. He also set four bases 90 feet apart, a remarkable decision that has proven to be ideal for the game. He invented foul lines, set the numbers of players on each side at nine, and limited a regulation game to nine innings. The nine players would have to bat in an order prescribed before the game. In short, he invented modern baseball. Cartwright was enthralled by baseball, but when gold was discovered in California he could not resist seeking his fortune. He went west in 1849. By 1852, he had become wealthy. He sailed for China but became badly seasick, and when his ship docked in Honolulu he went ashore. He soon fell in love with Hawaii, taught baseball to King Kalakaua, and built scores of baseball diamonds. He lived in Hawaii for the rest of his life.

People in New York City loved cockfighting, animal baiting, bare-knuckle boxing, wrestling and, for the wealthy, boat racing. They also avidly took to Cartwright's "New York game." When baseball came to New York, the city was America's largest, wealthiest, and most dynamic. In addition to their many popular violent sports, New Yorkers enjoyed harness racing, rowing, racquet ball, gymnastics, yachting, shooting clubs and horse racing. In 1823, more than 50,000 New Yorkers turned out to watch a horse race. Private clubs of upper-class people continued to support cricket, but working-class and middle-class people turned more and more to baseball.

By 1797, 14 years after the last British troops left the city, New York led the United States in imports and exports. After the War of 1812 and the opening of the Erie Canal in 1825, New York City led the country in immigrants, including many who had moved south from New England. There were also numerous immigrants, including growing numbers of impoverished Irish. In 1825, so many people were pouring into New York that the city had no vacant housing and more than 3,000 new housing units were under construction. Before 1840, rounders was still played alongside the "New York game," but between 1845 and 1860 the "New York game's" rules were standardized, and it rapidly grew in popularity among old New Yorkers and new immigrants alike. Unlike the "Massachusetts game," which required a team to score 100 runs before it could be declared the winner, making for games that often lasted all day, the "New York game" called for only nine innings of play with three outs per inning. The game usually lasted only two or three hours, a great advantage for the working men who played it during their lunch break, after work, or on Sunday. The same game was also played in several Canadian cities in the 1850s. By 1865, baseball was so popular in Montreal that an ordinance had to be passed to regulate its play in city parks.[19]

By 1855, there were 125 baseball teams in New York City. In 1859, Amherst beat Williams College by the amazing score of 75-32 in a nine-inning game.[20]   In 1860, the Brooklyn Excelsiors traveled to upstate New York, Baltimore, and Philadelphia to play against local teams, drawing crowds of more than 3,000. They won every game including one versus a Philadelphia team prophetically called the Athletics. Baseball was played in New Orleans as early as 1841, in San Francisco by 1858, and in Houston by 1861. It was played throughout the Midwest before the Civil War and also in some cities in the South.[21] Soldiers from both the South and the North – "Johnny Reb and Billy Yank" as they were known -- often played baseball in the quiet time between battles during the Civil War. They carried bats and balls in their knapsacks, but sometimes games were played with a barrel stave for a bat and a walnut wrapped in twine or yarn as a ball. Sometimes officers and men played on the same team, and their enthusiasm left no doubt that they were exhilarated by the game. The game was also played avidly in both Union and Confederate prison camps. In 1862, a game between Union soldiers in Hilton Head, South Carolina, drew an enormous crowd of some 40,000 spectators, most of them fellow soldiers.

In that same year, a crowd of 15,000 watched a game in New York on the same day that the bloody battle of Antietam was being fought in western Maryland.[22] Abraham Lincoln is known to have played baseball as a young man, and when a delegation of Republicans went to Illinois to tell him that he had been nominated as the Republican candidate for the presidency, they had to wait for some time because he was determined to have his next at bat before he would leave the game he was playing. Despite his intensely demanding presidential duties during the Civil War, he and his son, Tad, watched at least one complete game in 1862 in Washington, D.C. Holding Tad between his knees, Lincoln sat along the first baseline on some sawdust, often cheering loudly. When President Lincoln and Tad left, the crowd rose and gave them three loud hurrahs.[23]

In 1857, the nine-inning game rule was instituted, and in 1863 a ball caught on the first bounce was no longer an out as it had been before. Still, gloves were rarely used until 1875, and although catchers positioned themselves far behind the batters, they nevertheless often suffered badly bruised hands. Yet players were happy to play without gloves or catchers' masks. As George Ellard, organizer of a team in Cincinnati, proudly put it:

> We used no mattress on our hands,
>
> No cage upon our face;
>
> We stood right up and caught the ball
>
> With courage and with grace.[24]

The first gloves to be used, in 1875, were skin-tight leather, resembling modern golf gloves. Catcher's masks were first introduced that same year. A batter could still call for a pitch to be either above or below the waist, as had been allowed since the game's inception, and four balls were not a walk until 1889. But after 1884, when pitchers were allowed to throw overhand instead of underhand, as had previously been required, batters had great difficulty hitting the ball. To counter this undesirable result, in 1893 the pitching rubber was moved from only 45 feet to sixty feet, six inches away from the plate. The pitcher had to deliver the ball with his foot on a rubber.[25] In earlier years, pitchers could actually take a running start before delivering the ball. Also, unlike cricket, where every ball hit was in play, thanks to Alick Cartwright, baseball had first-base and third-base foul lines, with any ground ball hit outside these lines not in play. However, a foul ball was not counted as strike one or strike two until 1901.

In apparent response to these new rules, baseball's popularity grew rapidly, and although there were still 500 cricket clubs in the United States in 1859, by 1870, cricket, which had become popular in America not only as a sport but also as an object of betting was no longer widely popular.[26] Cricket was seen by New Yorkers as being too slow, because it was a game that could easily last for several full days. As the 1887 *Reach Baseball Guide* put it, cricket "was too slow a sport for the blood of young America."[27] It was also seen as a snobbish game played by and for upper-class Englishmen.[28] As a New Jersey newspaper commented in 1859, "Cricket is too solemn and deliberate a game for a Yankee, and Base Ball would seem too lively an exercise for Mr. Bull." Henry Chadwick, who was born in England but raised in the United States, added: "We, fast people of America, call cricket slow and tedious; while the leisurely, take-your-time-my-boy-people of England think our game of baseball too fast. Each game, however, just suits the people of the two nations."[29] In 1858, 1,500 fans in New York were the first people to actually pay to see a game of baseball.[30]

In 1845, burly 6 foot, 2 inch, 210 pound, Alick Cartwright, who loved to play the game and was an outstanding pitcher, set up a team called the "Knickerbockers," or "New York Club," on a former cricket pitch at Elysian Fields in Hoboken, New Jersey, only 15 miles from New York City.[31] The Knickerbockers wore blue pantaloons, white flannel shirts, and straw hats. They not only played the game, they engaged in extensive post-game feasting and drinking.[32] Their first game was played against a team from Brooklyn.[33] The single umpire who officiated the game wore a high, black silk hat, a Prince Albert coat and carried a cane. The countryside around Hoboken was enchanting. During the spring and summer, beautiful flowers bloomed everywhere, and there were many wild plums and grapes. Birds sang loudly, while geese, grouse, and wild turkeys were joined in the dazzlingly dense green forest by elk, bear, mink, otter, raccoons, beaver, moose, and even wolves. A game played in Hoboken in 1867 drew a crowd of over 40,000 fans who clung to trees, scaled roofs, and perched on fences before they excitedly poured onto the field ending the game in the first inning.[34] Baseball rapidly became so popular that the New York City press even began reporting the scores of high school games.

By 1870, almost half of all New Yorkers were foreign born; one-half of the immigrants were Irish, and one-third were German. These new immigrants took to baseball with great enthusiasm, just as Italian immigrants would do later. Even before the Civil War broke out, baseball was played by just about every kind of man, from well-paid professionals and artisans to factory workers and teenage boys.[35] Club teams grew rapidly made up of postal employees, firemen, jewelers, iron workers, plumbers, and every other kind of working men. All of the New York sporting weeklies proclaimed baseball "the national game" even before the Civil War. As one man recalled,

> "We had some merry times among ourselves; we would forget business and everything else, on Tuesday afternoons, go out into the green fields, don our ball suits, and go at it with a perfect rush. At such times, we were boys again. Such sport as this brightens a man up, and improves him, both in mind and body."[36]

Before the Civil War, African Americans had their own segregated teams in several large cities, and these teams continued to play during and after the war. With the war's end, increasing numbers of working class men played the game, which became even more dominated by rowdyism and gambling than it had been in prewar times. As early as 1860, these problems were so acute than an organization calling itself the National Association of Baseball Players (NABBP) based in New York, attempted to govern baseball, beginning by outlawing betting at games. However, it had no means of enforcing this edict and gambling only grew worse. Still, the game grew at a terrific pace. In 1870, one New York company produced 162,000 baseballs. One year later a New York Times reporter estimated that in 1871 the country would need another half million baseballs.[37]

And more and more people came to see the games. There were female spectators as well as men, and the men who came to games represented all classes, professions, and ages. Spectators often stood in the hot sun to watch a game. Flags and pennants flew from outfield fences; red, white and blue bunting decorated the grandstands, and brass bands played between innings. Because there were no changing rooms or showers at ballparks, players changed into their uniforms at their hotels, then rode in open horse-drawn omnibuses to the stadium, often singing their team song to the delight of fans, who applauded and cheered as they passed by.[38]   Drinking, gambling, rowdyism, and cheating were commonplace as bookies hawked odds, and there were betting booths at most ballparks.[39] This kind of open gambling ended in 1882 thanks to the insistence of William A. Hurlbert, the president of the new National League. However, post-game eating and drinking parties were not only commonplace, they often lasted until dawn.

For many working men, Sunday was the only day they were free to play in a ball game or to watch one, but due to the fervent demands of Sabbatarians, many cities forbade teams, including major league clubs, from playing on Sunday. New York City banned so-called "Sunday ball" until 1904, and even after Congress passed a bill in 1919 permitting baseball to be played on Sunday, several cities continued to ban Sunday baseball. Boston did not lift its ban until 1929, and the Sabbatarians were so strong in Pennsylvania that Philadelphia banned Sunday baseball until 1933, Pittsburgh until 1934.[40]

The first professional team was the Cincinnati Red Stockings in 1869. Playing five men from New York City, the team went undefeated against all opposition. "They wore flannel knickers, brilliant scarlet stockings, square-cut locomotive engineer hats and shirts laced at the throat with a cross-drawstring...."[41] They were so successful and so glamorous that they ignited the game. Newspapers sensationalized them, fans couldn't see enough of them, and even women flocked to their games. In 1869, the Red Stockings traveled 12,000 miles on trains, stagecoaches, and boats to play any team that would challenge them. During that year, 200,000 fans—or "kranks" as they were called then—paid to see them play. The team won 65 games, tied one, and lost none.[42] But as it became obvious that there were no teams able to compete with the Red Stockings, fewer and fewer spectators paid to see games, and the team was barely able to pay the players' salaries. The team became so impoverished that the Red Stockings were disbanded in 1871.

In 1876 -- the same year that General Custer and his men died at the Little Big Horn -- a formerly outstanding pitcher, Albert Goodwill Spalding, created the first professional baseball league, the National League. By this time, there were dozens of enclosed ball fields where admission was charged, and unlike the Red Stockings, the National League teams successfully attracted enough fans to pay their players and make a profit. Unlike earlier times, these games were seldom marred by arguments with umpires, by fights between players and spectators, or by gambling and "fixing" the games' outcomes. The league drew a whopping 343,750 paying fans in its first year.[43]

Sportswriter Henry Chadwick was born in 1824 to a prominent family in England, but at the age of 12 his family moved to Brooklyn, where some years later he became entranced by baseball after watching a game played in Elysian Fields.[44] As a devoted fan of the game, he soon after began to lambaste owners for mismanagement, just as he attacked the gamblers, drunks, and rowdies among fans and players, accusing them of disgracing the game. As early as 1874, Chadwick also published baseball slang terms that included "muffed balls," "assists," "balks," "daisy cutters," "fungoes," "grounders," "pop ups," "double plays," and "passed balls," among others.[45] Chadwick wrote the first baseball rule book, created the "batting average" and other statistics, including a box score very much like the one still in use. He also edited what he called *Spalding's Official Baseball Guide*, and served as chairman of the baseball rules committee.[46]

Chadwick readily acknowledged "rounders" as the ancestor of baseball. In 1907, however, former star player but by then a multimillionaire sporting-goods baron, Albert G. Spalding, created a committee of inquiry to determine the "true" origins of baseball. Believing that it was deplorable, if not downright treasonous, to acknowledge an English game as baseball's ancestor, Spalding accepted a letter written by an octogenarian claiming that Abner Doubleday, who later became a Civil War general, had actually invented the game at Cooperstown, New York, in 1839, the site of what later became baseball's Hall of Fame. There is not a shred of evidence to support this contention. For one thing, Doubleday spent the entire year of 1839 as a young cadet at West Point. No leave was permitted to young cadets. Also, his many diaries make no mention of baseball. As we have seen, the game was played widely in Massachusetts in 1791 and by George Washington's soldiers even earlier. Nonetheless, many Americans still believe that Doubleday invented the game.[47] In truth, no one invented baseball. It simply evolved.

NOTES

---

[1] Barzun (1954: 159).

[2] Cooper (1949: 506).

[3] Clune (1963).

[4] *Los Angeles Times*, February 24, 2003, D2; Henderson (1947).

[5] Beals (1933).

[6] Scarborough and Wilcox (1991: 197).

[7] Borhegyi (1980).

[8] Peterson (1973).

[9] Ibid., p. 38.

[10] *Lapta* means ball game or tennis.

[11] Alexander (1991: 3); Voigt (1983: xxv).

[12] Peterson (1970: 11-12); Henderson (1947).

[13] Ibid.

[14] New York Times, May 12, 2004.

[15] Los Angeles Times, May 12, 2004; Society for American Baseball Research (UK Chapter): Early bat-and-ball games www.sabruk.org/history/bat.html [hereafter cited as SABRUK].

[16] Hibbert (1987).

[17] Ibid., p. 370.

[18] Allen (1950: 337); Fischer (1989: 150).

[19] Prentice and Clifton (1995: 569).

[20] Rader (1992: 6).

[21] Kirsch (1989).

[22] Alexander (1991: 11).

[23] Voight (1983: 11-12).

[24] Durant (1973: 23).

[25] Rader (1992).

[26] Kirsch (1989: 38).

[27] Allen (1950: 24).

[28] Adelman (1986: 111).

[29] Kirsch (1989: 94).

[30] Seymour (1989: 24-25).

[31] Adelman (1986: 121).

[32] Astor (1988:2).

[33] DiClerico and Pavelec (1991).

[34] Ibid., p. 5.

[35] Riess (1999: 31).

[36] Kirsch (1989: 116).

[37] Ibid., p. 254.

[38] Rader (1992: 33).

[39] Durant (1973: 29).

[40] Riess (1999: 149).

[41] Astor (1988: 5).

[42] Ibid.

[43] Durant (1973: 251).

[44] Tygiel (2000: 17).

[45] Voigt (1983: 93).

[46] Springwood (1996).

[47] Ibid., pp. 5-7.

Chapter Two: Baseball in North America

While baseball took hold in America, it continued to spread overseas as U.S. naval officers and men took the game to various locales. As early as 1871, American officers on a U.S. warship easily won a game against a team of local residents in Callao, Peru. In 1888, a team of Chicago White Stockings and some other players and their wives, led by Albert G. Spalding, toured New Zealand, Australia, Sri Lanka, Egypt, Italy, France, and Britain demonstrating the game of baseball. Only the Australians displayed any keen interest in the game.[1] Some countries have only taken up the game during the past decade but others have played baseball for many years. Canadian teams, for example, were playing their own version of 5-base, 11-fielder baseball as early as 1838 in Ontario, and the "New York game" appeared in Canada in the 1850s. Baseball has flourished there ever since at all age levels, in schools, clubs, and leagues of all sorts including high quality professional ones. Baseball is also played by remote Indian tribes like the Chipewyan of the isolated village of Snowdrift in the Northern Territories, north of Alberta. During the summer, Chipewyan boys and single men from 16 to 30 play a game every evening at 8:30. Using a softball and a homemade bat, they play eagerly while many villagers look on.

Edmonton, Calgary, and Vancouver host triple-A teams in the Pacific Coast League; Ottawa hosts a team in the International League; and both Montreal and Toronto have been home to major league teams. Almost 200 Canadians have played in the major leagues, and many, such as George Selkirk, Reggie Cleveland, Larry Walker, and black pitcher Ferguson Jenkins have starred. The 6 foot, 5 inch Jenkins pitched in the major leagues from 1965 to 1983, winning 20 games a season seven times. Selkirk, who replaced Babe Ruth when he retired, hit .290 in nine seasons for the Yankees. The game in Canada has been played just as it has in the United States, except for the absence of overt racism against players of African ancestry. Jackie

Robinson began his professional career playing for Montreal when it was still a farm team for the Los Angeles Dodgers and the Canadian fans welcomed him warmly. When he proved to be a star player, the fans went wild over him. Thanks to an 11-1 win over Mexico in the 2003 Olympic Qualifying Tournament in Panama, Canada qualified for the 2004 Athens Olympic Games, the first Olympics that a Canadian baseball team ever played in. They were led by Justin Morneau, a Minnesota Twins minor league player, who hit five home runs during the tournament. He is now in the major leagues.

Meanwhile, baseball in the United States was attracting more and more ethnically diverse players. At the turn of the century, it was commonplace for Jews to be stereotyped as lacking physical courage, a curious perception given their remarkable success as boxers in England and America. Despite this stereotype, by 1900, 14 Jews had played in the major leagues, and there were also four Jewish managers and three Jewish owners. Later, the major leagues would welcome Jewish stars like Hank Greenberg and Sandy Koufax.

Contrary to the popular belief that Jackie Robinson was the first black player in the majors, catcher Moses Fleetwood "Fleet" Walker played in the major leagues in 1883, if only briefly, and several light-skinned, but part-African, Cubans also played in the majors. In 1905, New York Giants manager John McGraw told the press and the public that African American infielder Charlie Grant was actually a full-blooded Cherokee named Chief Tokohama. No one believed McGraw, and his attempt to break the color line for the Giants failed. Until Branch Rickey signed Jackie Robinson in 1946 to play for the Dodgers' Montreal farm team, where he hit .349 and stole 40 bases, almost all blacks were relegated to all-black Negro leagues. Even the brilliant pitcher Satchel Paige was excluded from the major leagues until after Robinson's path-breaking signing.

Of 720 entry-level players in the major leagues from 1910 to 1915, 39 percent were of British origin, 32 percent German, and 18 percent Irish, with 12 percent representing other ethnic backgrounds including several Native Americans, one Hawaiian, and a Canary Islander.[2] Of the players who entered the majors from 1916 to 1920, 36 percent were of British ancestry, 31 percent were German, and 19 percent were Irish.[3] Surprisingly, forty percent of all players came from white-collar families, one-third from manual labor backgrounds and only one-fifth from farmsteads.[4]

Many of these players, and still earlier ones, became nationally famous. One of the first to catch the nation's fancy was 5 foot, 10 inch, 180 pound Michael J. "King" Kelly whose great speed on the bases and his head-first slides enabled him to lead the league in stolen bases, 84 of them in 1887, when he also hit .394. Kelly's father came to America from Ireland to escape the deadly potato famine of 1845-1851. After settling in Troy, New York, marrying, and seeing his son Michael born in 1857, the elder Kelly served gallantly in the Union Army during the Civil War. Mike was orphaned in his early teens but began to play baseball in 1873 at the age of 15. He signed a professional contract in 1877 and soon became a star, his huge, floral mustache featured in many photographs.

Kelly would become most famous for his play in Boston, but he first starred in 1880 on the Chicago White Stockings with Cap Anson and a speedy outfielder, Billy Sunday, who later became a famous evangelist.[5] Kelly lodged in the elegant Palmer House, bet on horses, enjoyed vaudeville, and was a regular nightly visitor to saloons. At that time, Chicago had a population of one-half million, less than half the population of New York, and only two-thirds that of Philadelphia. Yet, thanks in part to Chicago's millionaire George Pullman, 22 railroads converged on the city. Electric lights arrived at the same time that Kelly did, and there were many thriving industries along with the excellent, inexpensive restaurants where Kelly ate and, all too often, drank himself into insensibility. Kelly's base-stealing became so famous that a hit song was called "Slide, Kelly, Slide":

Slide, Kelly, Slide!
Your running's a disgrace!

Slide, Kelly, Slide!
Stay there, hold your base!
If some one doesn't steal you,
And your batting doesn't fail you,
They'll take you to Australia!
Slide, Kelly, Slide!

Due to his heavy drinking, Kelly's career lasted only a decade. At the age of 36, alcoholic, penniless, and stricken with pneumonia, Kelly died. It is said that as he was being carried to the hospital, he slipped off the stretcher, then whispered these final words: "This is my last slide."[6] Billy Sunday wept when he learned of Kelly's death.[7] Ninety days after Kelly died, George Herman "Babe" Ruth was born.

Drinking was a problem for many other players as well. Native American players were often referred to as "drunken Indians." The first Native American to play in the major leagues escaped this insult by disguising himself as a white man. James Madison Toy was a Sioux Indian who played for Cleveland as early as 1887, but no one knew he was an "Indian." Louis Francis Sockalexis, the grandson of the Penobscot chief, was known to be an Indian, and he became the object of intense racial bigotry when he also played for Cleveland. He had been a brilliant outfielder in college at Holy Cross, and he also dazzled opponents, team-mates, and fans when he played for Cleveland. Unfortunately, he was a profound alcoholic whose addiction to whiskey was so public that he was blasted in the press as a "drunken Indian." His major-league career was short-lived, beginning in 1897 and ending early in 1899.[8]

At the turn of the century, nearly 9,000 children in South Carolina and 2,000 in Massachusetts were asked to name their favorite games. Boys in both places put baseball at the top of their lists. In 1921, the same question was asked of boys in San Francisco, and again baseball came out on top. But in 1959 in Ohio, boys listed baseball as only their ninth favorite game. In that same survey, girls in San Francisco listed baseball as their fourth favorite game behind tag, sewing, and bicycle riding, but girls in the other three surveys—Massachusetts, Ohio, and South Carolina—seldom mentioned baseball at all.[9]

As popular, talented and flamboyant as King Kelly was, the most dominant and well known pre-1900 player was Adrian Constantine (known as "Cap" or "Pop") Anson, a husky, tall, blond, blue-eyed man of English ancestry who was, for some reason, also known as "Swede." Anson was a racist who in his booming voice openly ridiculed blacks, whom he called "coons" and "chocolate-colored mascots." He gave no indication of great intelligence in other arenas either, as he did poorly in school as a boy and behaved imperiously at most times. Still, he played very well in the major leagues from 1871 to 1898, winning four league batting championships and failing to hit .300 only twice. He hit .352 as a 19-year-old rookie in 1871 and .395 as a 42-year-old veteran in 1894. He also served as a manager. Another prominent manager in these early days was a former catcher, 6 foot, 1 inch tall, 150-pound Cornelius McGillicuddy, or "Connie Mack," as he preferred to be known, who, unlike Anson, was a soft-spoken, kindly man, did not smoke, was a teetotaler, and never swore. During his playing days as a catcher, however, he did upset batters by intentionally tipping their bats with his glove.

Most remarkable of the early managers was John J. McGraw who stood only 5 foot, 7 inches and was slight-of-build as a young player, although he would later become quite pudgy. He became a star major leaguer with the Baltimore Orioles in 1894, hitting .340 and stealing 78 bases. He also became famous for his temper. He once punched an umpire after a game.[10] In 1899, at the age of only 26, he became the playing manager of the Orioles. He later moved on to manage the New York Giants where he won the pennant in 1904. Before he retired, he had won ten pennants and three World Series. Many thought him the greatest manager baseball had ever seen. One former player called him the greatest manager of all time because he knew how to handle men, being strict and demanding with some but kind and gentle with others.[11] Another called him "a great man, really a wonderful fellow, and a great manager to play for."[12] Although a heavy drinker who was also addicted to gambling, McGraw managed major league teams for 30 years, always doing so in uniform from the third base coach's box. Astonishingly, Connie Mack managed major league teams for 49 years, not retiring until 1950 when he was 88 years old. He always managed from the dugout wearing a business suit and tie.[13]

Like today's managers, these men had to deal with some extraordinarily difficult players. An early example was George Edward Waddell. A farm boy ignorant of all social graces, he quickly earned the nickname "Rube." Despite his exceptional ability to throw the ball past almost any hitter, he was forced to pitch in the minor leagues for several years before Connie Mack took a gamble and signed him. He promptly pitched a double-header, winning both games, then gleefully turned cartwheels on the mound. He went on to display extraordinary talent as a left-handed pitcher, but his off-the-field behavior continued to amaze onlookers. Uninvited, he would show up in saloons, put on an apron and tend bar, drinking heavily on the house. But he also happily played ball with kids on local Philadelphia playgrounds, and he loved to chase fire engines. He starred in a stage play until his second wife sued to attach his wages for nonsupport. Within the space of three days, he had three extraordinary experiences. First, he heroically prevented a potentially deadly fire in a crowded department store when he picked up a blazing oil stove and carried it outside. The next day, police charged him with assaulting and badly injuring his father-in-law. A day later, he was arrested for bigamy and jailed.[14]

Not long after, when a teammate was hit in the head by a pitch, everyone stood around not knowing what to do. Suddenly, Waddell picked up the unconscious player, carried him out of the stadium and hailed a cab that took them to a hospital. Then, still in uniform, he stayed by the man's bedside administering cold compresses until the player began to recover.[15] There were accusations that he had been bought by gamblers, but no evidence was ever produced. In the winter of 1912, "Rube" was visiting in Kentucky when floods raged. He voluntarily spent hours up to his armpits in near-freezing water stacking sandbags to reinforce levees. This ordeal left him with a severe lung infection that developed into tuberculosis, killing him at 37. [16] Another farm boy was Ohio's Denton True "Cy" (meaning "hayseed") Young, who came to the Cleveland Indians in 1890 and won 511 games by 1910, an average of 25 games a year. He had three no-hitters, one of them a perfect game, and, unlike Waddell, was a model citizen. Each major league's award for the best pitcher of the year carries his name, the "Cy Young Award."

McGraw called Honus Wagner the greatest player he had ever seen, and a man with "the quickest baseball brain" of all time.[17] Like his German immigrant father, Wagner went to work in a coal mine when he was only 12 years old, earning 70 cents for each ton of coal he loaded, but he also played baseball for numerous semi-professional and small professional teams. In 1900, he was signed by Pittsburgh, where he played until he retired, proving himself such a brilliant player that he led the National League in hitting eight times. He was also an outstanding shortstop and base runner. He was one of the first five players inducted into the Baseball Hall of Fame. The others were pitchers Walter Johnson and Christy Mathewson, along with Babe Ruth and Ty Cobb.

Known as the "Flying Dutchman," Wagner (born Hanus Vaagner) was one of many players of German ancestry to star in baseball. So did Babe Ruth (born Ruthe) and Heinrich Ludwig "Lou" Gehrig, who spoke fluent German but was seen by his fans as a true American hero. Many more recent players, such as Warren Spahn, Mike Schmidt, Andy Messersmith, John Smoltz, and Cal Ripken, Jr., were of German ancestry but were only seen as Americans by fans and teammates. Four Baseball Commissioners have also been of German ancestry – Ford Frick, William Eckert, Bowie Kuhn, and Peter Ueberroth. Several owners have had German ancestry as well, including George Steinbrenner, and so were several managers with Whitey Herzog and Buck Showalter probably the best known. There have been German-American umpires as well, such as Bruce Froemming and Harry Wendelstedt.[18] Italian Americans also starred in baseball. By 1936, there were 23 big leaguers of Italian ancestry. Later, Ernie Lombardi, Phil Rizzuto, Yogi Berra, and Joe DiMaggio would star.

In 1900, the same year that Wagner signed, the plate was officially changed from a 12-inch square to a 5-sided figure, 17 inches across, adding 200 square inches to the strike zone. As a result, hitting became much more difficult. Strikeouts rose by 50 percent while batting averages, home runs and runs-batted-in all fell to new lows. Of course, some of this decline was due to great pitching. Walter Johnson was a farm-boy from Idaho who threw side arm with such velocity that Ty Cobb said that his fastball "looked about the size of a watermelon seed and hissed at you as it passed."[19] Another outstanding hitter, "Ping" Bodie, spoke for many when he said of Johnson, "You can't hit what you can't see." Years after he retired, Johnson threw a silver dollar 372 feet across the Rappahannock River as George Washington was said to have done. Johnson was so mild-mannered that his worst expletives were "gee whillikins" and "goodness gracious." Christy Mathewson did not throw as fast as Johnson, but he was a superb pitcher for many years. In the 1905 World Series, he won three games by shut outs, something never done by anyone else. A graduate of Bucknell, he was a soft-spoken, gentlemanly man.

After Wagner, Tyrus Raymond Cobb was the next great everyday player. As a youngster in Georgia, his volatile temper was often in evidence. His father sought for his son higher things in life than baseball, but Cobb persisted in his love for the game, and his father's objections ended in 1905 when his wife killed him with a shotgun blast when he unexpectedly returned home one night. He was thought by many to have burst in on his wife that night because he suspected her of infidelity. It was a case of mistaken identity, she later insisted. Cobb soon became famous for his hitting, fielding and base-stealing which was marked by frequent spiking of infielders incautious enough to get in his way while trying to tag him. Cobb later wrote that he only twice intentionally spiked an opponent but mild-mannered Connie Mack called him the dirtiest player in the game. Both Mathewson and Cobb served in World War I as army captains in a chemical warfare unit. Mathewson was accidentally gassed, leaving him with a lung disorder that led to his early death.

Cobb signed with Detroit in 1905 where he played until 1928, retiring at age 42. He compiled a lifetime batting average of .367, the highest ever recorded. He led the American League in hitting 12 times, including nine years in a row, and in three seasons he hit over .400. By 1920, his salary was $50,000, the highest ever paid at that time, when the average major league salary was barely $5,000.[20] He also invested in a new product named Coca-Cola, and was said to have made a fortune by doing so. Whatever his financial condition, he continued to have brawls both on and off the field. In 1912, Cobb went into the stands to assault a heckler who happened to be physically handicapped. Officials suspended Cobb. In 1917, he spiked Buck Herzog of the Giants during an exhibition game, then beat him up in a bloody hotel room brawl. He also beat a black groundskeeper and when the man's wife tried to intervene, he beat her, too. Later, he beat a black man who complained when Cobb walked over his freshly poured asphalt. He sometimes carried a gun and threatened to use it. And Cobb baited his opponents viciously. He reviled the Yankees so brutally in 1924 that mild-mannered Lou Gehrig had to be restrained from fighting him.[21] At Cobb's death, sports writer Jimmy Cannon wrote, "He was the strangest of all our national sports idols. But not even his disagreeable character could destroy the image of his greatness as a ballplayer. Ty Cobb was the best. That seemed to be all he wanted."[22] He was unpopular with his teammates as well as his opponents. Only three people who had any association with baseball attended his funeral.

An Ohio youngster, George Sisler, graduated from the University of Michigan where he had been a brilliant pitcher who also hit and fielded superbly. Playing for the St. Louis Browns, he hit .407 in 1920 and .422 in 1922 before a sinus infection affected his vision and his skills eroded.[23] Second only to Cobb in these years was the Texan, Rogers Hornsby, who hit .424 in 1924, the highest in this century and compiled a lifetime batting average of .358, again second only to Cobb. Unlike Cobb, he was kind and gentle to umpires and opposing players alike. Unlike most players and managers at that time, he did not smoke, drink whiskey, or even drink coffee. He protected his eyes by staying away from the flickering light of the movies of that time. He never watched a single one. But he was a member of the Ku Klux Klan, and he often bet money at the racetrack, something that Baseball Commissioner Kenesaw Mountain Landis challenged him about until Hornsby pointed out that he could easily have lost more in the 1929 market crash than he ever did on horse racing. Playing for Boston, then Chicago, and later serving as manager of the St. Louis Browns and Cincinnati, he described himself this way: "I'm a tough guy, a gambler on horses, a slave driver and in general a disgrace to the game. I wish I knew why. I only wanted to win."[24]

In 1900 entrepreneur Byron Bancroft "Ban" Johnson, an irascible 300-pound lawyer and sports reporter, decided to create a second major league, the American League. He did so by signing players belonging to National League teams and moved American League franchises into National League cities. After three years of turmoil, the new American League stabilized. While great players and managers were coming and going, baseball's popularity rose and fell unpredictably. For example, when the Baltimore Orioles won the pennant in 1894, their fans went wild. The Reach Guide recounted the story:

> The team reached Baltimore on the evening of October 2nd by special train from Chicago. . . . From the time the train entered Maryland until it arrived at Camden Station [in Baltimore], the trip was one triumphal march. At Cumberland, thousands greeted the pennant-winners, and at Martinsburg, Harpers Ferry and Washington the scenes of enthusiasm were repeated. As the special train pulled into Camden Station, hundreds of track torpedoes were exploded, and a multitude limited only to the capacity of the surrounding streets cheered the players as they left the train. The players took carriages and led a procession of enthusiasts and rooters through the business district of the city, ending up at the Fifth Regiment Armory. The

line was divided into six divisions with floats and decorated wagons distributed throughout. Fireworks were discharged from an enormous platform-wagon. Mounted police and a band of music preceded the marshal and his aides mounted on horseback. Along the route of the parade, the houses were gorgeously decorated and illuminated. A terrific jam of humanity was on the streets from start to finish. When the armory was reached, there were more fireworks and the reception lasted nearly two hours.[25]

But Baltimore fans soon lost interest in their team, even though they continued to win. Winning, it seems, had become taken for granted. The only teams to win pennants in the years around the turn of the century were Baltimore, Boston and Brooklyn. The New York Giants were not winning (except in 1904), and their fans stayed away in large numbers. So it was in the country's other two largest cities, Chicago and Philadelphia. Even so, between 1909 and 1923, 15 massive concrete-and-steel baseball stadiums were constructed beginning with Shibe Park in Philadelphia and Forbes Field in Pittsburgh.[26]

And in 1913, New York Giants manager John McGraw and Chicago White Sox owner Charles Comiskey agreed to send the two teams across the United States and around much of the world on a tour paid for by Comiskey. It was the most extensive baseball tour ever undertaken. In the fall of 1913, the two teams and their entourages embarked on this venture, playing in 27 American cities before over 100,000 fans. Bill Klem was the home plate umpire. The teams included star players Sam "Wahoo" Crawford, Urban "Red" Faber, Tris Speaker, and Cristy Mathewson, but its most popular player was the Giants' Sac and Fox, native American Jim Thorpe, who had starred in track events during the 1912 Olympics in Stockholm and was the greatest athlete of his time. The teams also played in Tokyo, Shanghai, Hong Kong, the Philippines, Australia, Ceylon, Egypt, and several other major cities of Western Europe. The tour ended with a game in London, played before the King and 27,000 people. The English fans were not impressed. They were particularly contemptuous of the catcher for wearing what they called "armor." As one man said, "An English wicket keeper would not have a chest guard, a wire guard for his face, and a left glove that practically prevents injury to one hand."[27] The teams returned to the United States on the ill-fated luxury liner, the Lusitania, one year before it was torpedoed and sunk by a German submarine in 1915. The teams had traveled 35,000 miles. The tour was considered to be a great success, but the outbreak of World War I pushed news about baseball off the front pages.[28]

By 1916, the game was in such doldrums that the popular magazine, *Harper's Weekly*, published this diatribe against baseball by critic Louis Graves:

In an aimless spasmodic sort of way, a game played with a ball and bat had come into favor. . . . In an evil hour for this land of the free, some busybodies who ought to have been occupying their time in a better way, pounced upon this new game of baseball and decided it should be the national sport. . . .

The time had come when people demanded the privilege of sitting inert in great crowds and seeing a few less lazy human beings go through physical exercises. . . . They knew they wanted something and they easily hypnotized themselves into thinking that baseball filled the bill. It was all they had to choose, and they chose it.

The worst fault of baseball—and it is an unpardonable fault in any game that pretends to be a spectacle—is that it is not lively. For vivacity I would compare baseball with chess or billiards. It is somewhat less exciting than a spelling bee. . . .

. . . You go and sit through an hour and a half of dullness to get your one thrill. And you are lucky if the thrill comes then. . . .

Though unquestionably the most ardent rooters of baseball do go to see it played, I have found that a great number of citizens extol it as a patriotic duty. It's a habit—like rising for the Star Spangled Banner.

To put it briefly, baseball is the dullest of sports. I have never been able to understand why the clergymen want to prevent its being played on Sundays. There is so little about the game to distract one's attention that the grandstand is an ideal place for meditation and prayer.[29]

This perception of baseball was made even more negative by the so-called "Black Sox" scandal of 1919. Some players on the Chicago White Sox pennant-winning team were infuriated by their miserable wages and treatment at the hands of their notoriously miserly owner, Charles Comiskey. (Comiskey was the only owner to charge players for having their uniforms laundered.)[30] In response, eight of them conspired with gamblers to throw the World Series. Their "fix" was so obvious that they were quickly arrested and arraigned for conspiracy to defraud the public. Despite public confessions by several players, before a trial could take place, the players repudiated them. A sympathetic jury acquitted all eight players. Spectators in the courtroom roared their approval and several jurors joined spectators in carrying the accused players around on their shoulders. The jury members then joined the players in an Italian westside Chicago restaurant, where they celebrated until the small hours of the morning.[31] Although the gamblers who had conspired with the players were known, they were never even charged. However, the new Commissioner of Baseball, Kenesaw Mountain Landis, who had just been hired at the enormous salary of $50,000, more than seven times what he had been earning as a federal court judge, banned the players for life, ending the career of South Carolina country boy "Shoeless" Joe Jackson, one of the greatest hitters of all time. Jackson was in the prime of his career. The *Chicago Herald Examiner* published this famous exchange between Jackson, who could neither read nor write, and a small boy who approached him after his acquittal:

"Say it ain't so, Joe. Say it ain't so."

"Yes, kid. I'm afraid it is."

"Well, I never would have thought it," the boy said.[32]

Baseball fans were appalled by the Black Sox scandal, but thanks to the suppression of evidence, they were unaware that another 30 players appeared to have been engaged in fixing games. Landis' lifetime suspensions, however, eased the fans' minds, and the 1920s roared in with dazzling splendor. In 1924, a Columbia University student named Lou Gehrig left college after his sophomore year, signing a contract with the New York Yankees. In 1925, he replaced the injured veteran Wally Pipp, beginning his unbelievable playing streak of 2,130 consecutive major league games. Ten years earlier, "Babe" Ruth had come to the majors as a pitcher for the Boston Red Sox, winning 94 games and losing only 46 with an ERA of 2.28 and seventeen shutouts. While accomplishing these feats from the mound he also played right field and hit with power like no one else ever had. The two men would play together on the New York Yankees in the 1920s and early 1930s, making that team the most famous in baseball history.

The "Roaring Twenties" swept the nation into a seemingly limitless frolic, with scantily-clad young women dancing the Charleston and men and women of all sorts singing, dancing and drinking until all hours of the morning. These same Twenties brought baseball into the hearts of Americans as never before. The towering home runs of the "King of Swat," Babe Ruth, brought baseball alive. Fans flocked to see the Yankees play. And thanks to a livelier, "juiced up" baseball, many other players hit home runs as well. After the 1922 World Series was broadcast on the radio, Americans crowded around radios to listen to major league games, and fans across the country fervently read the sports sections of their tabloid newspapers and magazines. Newsreels showed baseball games as well. Fox Movietone News made newsreels so popular that by 1919 they had an annual audience of 30 million people.[33]

Raised in a Baltimore reformatory, the 6 foot, 2 inch Babe Ruth was so poorly educated that, while he spoke adequate German, he mangled English. However, his contagious grin, his home run records, and his insatiable appetite for hot dogs and beer, not to mention women, fascinated the nation. He often ate an eighteen egg omelet for breakfast along with huge slices of ham and many pieces of buttered toast, all washed down by five or six bottles of soda pop and several cups of coffee.[34] Even Ty Cobb took notice. "I've never seen such an appetite. He would start shoveling down victuals in the morning and never stop. I've seen him at midnight propped up in bed, order six huge club sandwiches and put them away along with a platter of pig's knuckles and a pitcher of beer. And all the time he'd be smoking a big black cigar."[35]

Widely seen as the greatest player ever, Ruth's flamboyance was matched by his home run records: 60 in one season and 714 for his career. In 1969, during the celebration of baseball's centennial, sportswriters and broadcasters voted Ruth the "Greatest Player Ever," a title that captured the spirit of the Twenties. However, his insatiable appetite for women—he typically slept with several different women during a single night—led to a number of lawsuits for paternity and child support, not to mention a host of venereal infections. On the 25th anniversary of Yankee Stadium, June 13, 1948, Ruth was invited to return and did so, thin, pale and weak, using a bat as a cane. It was a shocking sight for the capacity crowd. He died of cancer two months later at the age of 55.[36]

Although Ruth was the ultimate star, fans were fascinated by the powerful Yankees' lineup of the 1920s, calling it "Murderer's Row." In 1927, for example, Gehrig hit .373, Ruth, .356; Combs, in center field, hit .356; Meusel, in left, hit .337; and Lazzeri, at second, hit .309. Fans were especially taken with the talented, ever-smiling Lou Gehrig. Diagnosed with incurable and rapidly fatal *amyotrophic lateral sclerosis* in 1939—which would become known as "Lou Gehrig's disease"—Gehrig knew he had but a short time to live. When he appeared in uniform before 60,000 fans gathered to honor him at Yankee Stadium, his words not only brought tears to the eyes of many, they have lived to this day. As tears rolled down his cheeks, he said, "Today, I consider myself the luckiest man on the face of the earth."[37] Babe Ruth, long estranged from Gehrig, listened, then rushed forward to embrace him, and the two old teammates hugged each other as fans looked on in wonderment. Gehrig died less than two years later, two weeks before his 38th birthday.[38]

Shortly before Gehrig made his unforgettable "luckiest man alive" speech, Cincinatti's star catcher, 6 foot, 3 inch, 230-pound "Ernie" Lombardi, a man with hands so large that he could hold seven baseballs in each, suffered such a severe ankle sprain that he had to sit out the remainder of the year. He was replaced by 30-year-old Willard Hershberger. "Hershy" was popular with his teammates, but he was a deeply troubled man, haunted by the memory of his father shooting himself to death when Hershberger was a high school senior. After several losing games, Hershberger blamed himself for calling for the wrong pitches. When he was soon after late for a game, a friend went to his hotel room, convinced a maid to open Hershberger's door and found him on the floor of the bathroom in a pool of blood, his throat slit. Although shaken by this suicide, Cincinnati's players pulled themselves together and went on to win the pennant. Only eight days before Hershberger's suicide, *Baseball Magazine* had carried a flattering article about him.[39]

Despite the economic depression of the 1930s, baseball continued to have its stars. Gehrig and Ruth still hit with power, but some pitchers took a dominant role in the game. In 1930, the ball had been deadened and given higher stitches that made curveballs more devastating.[40] In the 1934 All Star game, left-hander Carl Hubbell struck out Babe Ruth, Lou Gehrig, Jimmie Foxx, Al Simmons, and Joe Cronin in order. Despite the exploits of many pitchers, by 1932 all but four teams were losing money, and teams cut players' salaries, including those of Ruth and Gehrig. Ruth was paid $80,000 in 1930, but by 1934, near the end of his career, he had been cut to $35,000. A year earlier, Commissioner Landis voluntarily took a $25,000 pay cut.[41] The minor leagues suffered even greater losses in attendance, and their payrolls were cut accordingly. From 1929 to 1932 the total national income fell by more than half, from $82.69 billion to $41 billion. Industrial production also fell by half, wages fell 60 percent, and some 15 million Americans were jobless.[42] But in 1935, baseball's first "night game" was played under the lights before a cheering crowd at Cincinnati's Crosley Field.

As the depression eased, the St. Louis Cardinals' J.H. "Dizzy" Dean (he was never sure whether his given name was Jerome Herman or Jay Hanna) dominated baseball in strikeouts. In 1934, he won 30 games, while his younger brother, Paul, often known as "Daffy," won 19 games and threw a no-hitter. The two brothers, who had grown up picking cotton in Arkansas, were never well paid as pitchers. At that time, Dizzy Dean was earning a salary of $7,500, but Paul was making only $2,000. Dizzy told the press, "I'm underpaid, but my brother is worse underpaid. I'll take the rap for myself, but my brother must have $2,000 more or we don't pitch."[43] The two brothers went on "strike," but, under pressure from owner Branch Rickey and Commissioner Landis, they soon came back and completed the season, much to the delight of St. Louis fans. When Paul pitched his no-hitter in the second game of a double-header after Dizzy had won the first game, allowing only three hits, Dizzy was upset, saying, "I wish I'd a known he was goin' to pitch a no hitter. I would of, too."[44] Fortunately for Dizzy, off-season barnstorming allowed him to earn four times his St. Louis salary.[45] Other stars did equally well during the off-season.

There were other great pitchers in the 1930s, including Grover Cleveland Alexander, Burleigh Grimes, "Dazzy" Vance, Ted Lyons, "Red" Ruffing, and Johnny Vander Meer, who pitched two no-hit, no-run games back to back in 1938. But no one captured fan interest as much as Bob Feller of the Cleveland Indians. An Iowa farm boy like "Cy" Young, Feller had a fastball that could reach 100 miles per hour. He started his first game for Cleveland in 1936 at the age of 17. The following year, he struck out 17 Athletics in a game, and in 1938 he struck out 18 Detroit Tigers. Although service in the U.S. Navy during World War II took three years away from his baseball career, he recorded 2,581 strikeouts, 12 one-hit games, and 3 no-hitters.

One of three brothers to play in the major leagues, Joe DiMaggio came to the New York Yankees in 1936. Raised in poverty in San Francisco, Joe learned to play on asphalt streets using a cut-down version of an oar from his father's fishing boat as a bat. A splendid fielder, as well as a powerful hitter, "Joltin' Joe" DiMaggio, who also was known as "the Yankee Clipper," replaced Lou Gehrig in the affection of Yankee fans. In 1939, he hit .381, and in that same year Ted Williams came to the majors with Boston. Despite DiMaggio's greatness, many consider Tris Speaker to be the greatest center fielder of all time. Playing from 1907 to 1928, Speaker's lifetime batting average of .344 is second only to Cobb's; Joe DiMaggio hit many more home runs than Speaker, 361 to 115, but he hit a lively ball while the ball Speaker hit was comparatively dead. Speaker was also a more dazzling fielder than DiMaggio and stole 433 bases to DiMaggio's 30.[46]

Baseball was played avidly by soldiers and sailors not only during the American Civil War, but also during the 1898 Spanish-American and all subsequent wars. Major league teams donated baseball gear, and star players demonstrated their skills for the troops. Baseball was considered so important to morale during World War II that when Joe DiMaggio asked to be sent to a combat unit rather than play baseball while serving in the army his request was denied. He continued to play the game for the enjoyment of his fellow soldiers. However, Bob Feller's similar request was granted by the navy, and he saw action aboard the battleship *Alabama*, which engaged in significant combat in the South Pacific.[47] After hitting .406 in 1941, Ted Williams flew as a combat fighter pilot in both World War II and the Korean War. The World War II years so depleted baseball rosters that the St. Louis Browns played a one-armed outfielder, Pete Gray, for 77 games in 1945, and the Cincinnati Reds pitched 15-year-old left-hander Joe Nuxhall.

Baseball not only sustained many American servicemen during their leisure time in World War II, some even played while the enemy was near at hand. During the 1944 invasion of Tulagi in the Solomon Islands, Marine Sergeant Dana Babcock stumbled upon what he first believed to be a pick-up baseball game amid the chaos of battle. One Marine had used a dead branch from a jungle tree as a bat, and the players ran the bases, hit home runs, got caught in rundowns, and argued with the umpire. However, Babcock soon noticed something that was more than peculiar: the Marines were playing baseball without a ball! The Marines could not locate anything resembling a baseball, so they proceeded to use a "ghost" ball, with the umpire calling balls and strikes as the pitcher delivered a phantom pitch. Sgt. Babcock felt that the game he witnessed proved that baseball was "deep in the hearts" of American servicemen.[48]

Henry Benjamin "Hank" Greenberg was an all-star high school first baseman in the Bronx. The Yankees offered him a contract, but rather than spend years behind Lou Gehrig waiting for a chance to play, he signed with Detroit. He refused to sit out on Rosh Hashanah and in 1934 hit two home runs to defeat the Red Sox on this Jewish holy day. Fans, including the Jewish community, applauded his decision. In 1939, he hit 58 home runs, only two short of Ruth's record. Drafted for military duty in 1941, he was discharged two days before the December 7 attack on Pearl Harbor. He reenlisted immediately and spent the remainder of the war with a B-29 bomber unit in the Burma theater, missing four and a half prime seasons of his baseball career. Despite this long absence from the game, in 1946, he led the American League with 44 home runs.

When Greenberg was growing up in the Bronx, he never heard any anti-Semitic comments. But as a baseball player, his ethnicity became an issue. Some of it was light-hearted, like this poem:

> The Irish didn't like it when they heard of Greenberg's fame
>
> For they thought a good first baseman should possess an Irish name.
>
> In the early days of April not a Dugan tipped his hat
>
> Or prayed to see a double when Hank Greenberg came to bat.

But it was not all light-hearted. As Greenberg wrote in his autobiography, "How the hell could you get up to home plate every day and have some son of a bitch call you a Jew bastard and a kike and a sheenie and get on your ass without feeling the pressure? . . . Being Jewish did carry with it a special responsibility."[49]

Sanford "Sandy" Koufax, another Jewish star player, was one of the finest pitchers ever to play baseball. Raised in Brooklyn, he signed with the Brooklyn Dodgers in 1955. After six mediocre seasons, he gained command of his overpowering fastball and dazzling curve to win the Cy Young Award three times and pitch four no-hitters. Unlike Greenberg, Koufax refused to pitch on the Jewish high holy days, and fans respected him for his faith. An arthritic left elbow forced him to retire at the young age of 30. Despite his early retirement, Koufax was elected to the Baseball Hall of Fame only four years later. There have been many other outstanding Jewish major leaguers, but Greenberg and Koufax are the most distinguished. There have also been Jewish owners, managers, and an umpire.

Professional baseball's color bar is well-documented. Branch Rickey signed Jackie Robinson to a contract with the Brooklyn Dodgers in 1946 and he played that season for Montreal. Many other great black players followed Robinson, and as we will see in subsequent chapters, many great black players starred in Latin America, especially Cuba and the Dominican Republic. It is not well known, however, that a few blacks played on white professional teams, including major league teams, long before Robinson was signed. Moses Fleetwood "Fleet" Walker and his brother, Welday, were light-skinned so-called "mulattos," who played on an otherwise all-white major league team in Toledo in 1884. But leading white players like "Cap" Anson refused to play against them. This, along with written death threats, ended their contracts after one year. Newspapers openly referred to Walker as "the coon catcher" and fans screamed "kill the Nigger."[50] Fleet was a brilliant catcher who wore a mask but did not use a glove. His hands were often bruised and bleeding as a result. His injured hands and a broken rib were used as an excuse not to renew his contract.[51] Three years later, however, African American George Stovey pitched briefly for Newark of the International League. Anson again forced the black player out of baseball. Fleet Walker, whose father was a doctor, had been educated at

Oberlin and the University of Michigan. He deeply detested racism and later in his life advocated the return of all Negroes to Africa. He also led a tempestuous life that included a trial for stabbing to death a white man. He was acquitted of that charge, but he was later convicted of allegedly stealing money from the federal mail. He served a one-year prison term.[52]

Bill "Hippo" Galloway played a few games for Woodstock, Ontario, in 1899. In 1900, John McGraw tried to recruit black second baseman, Charlie Grant, to his Baltimore Oriole team by passing him off as a Cherokee Indian. Charles Comiskey, among others, disclosed the deception. Although the expression, "the only good Indian is a dead Indian," was widely used, Native Americans were acceptable to most owners, players and fans. Lou Sockalexis pitched for Cleveland in 1897, and over the next 20 years, 30 other Indians also played in the majors. The two most successful early Indian players were catcher John "Chief" Meyers and pitcher Albert "Chief" Bender.[53] "Chief" was more a term of respect than derision, and both players accepted this nickname.

In all, nearly 100 Native Americans have played in the major leagues. More recent players with some Native American ancestry who starred in the major leagues were pitcher Gene Beardon, shortstop Bobby Bragan, second basemen Bobby Doerr and Napolean Lajoie, and pitchers Monty Stratton, Virgil Trucks, and Early Wynn.[54] Also, three relatively light-skinned Cubans of African ancestry played for Cincinnati in 1911—Tomas de la Cruz, Rafael Almeida and Armando Marsans—but darker-skinned Cubans were excluded.[55] Later, pitchers Hiram Bithorn from Puerto Rico and Alex Carrasquel from Venezuela also played in the majors despite their partial African ancestry.[56] And in 1944 a very dark-skinned Cuban pitcher, Tommy de la Cruz, pitched for Cincinnati. In all, between eight and ten Latin players with significant amounts of African ancestry played in the majors before Jackie Robinson. The fact that they spoke Spanish apparently served to disguise their race.

The vast majority of blacks in America played on racially segregated teams. During the American Civil War, for example, black soldiers in the Union Army played baseball on all-black teams.[57] Later, some universities had racially integrated teams. Actor Paul Robeson played on such a team at Rutgers in 1918. But, until the signing of Jackie Robinson, almost all Negroes played on all-black amateur and semiprofessional teams. In 1867, the all-black Excelsiors of Philadelphia marched to their games in full uniform behind a colorful and loud fife and drum corps.[58] The first fully professional black league, the Negro National League, began play in 1920. The league endured until 1949. Prior to the creation of this league by 6 foot 4 inch, heavy-set former star pitcher and later manager, Andrew "Rube" Foster, black semi-pro teams had been owned by whites, who kept most of the profits. Seven of the eight teams in Foster's Negro National League were owned by blacks. A second league, the Eastern Colored League, lasted from 1923 to 1928. The Negro American League began in 1937 and continued until 1960. The high point of the season was the Negro League "East-West" All-Star game, which began in 1933, drawing 20,000 fans. By the late forties, it drew over 50,000 fans.[59]

Soon after Jackie Robinson came up to the Dodgers in 1947, Negro League players followed him to the major leagues led by outfielder Larry Doby in July of that year and Hank Thompson a few days later. Among the most notable of these were Hank Aaron, Ernie Banks, Joe Black, Roy Campanella, Monte Irvin, Willie Mays, and LeRoy "Satchel" Paige. All of these men were later elected to the National Baseball Hall of Fame at Cooperstown. Nine other African-American players who were eventually elected to the same Hall of Fame played only in the Negro Leagues: James "Cool Papa" Bell, Oscar Charleston, Ray Dandridge, Martín Dihigo, Andrew "Rube" Foster, Josh Gibson, William "Judy" Johnson, Walter "Buck" Leonard, and John Henry "Pop" Lloyd. Many white major leaguers who saw them play believed "Rube" Foster to be the greatest pitcher of all time, Gibson the best hitter, Dandridge the greatest third baseman, and Dihigo the most talented all-around ballplayer ever to play.

Born and raised in dire poverty in Mobile, Alabama, "Satchel" Paige's actual surname was Page but, over time, its spelling somehow changed. He earned his nickname for his many attempts as a boy to steal the bulging satchels of white passengers at a train station.[60] After a tumultuous boyhood, Paige grew to be 6 feet 3 ½ inches tall but weighed only about 140 pounds when he began his career. He possessed an unhittable fastball and a delayed delivery in which he "hesitated" on top of his wind-up for so long that batters became disoriented. He once struck out the great Rogers Hornsby five times in one game, something this Texan, a member of the Ku Klux Klan, could not have found especially enjoyable. Satchel beat both Dizzy Dean and Bob Feller in exhibition games, and both Dean and Feller said that Paige was the best pitcher they had ever seen.[61] He was also a pilot and flew his own plane from game to game. He was famous for his endless pursuit of women and his sayings, such as, "Avoid fried meats which angry up the blood," "Avoid running at all times," and, most famous of all, "Don't look back. Something might be gaining on you."[62]

Many who played in the Negro Leagues believed that 6 foot, 5 inch, half-black, half-Indian "Smokey Joe" Williams threw even harder than Paige or Walter Johnson, but Paige was virtually unhittable. He pitched in the Negro Leagues for many years.[63] He was finally called to the major leagues by Bill Veeck of the Cleveland Indians in 1948 when he was somewhere in the vicinity of 42 years old. Over 72,000 fans crowded into the Cleveland stadium for his first game. In his first year, he won six, lost one and had a 2.84 ERA. He pitched for several years in the majors, including the 1952 season, with another Veeck team, the Kansas City Royals, winning 12 games with an ERA of 3.07 before spending three years with a Triple-A team. In 1956, when Bill Veeck became the owner of the Triple-A International League Miami Marlins, he once again called on Satchel Paige, who was then at least 50 years old. He won 11, lost only 4, and had an ERA of only 1.86, striking out 79 and walking only 28. An amazing performance! In 1965, at the age of about 60, he was called back to Cleveland to pitch in the major leagues one last time. After sitting in a wheelchair in the bullpen where a "nurse" served him coffee, he entered the game and pitched three scoreless innings before leaving the game to thunderous applause. [64] He was elected to the Cooperstown Hall of Fame in 1971. He died in 1982, largely ignored by his many children with whom he had long had rocky relationships.[65]

Despite strong support by black businesses, most black fans had such limited income that Negro League teams made little profit and salaries were very low. In an attempt to make a profit, these teams began to book any opponents they could including white semiprofessional teams, as they traveled across the East, Mid-west, and even the South. Teams traveled on old buses that had no bathroom facilities, often for six or seven hours at a stretch. Unwashed uniforms smelled foully. Typically, the men stopped to buy sandwiches for dinner, eating them as the bus traveled on. Because black players could not stay at white hotels, men frequently had to sleep on their buses, too, although sometimes they were able to locate rundown hotels for blacks or stay in the private homes of black baseball fans.[66] Barnstorming in the South was especially dangerous, as lynching was still a threat. Their lives were hard and salaries were low, but as several black players pointed out, baseball "beat pickin' cotton" for ten cents an hour, then the going wage.[67]

Racism continued to plague Negro League players. One man who had played for years in America was amazed by conditions in Canada when he later played there:

Off the field, Canada was like no place I'd ever been. Never did I imagine such a place even existed. Living and eating conditions were very much nicer. I never ran into a restaurant or a hotel that wouldn't take me. Nothin' up there like that. Canada was like paradise. You could go to any cafe you wanted. There was nowhere you couldn't go, nowhere you couldn't eat, no nothin' like that. After playing in Texas and Oklahoma and in the south, it was as different as night and day. You went wherever you wanted to go, and nobody bothered you. People didn't even look crossways at you. Even the police didn't bother you. The police up there didn't even have no pistols on them. All they had was sticks. It was just like heaven.[68]

In 1952, a black minor leaguer, Ed Charles, who would later go on to a fine major league career, was assigned to a team in Quebec City, Canada. "I'm used to having whites refer to me as 'nigger' and everything derogatory," he said. He had been sent to live with a family of white school teachers. "I felt a little uneasy with this family. I always thought I'd hear this magic word and they'd start referring to me as a 'nigger.' I was tense waiting for this. It never did come. I saw that they were very decent, genuine human beings.... It was an eye-opening experience for me."[69]

Some star black players even received special treatment under the law. Star pitcher Ferguson Jenkins, who was then playing for the Texas Rangers, was once arrested at the Toronto airport for possession of marijuana, hashish, and cocaine. Commissioner Kuhn suspended Jenkins, but the players' union protested and an arbitrator overruled Kuhn because Canadian authorities had deemed his offense "trivial," and Jenkins was allowed to plead "no contest" without jail time.[70]

Black women sometimes played baseball on black men's teams. In 1917, Pearl Barrett played first base for the Havana Red Sox, and in 1933 a Cleveland team had a female second baseman, Isabelle Baxter. As we noted earlier, Toni Stone played for the House of David, and although she was only five feet tall and weighed only 100 pounds, Mamie "Peanut" Johnson was an outstanding pitcher on several black men's teams. Johnson reported that she was extremely well treated by her male teammates, if not always by her male opponents.[71] She said that her teammates treated her with affection and respect and that their wives were not jealous of her: "I rode on the bus day and night, met everybody's wife, and had a good time. . . . I loved being a female on the team. I had twenty six wonderful brothers."[72]

In 1944 Bill Veeck attempted to buy the floundering Philadelphia Phillies and stock the team with stars from the Negro leagues. National League president Ford

Frick and Kenesaw Mountain Landis were so horrified when they heard of Veeck's intention that they pressured the Phillies into selling to another buyer.[73] Frick later openly bragged that he had prevented Veeck from "contaminating the league."[74] The year 1945 saw the end of World War II, but it did not change the major league's policy of excluding blacks from its teams including its minor league affiliates. Commissioner Landis often made public comments about this policy leaving no doubt that he firmly supported it. But in April, 1945, the elderly Landis stepped down. His replacement was Albert B. "Happy" Chandler, former governor of Kentucky. Soon after he took office, two journalists from a black newspaper asked him about the possibility of blacks playing in the majors. When these two men had asked Kenesaw Mountain Landis the same question years earlier, he had dismissed them curtly. Chandler's response was entirely different: "If a black boy can make it on Okinawa and go to Guadalcanal, he can make it in baseball."[75]

The only one of major league baseball's 16 general managers to act on Chandler's words was the Brooklyn Dodgers' president Branch Rickey. Rickey had opposed racial discrimination since early in the century when, as the young coach of Ohio Wesleyan University's baseball team, he tried to check his players into a South Bend, Indiana, hotel room only to be stunned when he was told that his star catcher, "Tommy" Thomas, who was black, could not be "registered." Thinking quickly, Rickey proposed that Thomas sleep in his room without being registered. The desk clerk agreed. After registering the rest of his players, Rickey went to his room, to find Thomas "crying as though his heart would break. His whole body was racked with sobs. . . . He looked at me and he said, 'It's my skin. If I could just tear it off, I'd be like everyone else. It's my skin. It's my skin, Mr. Rickey!'"[76] Soon after Chandler made his position known, Rickey signed Jackie Robinson.

Born in Georgia, the grandson of a slave and son of a sharecropper, Jack Roosevelt "Jackie" Robinson was the youngest of five children. His father abandoned the family when Jackie was 6 months old, and his mother supported her children by working as a domestic in an all-white neighborhood in Pasadena,

California, where they managed to rent a home. As a boy, Jackie played on all-white teams, yet his family lived in poverty, and he endured continual racial slurs and taunts. His older brother, Mack, suffered similarly but, nevertheless, made the Olympic team in 1936 and won a silver medal in the broad jump in the Berlin Olympics. When Mack returned to Pasadena, there was no hero's welcome, and the only job the college-educated Olympian could find was as a street sweeper or ditch digger.[77] When African American sprinter Jesse Owens, the star of those Olympic games, returned to New York, the only hotel that would rent him a room was in Harlem.

After becoming a four-sport star at UCLA—a brilliant basketball player, a superb running back in football, and a talented track athlete, as well as a baseball player – Jackie Robinson played some black professional baseball before entering the army, where he graduated from officer's candidate school as a second lieutenant. Robinson was soon after court-martialed for his refusal to move to the back of a bus in Fort Hood, Texas. After his acquittal, following a four-hour trial, he was given an honorable discharge. Jackie played in the Negro League in 1945. Before choosing Robinson to break the major league "Color bar," Rickey had considered signing outstanding, but aging and hard-drinking Cuban pitcher Silvio García. But when he asked García what he would do if a white American slapped his face, the Cuban snarled, "I kill him."[78] Although hardly one to suffer racism meekly, Robinson told Rickey, "If you want to take this gamble, I will promise you there will be no incident."[79] Robinson also did not smoke, drink, or womanize. In that same year, the Negro League's Cleveland Buckeyes surprisingly signed a 5 foot, 7 inch white pitcher, Eddie Klep. Neither the white nor the Negro press made anything of this action, and although he pitched well in his first start, Klep was inexplicably released after only one game. His release was not mentioned in the national newspapers, but neither was his imprisonment for theft, assault, and drunkenness, behaviors that had been a part of his life both before and after his release.[80]

In part because Robinson convinced Rickey that he was willing to turn the other cheek, Rickey signed him instead of Garcia, sending him to Triple-A Montreal in 1946 where despite predictions of failure by several Negro League players who had seen him play, he led the league in hitting, with an average of .349, and stole 40 bases. Before the season began, Rickey told Montreal's manager, Mississippian Clay Hopper, that he thought Robinson was "super human." Hopper looked startled, then asked, "Do you really think a nigger's a human being?" [81] When the season ended, Montreal fans rushed onto the field to carry Robinson off in honor, and a contrite Hopper told Rickey that Robinson was "the greatest competitor I ever saw, and what's more, he's a gentleman."[82]

When it became known that Rickey intended to bring Robinson up to the Dodgers in 1947, all 15 of the other major league teams voted not to permit Rickey to do so. Happy Chandler pointedly ignored them. The Dodgers' Dixie Walker, a fine outfielder from Alabama, brought a petition he had initiated to Rickey demanding that Robinson not be brought up, but Pee Wee Reese, also a Southerner, refused to sign it. When manager Leo Durocher heard about the petition he called a team meeting at midnight, then angrily berated those who had signed it, telling them that anyone who did not want to play on the same team as Robinson would be traded away. He added, "This fellow is a great player. He's gonna win pennants. He's gonna put money in your pockets and mine. . . . Unless you wake up, these colored ball players are gonna run you right out of the park. . . . Fuck your petition . . . Go back to bed."[83]

In 1946, six African-Americans were lynched in the United States. There were only two blacks in Congress and no major city had a black mayor.[84] In Athens, Georgia, over 100 physically impaired and elderly black protesters were knocked down and trampled.[85] Despite this racial tension, in 1947 Robinson moved up to the Dodgers, where he hit .297, stole 29 bases and led the team to the World Series. Although Hank Greenberg publicly supported Robinson in 1947, as did major Jewish organizations including the Anti-Defamation League, racism plagued Jackie

Robinson during his early days in the majors and never entirely ended. Opposing payers taunted him with jeers of "Jungle Bunny" and "Snowflake." Major league players on three National League teams, the Pirates, Phillies, and Cubs, voted to strike when the 1947 season opened, but the other teams refused to join them. Death threats in Cincinnati were so serious that the FBI stepped in to protect Robinson.[86] When the season began, teams taunted him mercilessly, led by the Phillies' racist manager, Ben Chapman. When the Cincinnati Reds would not control their racist taunts during a game, the Dodgers' shortstop, Pee Wee Reese, called time then walked over to Robinson and put his arm around his shoulder, and the two men stared quietly at the Cincinnati bench. The crowd audibly gasped, and the taunting stopped.[87]

Robinson was Rookie of the Year in 1947, and Brooklyn held a tickertape parade on the day he received the award from J.G. Taylor Spink, owner of *The Sporting News*. There were tears in Robinson's eyes.[88] He won the National League MVP Award in 1949. A superb base runner, he had a .311 lifetime batting average, led the Dodgers to six pennants, and was elected to the Hall of Fame in 1962, the first year that he was eligible.[89] Despite Robinson's success, some teams were in no rush to sign a black player. The Phillies did not play a black man until 1957, and Detroit did not play one until 1958. The New York Yankees were among the slowest of all teams, despite the precedent set by the home-city Dodgers and Giants, who signed several blacks. The Yankees actually turned down an opportunity to sign Willie Mays, and their first black signee was Elston Howard in 1955, nine years after Robinson came to the Dodgers. Most black players were not well paid, either. When Hall of Fame player Monte Irvin left the Newark Eagles of the Negro League to sign with the Giants, he took a pay cut from $6,500 to $5,000 a year.[90]

Robinson made only $5,000 in 1947, and his highest salary was $42,000 in 1956 when he retired. After his retirement, no team offered him any kind of position in baseball. Instead, he worked in the food industry and later served as a special assistant to New York governor Nelson Rockefeller. And in 1956, the year of his retirement, he won the prestigious Spingarn Medal, awarded annually "for the highest achievement of an American Negro." He had worked zealously for the NAACP before his untimely death in 1972, but he found them too conservative. He rejected most Democrats because of the heritage of Southern racism, instead choosing to support Republicans he thought sympathetic to civil rights.[91] When Robinson died in 1972, Pee Wee Reese was one of his pall-bearers. He appeared on a U.S. postage stamp issued in 1982 as a part of the "Black Heritage" series.

Soon after Robinson left the game, African American Curt Flood became an outstanding outfielder for the St. Louis Cardinals. In 1969, after being sold to the Philadelphia Phillies, Flood challenged the "reserve clause" that held players in perpetual bondage to their owners. In 1972, the Supreme Court ruled against Flood. Desperately in need of income, he played 13 games that year before vicious taunts and several written death threats drove him out of the game. He later said, "I am pleased that God made my skin black, but I wish he had made it thicker."[92]

A few years after Flood's misery, black pitcher Dock P. Ellis, Jr. became such an outspoken, proud opponent of racism that black magazines like *Jet* and *Ebony* wrote many stories about his refusal to turn his cheek when white racists attacked him, usually by hate mail rather than in person. He went so far in his quest for individuality as to wear hair curlers under his cap while in uniform before games began. White sports pages happily criticized the brash pitcher, calling him a "militant," but the black media adored him not only because of his anti-racist stands, but also because he spent his leisure time working on projects for needy black people—helping black youth, rehabilitating convicts, and fighting sickle-cell anemia.[93] He was also an excellent pitcher for the Pittsburgh Pirates.

Other outstanding black pitchers included Don Newcombe, Dwight Gooden, Bob Gibson, and Vida Blue, and there were exceptional catchers, too, such as Roy Campanella and John Roseboro. However, thanks to an undercover practice called "stacking," very few blacks were brought to the majors as pitchers or catchers. There were many brilliant black infielders including Jim Gillian, Joe Morgan, and

Derek Jeter, and Maury Wills, who broke Ty Cobb's stolen base record of 96 with 104 of his own in 1962. Black outfielders have been especially talented, from Lou Brock, Larry Doby, and Don Baylor to the brilliant Willie Mays and Henry Aaron, who broke Ruth's all-time homerun record. In the mid-1970s, as "Hank" Aaron came closer and closer to eclipsing Babe Ruth's career home run record, he received so much hate mail including death threats to his family that he had to hire bodyguards. The FBI also protected him. Despite this racist barrage of threats, Aaron hit 755 home runs before retiring in 1976. Black outfielder Barry Bonds now holds the single season home run record of 73, which he set in 2001. Frank Robinson, another fine player, became the first black major league manager in 1975, and Emmet Ashford the first major league black umpire in 1966.

Women in nineteenth century America did not have the right to vote, could not own property after marriage, could not initiate divorce, and were seldom allowed to have a college education. But surprisingly, many of them did find a way to play baseball. In women's search for education, elite women's colleges were founded, with Vassar opening its doors in 1865, followed by Smith and Wellesley a decade later. The founders of Vassar strongly believed that exercise benefited women, and all Vassar's students were required to carry out rigorous calisthenics. Golf, tennis, and bicycling became popular, too, and baseball followed. By 1866, women at Vassar were playing baseball and, when Smith and Wellesley soon after opened, women played there as well. However, a young woman playing at one of these colleges in the 1870s was required to wear so many layers of clothing that her attire weighed 30 pounds. After hitting a ball she had to lift the long train of her skirt, then drape it over her arm before she could run to first.[94] Appalled by this absurdity, young Amelia Bloomer designed and wore loose-fitting "Turkish" trousers that quickly became known as "bloomers," and so many women baseball players adopted this uniform that women's teams became known as "bloomer girls." They often competed against men.

Women not only played baseball against men, some umpired men's games. At the turn of the century, Amanda Clement, 5 foot, 10 inches tall, pretty and highly athletic, umpired men's baseball games. She was liked and respected by the players even though she did not hesitate to eject any player who argued with her calls. She succeeded despite the menacing reality of fans' shouted threats to "kill the umpire." Several major league umpires were severely beaten, and some minor league umpires were actually killed.[95] As was then the practice, only one umpire worked each game, so Clement umpired from behind the mound, where she could call runners out or safe on the bases as well as call balls and strikes. Working part-time, she earned $1,000 a year, while 96 per cent of American working men earned less than $2,000 a year working full-time. She used the money she earned by umpiring to put herself through college.[96]

In 1890, promoter W.S. Franklin put together a team of what he called "bright and buxom" young women ballplayers, known as the Young Ladies Baseball Club #1. They played against men's town, semiprofessional and minor league professional teams across the country, usually winning easily.[97] They won in part because there were many talented women on the team, but also because early women's teams like this one used a few talented male players who actually wore wigs and dressed like women, usually to pitch, catch, and play shortstop. In fact, two Hall of Fame major leaguers started their baseball careers disguised as "bright and buxom" women. One was pitcher Smokey Joe Woods, the second was none other than second baseman Rogers Hornsby who later went on to compile the highest single-season batting average in twentieth century major league history in 1924, hitting .424.[98]

"Josie Caruso," whose real name was Josephine Parodi, played first base on a male semiprofessional team. She was so pretty and full-bosomed that she attracted a photographer and became a national celebrity when she appeared in a newsreel shown in theaters across the country. Although she was said to have played first base as well as any man, she played only three years before leaving the game to marry and have children.[99] During the early 1900s, several other women were such talented baseball players that they played on men's semiprofessional and professional teams. In 1903, Maud Nelson pitched against a man's team; in five innings, she had three hits of her own and struck out seven. Alta Weiss was a star pitcher for a men's team in Ohio from 1907 to 1922. She had a fastball, curve, knuckleball, sinker, and spitball. A trim, attractive woman, she chewed gum to stimulate her saliva for the spitball. Like her father, she went on to become a medical doctor.

Lizzie Murphy, the daughter of a mill hand, played first base professionally both with and against men from 1918 to 1935. In 1922, she played against major league teams in benefit games at least twice. During the 1930s, 5 foot, 7 inch, 130-pound pitcher, Virnie Beatrice "Jackie" Mitchell, played for a minor league men's team, as well as the House of David, a famous men's barnstorming team. In 1931, she pitched in an exhibition game against the New York Yankees, using her "mean drop pitch" to strike out Babe Ruth and Lou Gehrig back to back. In his customary autocratic manner, Commissioner Landis promptly banned her from professional baseball, insisting that women were too frail to play the game, but she continued to play semiprofessional baseball for years. During the 1930s and 1940s, several other women played briefly for minor league teams. As recently as 1948, "Bullet" Betty Evans created a sensation when she struck out six of nine Portland batters in the men's Triple-A Pacific Coast League.[100]

In 1934, promoters offered Mildred Ella "Babe" Didrikson, the daughter of Norwegian immigrant parents, $500 a night, a large sum of money at that time, to pitch in minor league exhibition games. Didrikson was a faster runner that most men—she was a double gold-medal winner in track at the 1932 Olympics—and she could also hit with power, as her nickname, "Babe," indicated. But even though she could throw a baseball over 300 feet, she was not a skilled pitcher and was hit hard. She soon gave up baseball for a great career as a professional golfer.

Dorothy Kamenshek, who played on a women's professional baseball team, was not simply outstanding by women's standards. Wally Pipp, the great-fielding New York Yankee first baseman, was in awe of her, declaring that she was the "fanciest-fielding first baseman I've ever seen, man or woman."[101]   In 1928, Margaret Gisolo played American Legion baseball on an otherwise all-male team. She played second base and pitched so well that a newspaper wrote, "She can hit, field and run better than most boys her age."[102]   In a seven-game tournament, she hit .429 and had 38 fielding plays without an error. The newspaper reporter added this: "Margaret Gisolo shined with unusual brilliance around the keystone sack, making two sensational catches of line drives, and featuring in one double play."[103]

Margaret became a national celebrity, with newspapers across the country carrying articles about her, and Movietone News prepared a sketch about her that appeared in newsreels in most theaters. The American Legion wasted no time in responding. It barred all girls from playing baseball claiming that it could not afford to pay for chaperones to protect all the women who wanted to follow in Gisolo's footsteps. Margaret was not the only girl to star on boys' baseball teams. Alice Backman became a star on a boys' high school team in Indiana, and a 15-year-old New Yorker, Carmel Yull, made the West Side Rangers team. And 5 foot, 10 inch, left-handed pitcher, Ila Borders, played on men's professional teams so skillfully that her jersey hangs in the Baseball Hall of Fame in Cooperstown.[104]   One sportswriter was so impressed that he wrote about these girls under this headline: "Girls Usurping National Sport: Suffrage Now Extends From Ballot Box to Baseball Diamonds."[105]

In 1943 with professional baseball's rosters decimated by the Second World War (90 percent of all major league players served in the military) Chicago Cubs owner P. K. Wrigley, and even President Roosevelt, feared that major league baseball might have to be suspended. To counter this threat, Wrigley decided to found what he called the All-American Girls' Softball League (AAGSBL) in Midwestern cities, in part to rekindle America's interest in baseball but also to boost the morale of factory workers in the war effort. He chose softball because he did not believe that women were athletic enough to play baseball, and softball in America had become so popular that in 1939 it was estimated that 60 million people watched softball games, 10 million more than watched baseball.[106]

Women who played softball at that time were seen by most people as masculine, even lesbians. Wrigley hoped to sell the AAGSBL as wholesome, all-American family entertainment. He recruited voluptuous players, made their uniform skirts short, barely covering red satin underpants, and had them attend a charm school with the famed Helena Rubenstein, where they learned to epitomize femininity.[107] They could not drink alcohol or smoke tobacco, had to wear lipstick and dress attractively at all times in public, and they were always accompanied by chaperones wearing navy blue uniforms like those then worn by airline hostesses. A fine of $50 was imposed on any woman who appeared "unkempt" in public. The chaperones were needed to overcome the promiscuous image created earlier by Maxie Rosenbloom's team known as Slapsie Maxie's Curvaceous Cuties and by Barney Ross's Adorables. AAGSBL teams had names such as the Racine Belles, Fort Wayne Daisies, Kalamazoo Lassies, Grand Rapids Chicks, Chicago Colleens, Springfield Sallies, and Rockford Peaches.

AAGPBL teams were managed by men including former major league manager Max Carey. To the surprise of Wrigley, these men encouraged their girls to play "hardball," not softball, and by 1947 they were pitching overhand with regulation baseballs from a regulation pitching distance on baseball-sized diamonds.[108]

During its twelve years of existence, over 500 players played in the league, always managed by men, and always competing fiercely.[109] These women played the game hard, often suffering painful "strawberries" from sliding hard, because of their bare legs. They played the game with dedication, and the routine of their lives was neither easy nor glamorous. As one recalled, "After a double-header, we'd shower, get dressed, travel all night in the bus, get to our hotel at 8 or 9 in the morning, shower, play two games of baseball in 110 degrees of heat, then do it all over again the next day."[110] The league drew one million paid attendance fans as late as 1948, but attendance soon dwindled, Wrigley lost interest, and the league folded in 1954. In 1992, a popular movie about the AAGPBL, *A League of Their Own,* featured Tom Hanks and Madonna.

Jennie Finch, a 6 foot, 1 inch thin blonde softball pitcher set an NCAA record in 2002 by winning 60 consecutive games for the University of Arizona. In the Pan Am Games of 2003, she beat Canada 1-0, giving up only one hit and striking out ten. Later that year, she put on pitching exhibitions at Southern California major league ballparks, pitching to major leaguers before games. Her fastball was consistently timed at 71 miles per hour, but from the softball mound only 43 feet from the plate, it was the equivalent of over 90 miles per hour, and it also rose dramatically. Ten major leaguers agreed to bat against her. Only one of them managed to hit so much as a ball fair. Los Angeles Dodger catcher, Paul Lo Duca, said, "She's nasty. I caught her in the bullpen...and I could barely catch it. It's just unbelievable how hard she throws from that distance."[111]

After Margaret Gisolo starred in Little League ball in 1928, Little League baseball was restricted to boys until 1974 when, after parents threatened a lawsuit, and the Little League again allowed girls to compete. Since that time, thousands of young girls have played Little League baseball along with boys. Many have done so superbly. In 1989, 9-year-old Brianne "Breezy" Stephenson pitched nine games for the Malden, Massachusetts "Mohawks." In 36 innings, she gave up no runs, only two hits and struck out 98 batters. She also batted an incredible .685 and hit 12 home runs.[112] However, by the late 1990s, there were only 8,000 girls in Little League, 28 girls for every 10,000 boys, and only 1,000 girls were playing Babe Ruth League Ball.[113]

Beginning in 1977, another woman, Pam Postema, umpired minor league men's baseball games for 13 years, the last six of them in the Triple-A Pacific Coast League. Although she was invited to umpire the annual Hall of Fame game at Cooperstown as well as major league spring-training games in 1988, she was not promoted to the major leagues and at year's end was released. In 1992, she published a book, *You've Got to Have Balls to Make It in This League,* in which she praised the several male umpires and a few players who had helped her. But her conclusion was embittered: "Almost all of the people in the baseball community don't want anyone disrupting their little male-dominated way of life. . . . And I'll never understand why it's easier for a female to become an astronaut or cop or firefighter or soldier or Supreme Court justice than it is to become a major league umpire."[114] Despite Postema's ordeal, there are now professional women's baseball leagues in several countries, including the United States, India, Australia, Hong Kong, Canada, and Japan, and women's teams play in international tournaments.

As a poet and baseball fan, Donald Hall wrote that baseball is fathers and sons playing catch. It is also fathers and sons sharing emotions about the game. Hall remembered a time, he thought it was in 1941, when he was in a car with his father and mother listening to Red Barber broadcast a crucial game between the Dodgers and Giants. Hunt's father was a devoted Dodgers fan, but his favorite player was the Giants' veteran left-handed pitcher, Carl Hubbell. The Dodgers were trailing when Hubbell entered the game, but Pee Wee Reese hit a home run, and the Dodgers won. Hunt, who was only 11 years old at the time, clapped and cheered: "Then I hear my father's strange voice. I look across my mother to see his knuckles white on the wheel, his face white, and I hear him saying, 'The punk! The punk!' With astonishment and horror, I see that my father is crying."[115] That is what baseball can mean to fathers and to sons. What it means to mothers and daughters today is less clear, but a bond is growing.

Older baseball fans will never forget managers like Connie Mack, John McGraw, Casey Stengel, Bucky Harris, and Leo Durocher, or owners like Branch Rickey, Clark Griffith, Bill Veeck, Philip Wrigley, Tom Yawkey, Horace Stoneham, and Walter O'Malley. No fan can forget the actions of Commissioner Kenesaw Mountain Landis, or even Happy Chandler, Bowie Kuhn, Ford Frick, or today's Allan H. "Bud" Selig. And, of course, there were many star players not mentioned here whose achievements will never be forgotten: Mickey Mantle, Roger Maris, Eddie Mathews, Duke Snider, Willie McCovey, Warren Spahn, Don Drysdale, Al Kaline, Harmon Killebrew, Willie Stargell, Maury Wills, Tom Seaver, Pete Rose, Stan Musial, Gil Hodges, Ralph Kiner, Rod Carew, Chuck Klein, Bob Lemon, Ted Lyons, Gaylord Perry, Mickey Cochrane, Charlie Gehringer, Dwight Gooden, Rollie Fingers, Dazzy Vance, Bill Dickey, Whitey Ford, Bill Terry, Jimmie Foxx, Goose Goslin, Joe Morgan, Jim Palmer, Gurt Gowdy, Mike Schmidt, Steve Carlton, Lefty Grove, Carl Yastrzemski, Larry Doby, Red Schoendienst, Yogi Berra, and Johnny Bench. The list is endless. And the list of Hall of Fame members includes over 100 additional names. In his book, <u>My Prison without Bars</u>, published in January, 2004, baseball's all-time leader in base hits, Pete Rose, admitted that he had bet on games he had played in or managed. The book became an immediate bestseller, but his confession is unlikely to lead to his admission to the Hall of Fame, as he had apparently hoped.

Home run records like those of Mark McGuire and Barry Bonds fascinate fans, and so do no-hit pitching performances. Few older fans will forget the "shot heard round the world" in 1951 when New York Giant Bobby Thomson hit a ninth-inning three-run homerun to turn an apparent 4-2 Giants loss into a 5-4 win over the Brooklyn Dodgers for the National League pennant. Football may well capture the interest of more Americans than baseball does. In 1985, professional football edged out baseball as America's most popular sport by 24 percent to 23 percent; today, that margin has risen to 27 percent for football against only 14 percent for baseball.[116] Yet, baseball attendance has grown despite the fact that fans were horrified and angered by the baseball strikes of 1972 and another in 1981 that cancelled half the season and that year's World Series. In 2001, almost 33 million fans attended American League regular season games, and 37 million attended National League regular season games. Hundreds of thousands more attended divisional playoff and World Series games. Almost 30 million more paid their way in to see games played by the more than 100 minor league teams in cities across the United States and parts of Canada. It is not known how many people watched games on television. And attendance rose slightly in 2002, 2003, 2004, and 2005.

Baseball is so much a part of American culture that even youngsters know and use its jargon. A good fielder can "really pick it." Legs are "wheels." A bad fielder has "bad hands" or "stone hands." A hard line drive is a "frozen rope" or a "blue darter." "Hose" means arm, "tweener" is a ball hit between fielders, "loosen him up" means to throw a pitch inside on a batter, and "chin music" is a pitch thrown near a batter's chin. When a coach or manager tells a player to sit down, he is likely to say, "go grab some bench," and when a pitcher seems to be losing his command, a coach may shout, "Have an idea out there!" A pop fly that falls in for a hit is a "bloop" or a "Texas-leaguer," an error is a "boot" or a "muff," a base-on-balls is a "free pass," and a strike out is a "whiff." Third base is the "hot corner," a left-handed pitcher is a "southpaw," a catcher is a "backstop," to "lay one down" is to bunt, and a "can of corn" is a high flyball that is easily caught. Players and fans alike resort to all manner of lucky rituals to ensure victory. Players all know that it is bad luck to step on a foul line while taking the field or leaving it. Pitchers often touch the rosin bag before every pitch or pull the bill of their cap. And batters warm up in highly ritualized fashion. Players and fans alike also try to control the game's outcome by the clothes they wear or the food they eat.[117]

Early in the twentieth century, as many kids played ball in the alleys of big city tenements as on actual diamonds. Today, there are diamonds almost everywhere across the country, even in big cities. And although youngsters still play catch with their fathers and other children of their age, before they turn 12 they can play in organized Little Leagues. When they grow too old for these leagues, there are Babe Ruth Leagues, American Legion teams and high school leagues. Most junior colleges and universities field teams, too, as do work-based semi-professional leagues and the armed forces. There are nearly 200 professional minor league teams with nearly 5,000 players and there are 750 major leaguers on 30 teams.

More than 200 of these 750 major league players are from Latin America, with others from Asia, Australia, Canada, Japan, and Korea. One big leaguer was even a Basque. Basques from the Pyrenees in France and Spain came to California in large numbers in 1849 as part of the Gold Rush. Few found gold, and most of the population moved to Southern California, where they became successful sheep herders. Later, they also became ranchers, dairy farmers, and all sorts of businessmen. Their most cherished sport was handball, and courts were built all over Southern California.[118] However, some Basques also played baseball, and one of them, Andy Etchebarren, became the starting catcher for the Baltimore Orioles in the 1960s.

During the winter of 2002, the New York Yankees signed Japan's star outfielder and power hitter, Hideki Matsui, along with Cuba's defecting star pitcher, Alex Contreras, to huge, multi-year contracts. In 2002, *Baseball America* listed the top 30 minor league prospects for each major league team. Of these 900 prospects described, 204 were from foreign countries. The Dominican Republic led with 118, Venezuela was next with 41, followed by Mexico with 10, Australia and Korea with 9 each, Taiwan and Japan with 5 each , Puerto Rico and the Netherlands Antilles with 2 each, and Nicaragua, New Zealand, and Cuba with 1 apiece, the Cuban being a defector.[119] As these numbers so eloquently tell us, the American game has reached out to players from many other countries. And as we shall see, it has taken root in these countries with exceptional vigor.

What *Baseball America* wrote in 1908 came to reflect the feelings of people in many parts of the world:

Baseball's chief clutch on the heartstrings of its devotees is the fact that it is played on the square, first, last and all the time. Baseball is an honest game. It is a clean game, played by little boys on the corner lots, and big boys on the well-kept grounds of the various leagues. It is played out in the sunshine where the blue sky looks down on the green grass....Baseball is our one best pastime. We play it when schoolboys. We go to see it when we come to middle age. We send our boys and our office boys when we are grown old and fat and gouty. And when we have crossed The Home Plate, as some day we must, and when the children of our children fill the stands where once we cheered, perhaps our spirits shall be spectators.[120]

And we should not ignore the fact that while the average salary of a major league player in 1920 was only about $5,000, in the year 2003, it was $2.5 million! Philadelphia Phillies outfielder Pat Burrell hit .282 with 37 home runs and 116 runs-batted-in in 2002, a fine but hardly sensational record. On February 3, 2003, he signed a $50 million, six-year contract. In 2002, the New York Yankees major league payroll was a record-setting $138 million. In 2003, this amount increased to over $150 million. In that same year, Atlanta Braves pitcher Greg Maddux earned $14.75 million, and the Boston Red Sox star pitcher, Pedro Martinez, earned $17.5 million in 2004. Sammy Sosa has a four-year contract worth $70.5 million, almost $18 million per season. But Sosa's salary pales in comparison to that of Boston Red Sox outfielder Manny Ramirez, who has an eight-year contract at $20 million per year and Detroit's outfielder, Maglio Ordoñez, who has a five-year contract for $75 million. Super-star Texas Ranger shortstop Alex Rodriguez had a ten-year contract at $25.2 million a year, even before he was traded to the Yankees in 2004. And, most remarkable of all, in 2005, 41-year-old left-handed pitcher Randy Johnson signed a two-year contract extension with the New York Yankees for $32 million.

Baseball in the United States major leagues is an impressive success story for its players and their families. Players are not only idolized by many fans, they are paid lavishly. But what about the rest of the world? As we will see, there is tremendous variation in how the game is played, how fans enjoy it, and how players benefit financially and psychologically from their efforts. We begin our exploration of global baseball by looking at baseball in Asia.

64

[1] Springwood (1996: 38).

[2] Burk (1994: 204).

[3] Ibid., p. 223.

[4] Ibid.

[5] Durant (1973: 31).

[6] Astor (1988: 15); Appel (1996); Reilly (2000: 6).

[7] Durant (1973 32).

[8] Fleitz (2002).

[9] Sutton-Smith and Rosenberg (1961).

[10] Astor (1988: 71).

[11] Ritter (1966).

[12] Ibid.

[13] Wallop (1969: 131).

[14] Astor (1988: 84).

[15] Ibid.

[16] Ibid.; Levy (2000).

[17] Ibid., p. 49.

[18] Gerlach (1998).

[19] Ibid., p. 91.

[20] Burk (2001: 308).

[21] Ibid., p. 91.

[22] Astor (1988: 92).

[23] Astor (1988: 130).

[24] Ibid., p. 135.

[25] Wallop (1969: 90-91).

[26] Rader (1992: 85).

[27] Collier's, April 4, 1914, p. 9.

[28] Elfers (2003).

[29] Wallop (1969: 100-101).

[30] Alexander (1991: 128).

[31] Rader (1992: 105).

[32] Wallop (1969: 177).

[33] Tygiel (2000: 65).

[34] Creamer (1974: 320).

[35] Wallop (1969: 189).

[36] Creamer (1974: 29).

[37] Baseball Magazine, June, 1939, p.29.

[38] Robinson (1991).

[39] Alexander (2002: 297).

[40] Alexander (1991: 157).

[41] Obojski (1980: 1).

[42] Alexander (2002: 15).

[43] New York World Telegram, June 5, 1934.

[44] Durant (1973: 189).

[45] Burk (2001: 55).

[46] Durant (1973: 104).

[47] Bullock (2000: 83).

[48] Stars and Stripes (Mediterranean Edition), March 11, 1944.

[49] White (1996: 262-263).

[50] Gendin (1998: 25).

[51] Zang (1995: 45).

[52] Ibid. p. 85.

[53] Riess (1999: 192).

[54] Powers-Beck (2001).

[55] Chadwick (1992: 29).

[56] Bjarkman (1994: 1).

[57] Ibid., p. 19.

[58] Rader (1992: 6).

[59] Rogosin (1983: 25).

[60] Ribowsky (1994).

[61] Ibid., p. 15.

[62] Wallop (1969: 218).

[63] Holway (1988: 61).

[64] Chadwick (1992).

[65] Ribowsky (1994).

[66] Chadwick (1992).

[67] Ibid.

[68] Ibid., p.167.

[69] Adelson (1999: 20).

[70] Burk (2001: 237).

[71] Ardell (2001: 185).

[72] Ibid.

[73] Veeck and Linn (1965).

[74] Veeck (1962: 172).

[75] Golenbock (1998: 14).

[76] Mann (1957: 216).

[77] Dreier (2001: 44).

[78] Pettavino and Pye (1994: 33).

[79] Rader (1992: 142); Gerlach (1998).

[80] Gerlach (1998).

[81] Golenbock (1998: 16).

[82] Ibid.

[83] Durocher and Linn (1975: 205).

[84] Kahn (2001: 40).

[85] New York Times, August 11, 1946, p.12.

[86] Burk (2001:102); Norwood and Brackman (1999).

[87] Dreier (2001: 40).

[88] Golenbock (1998: 20).

[89] Dreier (2001).

[90] Rogosin (1983: 217).

[91] Rampersad (1997).

[92] Ibid., p. 62.

[93] Hall (1976).

[94] Gregorich (1993: 3).

[95] Thorn (1974: 18).

[96] Gregorich (1993: 18-19).

[97] Berlage (2001: 240).

[98] Ibid., p. 240-241.

[99] Berlage (1994: 58).

[100] Beale (1957: 29).

[101] Ibid., p. 92.

[102] Berlage (1994: 94).

[103] Ibid.

[104] Christian Science Monitor, August 31, 1999.

[105] Berlage (1994: 95).

[106] Ibid., p. 244.

[107] Ibid.

[108] Pratt (1993: 53).

[109] Ibid., p. 56.

[110] Berlage (1994: 141).

[111] Los Angeles Times, August 8, 2003, D1, 13.

[112] Gregorich (1993: 205).

[113] Light (1997: 793).

[114] Gregorich (1993: 196).

[115] Hunt (1985: 32-33).

[116] Baseball America, December 22, 2002, p. 3.

[117] Gmelch (1999).

[118] Eagle (1979).

[119] Collis and Lingo (2002).

[120] Wallop (1969: 51).

Chapter Three: Baseball in Asia

During the latter part of the nineteenth century, both the British and Americans insisted with all their might that devotion to vigorous sporting activities—a life of "manly vigor" as many of them put it—was the key to "true national greatness," as Theodore Roosevelt declared.[1] Earlier, the Duke of Wellington had assured the world that the battle of Waterloo had been won on the playing fields of Eton, where sporting contests like football and rugby had honed the self-reliance, strength, endurance, and courage of male Britons. Americans of all sorts ascribed the same manly attributes to playing the game of baseball.

When U.S. Commodore Matthew Calbraith Perry's so-called "Black Ships" forced Japanese ports to open to Western trade in 1853, the Western world beheld a physically small people who, except for a few muskets and ancient brass cannons, were armed only with swords. During her nearly 300 years of feudal isolation from Western and Christian influence, Japan had destroyed her navy, as well as her firearms, in an attempt to disarm the common people who were seen by the Samurai as threatening their rule. Faced first by American, and later, by British ships with powerful cannons, along with sailors and marines armed with deadly rifles, Japan had no choice but to open six of her coastal ports in the Yokohama area near Tokyo to European trade. While the Meiji Restoration attempted to once again acquire Western weaponry and technology, not only could American, British, and other European ships recoal in these ports, they were also able to sell their goods there. Many Europeans, most of them from Britain, flocked to these ports as residents, merchants, military personnel, and visitors who had complete authority over all civil and criminal matters in those places. Within ten years, they had built homes, hotels, shops, "international" sporting clubs, public parks with lawns for croquet, and playing fields for cricket and baseball.[2]

As soon as they arrived, the white men in these so-called "treaty ports" devoted themselves to sports with apparently even more zest than they had displayed at home. Whether the sports were crew, rifle shooting, cricket, tennis, or baseball, the Britons and Americans engaged in them with a vigor that they believed made Japanese sporting customs and activities seem feeble by comparison. It was commonplace for these Europeans to look down upon the Japanese as not only a small people, but also a pusillanimous one. They were seen as a nation whose men flew kites, studied flower arrangement, enjoyed toy gardens, and carried fans. They were disparaged by Europeans as "effeminate."[3] Clearly, the whites sniffed, the Japanese were incapable of excelling in manly team sports like rugby or baseball.[4]

Albert G. Spalding spoke for most Americans when he wrote that baseball had "all the attributes of American origin [and] American character"; indeed, he said, it was "the exponent of American Courage, Confidence, Combativeness, American Dash, Discipline, Determination; American Energy, Eagerness, Enthusiasm . . . ; American Vim, Vigor, Virility."[5] To play baseball, in other words, was to exude those manly virtues that were singularly characteristic of the United States.

Despite this widespread contempt for Japanese athletic abilities, early in the 1870s a young American named Horace Wilson, who was a professor at a Japanese university in Tokyo, not a resident of a Yokohama treaty port, taught baseball to Japanese students who initially played in kimonos and wooden sandals and called the game *beisu boru* and *yakyu*.[6] While Americans played baseball on their Yokohama treaty-port diamonds unaware of any Japanese interest in their sport of choice, an Englishman, F. William Strange, who had become enthused about baseball, also taught the game to his students at Tokyo University. Strange became the first person to write down the rules of baseball for the Japanese in a book entitled *Outdoor Games*. His book championed baseball as the national game of the American people, one that demanded "mental ability" and "manly qualities." Despite Strange's endorsement, baseball did not become terribly popular among the Japanese until the 1890s.

Even before baseball was played in Japan, it was being introduced in China. In 1836, Massachusetts merchants in Canton formed the "Union" baseball club, which played against British residents.[7] As early as 1863, the Shanghai Base Ball Club was formed by the few hundred Americans living there. In 1872, at the urging of Rong Hong, a Chinese Mandarin who had graduated from Yale, the Qing Dynasty sent a group of 120 male students to study in what was called the Chinese Educational Mission in Connecticut, where they lived with local American families and went to school to learn Western science and the English language as part of China's so-called "self-strengthening movement." Wearing ankle-length, brocaded silk gowns and their hair in long queues, as Confucian scholars of that time were required to do in order to demonstrate loyalty to their Manchu rulers, they immediately became objects of derision by American boys. In response, the Chinese students not only adopted American culture and clothing, they also formed what they called the "Orientals" baseball club and began to play the game with great zest and skill. Eventually, one of their supervisors wrote to the Chinese government complaining not only about the students' Americanization but also their growing rejection of Chinese culture.[8] He was distressed because they had not only played baseball, but they had also shed their silk robes, cut off their queues, and had begun to dress and behave like Americans.

To prevent them from becoming even more Americanized, the students of the Chinese Educational Mission were summoned home from the United States in 1881. The American-educated students who returned to China introduced a modern navy and sophisticated shipbuilding techniques, the long-distance telegraph, special mining skills, and the Beijing-to-Mongolia railway, an engineering marvel. On their journey home, they stopped in San Francisco. While they were waiting for a ship to take them home to China, an all-Caucasian

Oakland baseball team tauntingly challenged them to a game. "But the Oakland nine got the shock of their lives as soon as they attempted to connect with the deliveries of the Chinese pitcher; the fans were equally surprised at the strange phenomenon—Chinese playing their national game . . . Unimaginable! All the same, the Chinese walloped them, to the great rejoicing of their comrades and fellow countrymen."[9] The Americans were simply stunned. By 1895, three schools in China—St. John's University of Shanghai, Tongzhou College of Beijing, and Huiwen College of Beijing—had organized baseball programs, and they competed against one another.

In 1873, while the Chinese were learning baseball in America, Albert Bates, an American teacher at Kaitaku University in Tokyo, organized the first formal baseball game in Japan. Players ran the bases in wooden sandals.[10] Five years later, railway engineer Hiroshi Hiraoka, an ardent Boston Red Sox fan from his days as a student in the United States, organized the first Japanese baseball team, the Shinbashi Athletic Club Athletics. Students at a number of elite preparatory schools for Japan's national university became entranced with baseball and devoted themselves to mastering the necessary skills to excel at it. In 1891, the most prestigious of these schools—First High School (Ichikō) of Tokyo—challenged the Americans of the Yokohama Athletic Club to a game of baseball. The Americans not only arrogantly refused to play the Japanese for five consecutive years, they rudely derided the Japanese youngsters as culturally and physically incapable of contesting a game with them.

One of the Ichikō students wrote, "'The foreigners in Yokohama have established an athletic field in their central park into which no Japanese may enter. There, playing by themselves, they boast of their skill in baseball. When we attempt to challenge them, they refuse, saying, 'Baseball is our national game' or 'Our bodies are twice the size of yours.'"[11] This kind of insulting rejection only made the Japanese students more determined. Ordered to "practice until you die," as they put it, they frenziedly engaged in day-long practices that came to be called "bloody urine" because players would actually vomit blood or pass blood in their urine.[12] They were not allowed to smoke, drink beer, date girls, or even swim, an activity that was thought to develop the wrong muscles. Undaunted, they continued their all-day practicing as well as their challenges to the Americans, and five years later, thanks to the intervention of an American teacher of English at Ichikō, W. B. Mason, the Americans agreed to a game in May 1896.

When the young Japanese arrived for their game on the Yokohama field, many American spectators greeted them with jeers and howls. Although so shaken by this rude reception that they appeared to be bumblers during the pre-game warm-up, when the game began the Japanese youngsters quickly dominated the older American players, thrashing them by the shocking score of 29-4 while the American spectators sat in stunned disbelief. After the game, the Ichikō students returned home to a raucous welcome, complete with *banzai* chants, loud choruses of the national anthem, and overflowing cups of *sake*. The student president proclaimed, "This great victory is more than a victory for our school; it is a victory for the Japanese people!"[13] Thanks to widespread Japanese newspaper coverage, the Ichikō boys were instant national heroes.

A few days later, the Americans demanded a rematch. Bolstered by players from the crews of two American destroyers that were anchored nearby, the American men again met the Ichikō boys on the Yokohama field. Once again, the Japanese routed the Americans, this time by a score of 32-9. As before, the Ichikō players were grandly fêted by a huge throng of fans and praised by an adoring press. While the Japanese celebrated, the Americans made excuses, claiming that unlike the older Americans who had to work during the day, the Japanese school boys had ample time to practice. They also argued that the "spare figures" of the Japanese gave them an unfair advantage. Paradoxically, what had long been a sign of Japanese physical weakness had now become an asset![14]

An Ichikō student writing in the 1896 annual report of the Ichikō Baseball Club, demonstrated the intensity of feeling about baseball among the Japanese: "'The Americans are proud of baseball as their national game just as we have been proud of judo and kendo. Now, however, in a place far removed from their native land, they have fought against a 'little people' whom they ridicule as childish, only to find themselves swept away like falling leaves. No words can describe their disgraceful conduct. The aggressive character of our national spirit is a well-established fact, demonstrated by the Sino-Japanese War (which Japan had crushingly won) and now by our great victories in baseball'."[15]

Later that same month, the Americans in Yokohama sent a team exclusively composed of sailors from the cruiser U.S.S. *Detroit*, to play a game on the Ichikō campus, where the sailors were startled to find nearly 10,000 spectators squeezed together around the ballfield. Both Japanese and American dignitaries attended as well. With bands playing and the crowd roaring, the Japanese boys thumped the embarrassed Americans 22-6. Thoroughly humiliated, the Americans next put together a team of sailors from several ships including the U.S. Navy's flagship, the battleship U.S.S. *Kentucky*. One of the sailors on this team had previously played baseball professionally, and the Americans won a spirited contest, 14-12. This time, the American spectators applauded the Japanese sincerely, and the Japanese were pleased. From 1897 to 1904, the Yokohama Americans and Japanese high school students would meet in nine more games, with the Japanese losing only one of these, a close 6 to 5 game. One Japanese victory was 4-0, while two others saw scores of 34-1 and 27-0.[16]

The following triumphant lyric was adopted as Ichikō's fight song:

Among the literary and martial arts pursued
In the righteous air of First Higher School,
Baseball stands especially high
With its spirit of honor that refused to die.

. . . Enduring all hardships, we practice the game
While the years have seen many a foe.
Come to our schoolyard where strong winds blow
Upon touching the sleeves of our armored knights.
We turn them away, speechless with fright.
The valorous sailors from the Detroit, Kentucky, and Yokohama
Whose furious batting can intimidate a cyclone
Threw off their helmets, their energies depleted
Behold how pathetically they run away defeated.
Courageously, we marched twenty miles south
To fight the Americans in Yokohama
Though they boast of the game as their national sport
Behold the games they have left with no score.

Ah, for the glory of our Baseball Club!
Ah, for the glitter it has cast!
Pray that our martial valor never turns submissive
And that our honor will always shine far across the Pacific.[17]

After the Russo-Japanese War ended in 1905 with devastating Japanese victories in battle, but frustrating losses at peace talks held in the United States, several Japanese university teams, including those from Waseda and Keio University, were invited to visit America and play American college teams on the West Coast while teams from the Universities of Washington and Wisconsin, as well as Stanford University and the University of Chicago, visited Japan. The teams from Washington and Wisconsin had been badly defeated, so before the team from Chicago left for Japan, they practiced harder than ever. They landed in Yokohama in a pouring rain, but a large crowd was there to welcome them. The players rode rickshaws to the station, where they took a train to Tokyo. After practicing for several days before throngs of kimono-clad spectators, the Americans played their first game against a team from Waseda University. The crowd rose to salute them, then settled back on their heels to watch the game. There were no women among them, as it was not considered proper for women to attend baseball games.

The games in Tokyo were hard-fought, but the players were friendly and the spectators applauded good plays by the Americans. The Chicago University team won all seven games before taking a train 250 miles south to Osaka, where they were welcomed by a brass band, then grandly received with receptions, dinners, banquets, dances, and theater parties. Crowds of about 30,000 watched the Americans play three games against Keio University. Again the Americans won every game. The Japanese spectators waved to the Americans as they steamed out of Kobe harbor on their way home, a huge crowd cheered, and a band played "Auld Lang Syne."[18]

Baseball spread elsewhere in Asia as well. In 1879, Dr. Sun Yat-Sen went to college in Hawaii where he learned to play baseball. He later taught the game to his revolutionary Chinese troops. In 1906, baseball was first played in Korea by YMCA staff and students of the German Language Institute. One year later, China's first official intercollegiate game was played in Beijing between Tongzhou and Huiwen universities. The following year, a team comprised of major leaguers and players from the Triple-A Pacific Coast League toured Japan to promote the Reach Sporting Goods Company. The American professionals won all 17 of the games that they played against Japanese college teams. In 1909, 25 Korean students studying in Tokyo formed a baseball club while home on leave and handily defeated a team of foreign missionaries. The following year, the University of Chicago baseball team traveled to the Philippines and won three of four games against local squads.

That same year, a game between Hansong High School and Hwangsong Christian School became known as the official "foundation" of Korean baseball. The game was umpired by an American and a Japanese and was watched by a crowd large enough to convince Korean newspaper reporters that baseball had moved from a fringe activity to a mainstream sport. Two years later, in 1911, Sun Yat-sen's Chinese revolutionary party, the Tongmenghui, organized a baseball association in Changsha, the capital of Hunan Province, on the eve of the Chinese Revolution. The so-called Changsha baseball team served, among other things, as a cover to teach young men how to throw hand grenades. As early as 1913, baseball had spread across much of China, and some teams played in international tournaments.

In 1912, Waseda University sent the first Japanese collegiate baseball team to visit the Philippines. Waseda, a perennial powerhouse in Japan, won only two of five games in the Philippines. The following year, the New York Giants and Chicago White Sox played three games in Japan on the first leg of their famous world tour, and they went on to play in the Philippines, China, and Hong Kong. In 1914, the first Far Eastern Games were held in Manila. Baseball was part of the competition, and Japan won the championship. At the same time, an American missionary, Willard L. Nash, serving as director of physical education at China's Suzhou University, helped organize six schools into the East China Intercollegiate Athletic Association. St. John's of Shanghai won the baseball championship the first year. From 1923 to 1927, St. John's sent teams to compete in Japan. At this time, Liang Fuchu went to school in Japan, where he learned baseball before returning to China to found a team he called the "Pandas." In the 1950s, Marshal He appointed him to coach newly formed teams of Mao Zedong's People's Liberation Army.

In 1917, Japan won the baseball competition at the third Far Eastern Games in Tokyo. In 1919, the Philippines won the baseball medal at the fourth Far Eastern Games in Manila. It was the first of four consecutive baseball titles that the Philippines would win. Japan won in 1927, but the Philippines won again at the 1930 Far Eastern Games in Tokyo. In 1922, a team of future Hall of Famers, including Casey Stengel, Herb Pennock, and Waite Hoyt, became the first American professional team to lose to the Japanese when they were beaten 9-3 by the Mita Club. The following year, the University of Chicago team toured Japan, winning seven games and losing seven. Their coach, Nels Norgren, commented that baseball was "more the national sport of Japan than it is of America," a remark that would become famous.[19]

In 1927, the Royal Giants from the Negro League toured Japan and went 23-0-1. How the black Americans were treated by the vanquished Japanese is not recorded. During 1931, Hall of Famers Lou Gehrig, Frankie Frisch, Lefty Grove, Rabbit Maranville, and Mickey Cochrane were among the Major League All Stars who compiled a 17-0 record on a tour of Japan. In 1934, Babe Ruth joined a team touring Japan sponsored by the newspaper *Yomiuri Shimbun*. Sixty-five thousand fans thronged Jingu Stadium in Tokyo to see the first game. Although the aging Ruth was nearing the end of his career with the Yankees, he hit 14 homers during the tour, batted .408 and his team won all 16 games. A middle-aged Japanese man walked 80 miles to watch the U.S. team play the All-Nippon Stars. He carried a Samurai sword that he intended to present to the first U.S. player who hit a home run. Earl Averil, not Ruth, won the sword.[20]

The highlight for Japanese fans was when a Japanese pitcher, Eiji Sawamura, struck out Charlie Gehringer, Babe Ruth, Lou Gehrig, and Jimmie Foxx in succession. Sawamura, who was outspokenly anti-American, later visited the United States and was offered a contract by the Pittsburgh Pirates. He refused, saying:

My problem is I hate America and I cannot make myself like Americans. I'm not good at the language, I can't eat as much rice as I wish when I'm there, and the women are too haughty. In America, you can not even tie your shoestrings if there is a woman around. People like myself cannot possibly survive in an environment where such uncomfortable customs exist.[21]

Sawamura was killed in World War II during the Battle of the Ryukyus when the ship on which he served was torpedoed by an American submarine.

In 1924, a two-week national high school tournament was initiated in Japan with each of the country's 47 prefectures entering a team. The tournament quickly became immensely popular. Today, while mini-skirted pom-pom girls lead fans in cheers, young high school fans scream emotionally for their team, and parents shout as well. Many others sit at home, in coffee shops, or tea rooms, watching the televised games. For the past decade, close to one million fans have attended games in this tournament each year.[22] Said to be the "ultimate crucible of youth," the tournament's games were played in the steel and concrete Koshien Stadium. The stadium was called the "temple of purity," while the ballfield itself was considered to be nothing less than sacred. The first national high school tournament game played in Koshien Stadium drew 85,000 fans.[23]

Japanese girls and women were slow to take up baseball. In 1892, the Bloomer Girls toured Japan, although there were no Japanese women's teams, and they had to play against men's teams. In 1925, another women's team, the Philadelphia Bobbies, toured Japan, also playing against men's teams. They lost badly, and crowds dwindled so greatly that they could not earn enough money to pay their way home. A British philanthropist eventually paid their fares to America but, during a storm, one of the women was swept overboard, and no trace of her was ever found.[24]

Tours of Japan by United States men's teams continued, however, and one of these teams featured Boston Red Sox catcher Morris "Moe" Berg who, although raised in a poor Ukrainian immigrant family, had received a B.A. from Princeton, studied at the Sorbonne, then completed a law degree at Columbia, finishing second in his class. In addition to his athletic skills, he was nothing less than a genius with languages, speaking 12 of them well, including Sanskrit and Japanese. His Japanese was so fluent that he once corrected a Japanese reporter's grammar. Despite this embarrassment, the Japanese press loved him.[25] Just before World War II, he spied on Japan during a baseball tour of the country. Berg went to St. Luke's Hospital in Tokyo, one of the tallest buildings in the city, ostensibly to visit a patient, but instead he climbed onto the roof and photographed the city with his 16-millimeter movie camera. He made this film available to Colonel Doolittle for planning his famous retaliatory bombing raid on the city soon after the Japanese attack on Pearl Harbor, but it is unclear how useful the film proved to be.[26]

In 1936, the Japanese Professional League was formed. One of these teams, the Tokyo Giants, came to the United States for part of their spring training and played two games in April against Tulsa. In 1941, a few months before the attack on Pearl Harbor, the militarists who controlled the Japanese government tried to disband Japan's professional league after just 84 games. In their eyes, baseball had suddenly become an American game that was anti-Japanese and should be closed down.[27] They also insisted that nicknames such as "Tigers," "Giants," and "Senators" be removed from players' jerseys and replaced by Japanese names. Nevertheless, the game continued in Japan through most of 1944, ending only late that year when American fire-bombing became too intense to permit fans to safely attend the games.

During the war years of 1941 to1945, baseball was also played across war torn Asia by U.S. troops and among U.S. captives in Japanese prisoner of war camps. After the war, baseball soon returned to Japanese cities. Using a vast secret fund of cash and valuables the Japanese army had seized throughout Asia, General Douglas MacArthur cleaned out and repaired Japanese baseball stadiums, built new ones, and channeled money to potential baseball magnates.[28] The game once again began to flourish, and some Japanese teams once again called themselves "Giants" and "Tigers."[29]

In 1949, Lefty O'Doul led the San Francisco Seals of the Pacific Coast League on a ten-game tour of Japan. The Seals won nine of ten games and attracted 430,000 fans. Many, including General MacArthur, believed that the O'Doul tour had broken postwar tension and created a new basis for friendship between the two countries.[30] The following year, Japanese professional baseball adopted a two-league system modeled on the U.S. major leagues.[31] The Central League, dominated by the Yomiuri Giants, was opposed by the Pacific League. Japanese women began to play the game after the war, and in 1949 the Romance Bluebirds, a women's professional baseball team, was formed. Currently, over 200 female baseball teams play in high school, college, and recreational leagues in Japan. There is also a national women's team, Team Energen, that has played superbly in international competition.

Foreign players entered Japanese baseball as well. In 1952, the St. Louis Browns lent two black minor league players to the Hankyu Braves of the Japanese Pacific League. The Harlem Globetrotters sent third-baseman John Britton and pitcher Jim Newberry to Japan in a "lend-lease" deal that benefited both Japan and the United States. Soon, each Japanese team was permitted to sign three foreign "imports," and almost all teams did so. Currently, there are 60 foreign players on Japanese major league rosters, most of them from the United States.

Other Asian countries also expanded their baseball activities. In Maoist China in 1959, more than 30 provincial, military, and city teams took part in the first New China Baseball Tournament. In 1963, Korea established itself as a force in baseball by defeating Japan to win the fifth Asian Amateur Baseball Championship. In 1964, Masanori Murakami became the first Japanese-born player to reach the American major leagues when he made the roster of the San Francisco Giants. In 1969, Taiwan competed in the Little League World Series for the first time, and they astonished their opponents by winning the championship. In 1974, the San Francisco Giants signed Tan Shin-ming, a Taiwanese pitcher. He pitched that season for the Class-A Fresno Giants and was the first Taiwanese to play professionally in the United States. However, he was not able to advance to the major leagues.

Although the People's Liberation Army had come to love baseball, "The Great Leap Forward" of the early 1960s, followed by the "Cultural Revolution," temporarily put an end to organized baseball in China although some Red Guards played in secret, posting look-outs to be certain they were not seen.[32] In 1975, baseball was officially "rehabilitated" in China after the Cultural Revolution. The People's Republic of China hosted its first official baseball tournament, the Beijing International, for 11- and 12-year-old boys. After the 1984 Olympic Games, China decided that it wanted to play baseball in the 1988 Olympics. Its first problem was the lack of an appropriate field for play and a stadium for fans. In response to a Chinese government request in 1984, the Los Angeles Dodger's owner, Peter O'Malley, visited the proposed site for this field at Tianjin, 60 miles southeast of Beijing. O'Malley not only volunteered to pay for the field's construction, he also sent two of the Dodgers' coaches to China to teach baseball. The following spring several Chinese coaches and players were invited to the Dodgers' spring training camp at Vero Beach, Florida.[33] The O'Malley field, which would be used exclusively for baseball, was completed in 1986. A four-league system was established for ages 9-11 ("dragon's tail"), 12-15 ("dragon's belly"), 16-19 ("dragon's belly-upper") and adults ("dragon's head"). Play was well under way by 1991 when the Asian Games were held, but China finished fifth, failing to qualify for the Barcelona Olympic Games of 1992.[34]

In 1988, the Tokyo Dome with a retractable roof opened, modeled after the Metrodome in Minnesota. Two years later, the Chinese Professional Baseball League began play in Taiwan, and North Korea was accepted for membership in the International Baseball Association. In 1992, a team from the Philippines won the Little League World Series at Williamsport, Pennsylvania, but was disqualified three weeks later for using illegal players. It was found that the manager and at least 8 of the 14 team members had been recruited from outside Zamboanga, the area they were supposed to represent. What is more, many of the Philippines' Little League and Pony League players were found to be above the age limit. In 1993, the Los Angeles Dodgers visited Taiwan for a three-game friendship series. In the same year, ten teams in Thailand competed in that country's first baseball championship.

In 1994, Thailand and Mongolia made their international baseball debuts at the Asian Games in Hiroshima. These two countries had only begun to play baseball in 1991, after a Japanese cultural exchange group donated 2,000 used gloves to Mongolia and a Japanese-Thailand joint-venture company donated equipment to Thai boys. Neither country has a baseball stadium, but teams play the game frequently on soccer fields. Even though both Thailand and Mongolia were thrashed by huge scores in Hiroshima, Japanese schoolboy spectators, who were taken to the games on chartered buses, cheered them and waved small flags.

In 1994, Korean pitcher Chan Ho Park, who Westernized his name by putting his family name last, made the opening-day roster of the Los Angeles Dodgers. Park was the first native Korean to reach the major leagues. He is still pitching well for the Texas Rangers in the American League. The following year, the Dodgers signed Japanese star pitcher Hideo Nomo to a major league contract. Nomo went on to win the National League Rookie of the Year Award that year. After pitching well for the Dodgers, he went to the Boston Red Sox, then returned to Los Angeles, where he was once again a starting pitcher for the Dodgers. And left-handed pitcher Kazuhisa Ishii is still pitching well for the Dodgers.

Baseball began to be played in Hong Kong three decades ago, and today there are 25 to 30 adult teams and 25 youth teams. Games are played on soccer fields because there are no baseball fields.[35] Hong Kong teams compete against teams from China and Taiwan, and the game is growing in popularity. In 1988, a foundation was laid for Mongolia's first baseball stadium in Ulan Bator, and play soon followed. During the 1990s, baseball was played across much of China. In 1996, for the first time, a Japanese professional team traveled to China to play two games against the Chinese national team. Other Japanese teams later toured China as well, and the United States sent coaches there on several goodwill missions. In 2001, the Chinese Baseball League (CBL) was initiated in four large cities. Owned by the government, the CBL proposed to pay its players well and the CBL's games are carried on national television.[36] In 2002, Chao Wang, a 6 foot, 5 inch, 17-year-old pitcher, became the first Chinese-born player to be signed by an American major league team, the Seattle Mariners. His mother played fast-pitch softball, and his father played baseball. Several other Chinese players are being scouted by the Mariners.[37]

In November, 2003, America's Major League Baseball (MLB) and its fledgling counterpart, the China Baseball Association, announced that they would join to promote baseball across China in preparation for the 2008 Beijing Olympics. American collegiate and professional coaches will go to China to coach young players, and top Chinese coaches will travel to America to study major league clubs. Chinese umpires will also receive training. Also, MLB will scout in China, locating the top Chinese players and preparing them for professional baseball, either in China or the United States.

In 1997, a dispute over television rights led to the formation of a second professional baseball league in Taiwan, known as the Taiwan Major League. Soon after, three of Taiwan's most famous professional baseball stars, including two-time MVP pitcher Kuo Chin-hsing and a teammate, confessed to charges that they rigged games for gambling syndicates. In all, 22 players were convicted of throwing games and were suspended. Gangsterism and big money gambling, called "black gold," were a way of life in Taiwan, with an estimated $2 billion bet on baseball games over the telephone alone each season.[38] Taiwan also announced that it was withdrawing from competition in the Little League World Series because it felt unable to comply with a rule limiting the number of players from each school district. However, in 2001, Taiwan resolved this dispute and agreed to hold the 34th World Club Baseball Tournament, hosting 16 youth teams from Japan, Korea, Holland, Italy, Canada, Panama, Australia, Cuba, Nicaragua, France, Russia, the Dominican Republic, and the Philippines. After years of squabbling and refusing to cooperate, in 2003, Taiwan's two professional leagues agreed to merge. Also in 2003, the Los Angeles Dodgers signed Taiwanese infielder Chin-Lung Hu to a contract that included a $2 million signing bonus.[39] Because China refuses to recognize Taiwan as an independent nation and lobbies international bodies against recognizing the Taipei government, Taiwan's baseball team competed in the 2004 Athens Olympics as "Chinese Taipei."

In 1998, in the midst of an Asia-wide economic downturn, South Korean viewers voted against having national broadcasters purchase rights to live television coverage of Los Angeles Dodgers baseball games. The move saved $3 million in foreign exchange but meant that Koreans were unable to see live coverage of the wildly popular pitcher Chan Ho Park until a small cable network picked up the telecasts. In 1999, the Arizona Diamondbacks activated Korean pitcher Byung-hyun Kim, then a 20-year-old sidearm rookie who is still pitching well in the major leagues. In 2001, outfielder Chin-Feng Chen signed with the Los Angeles Dodgers and became the first Taiwanese position player to appear in a professional game in the United States. He batted .316 (161 for 510) in 131 games for Class-A San Bernardino (California) and led all Dodger minor leaguers with 31 home runs and 123 RBI. In 2003, he played for their Triple-A team, Las Vegas, and hit 26 home runs and batted .281. He went to spring training with the Dodgers in 2004 but opened the season in Las Vegas. He also went to spring training with the Dodgers in 2005 but did not make the major league roster.

In 2000, the New York Mets and Chicago Cubs opened the National League season with a pair of games at the Tokyo Dome in Japan, the first time a regular season major league game had been played outside North America. Both games drew sellout crowds of 55,000. In that same year, Kazuhiro Sasaki joined the Seattle Mariners and recorded 37 saves, third best in the American League, leading the Mariners into the playoffs and winning American League Rookie of the Year honors. In 2003, the Oakland Athletics and the Seattle Mariners, led by Ichiro Suzuki, were scheduled to open the American League season in the Tokyo Dome to a sellout crowd. Due to the war in Iraq, however, both teams chose to remain in the United States for safety sake.

The U.S. Olympic baseball team, managed by former Los Angeles Dodger manager Tommy Lasorda, upset Cuba to win the gold medal at the 2000 Sydney Olympics, and South Korea defeated Japan 3-1 in an emotional game to win the bronze, South Korea's first Olympic medal in baseball. During 2001, Asian players were common and becoming increasingly dominant in professional baseball in the United States. Outfielder Ichiro Suzuki, whose father taught him the game when he was seven, became a seven-time batting champion in Japan. He joined Sasaki with the Seattle Mariners in 2000, signing for $12 million.[40] He got a base hit in each of his first 12 games. Japanese fans dubbed Ichiro and Sasaki the "Seattle Samurai." The majority owner of the Mariners is Nintendo, the Japanese manufacturer of video games. Hideo Nomo pitched a no-hitter for the Boston Red Sox and only weeks later missed a second no-hitter on a controversial call. A second Japanese position player, outfielder Tsuyoshi Shinjo, broke into the starting lineup with the New York Mets and became a fan favorite in New York.[41] In late 2003, Japanese all-star shortstop Kazuhiro Matsui also signed with the Mets. He became the Mets starting shortstop in 2004. And Hideki Matsui, nicknamed "Godzilla," is a star power-hitting outfielder for the New York Yankees. New York and Tampa Bay opened the 2004 season with two games in Tokyo in front of crowds of 55,000. Matsui hit a home run, and the fans went wild.

Although baseball owed its birth in Asia to American sailors, educators, and missionaries, it was the Japanese who spread the game across Asia. Sometimes this happened through colonization, or even in prisoner-of-war camps, but Japan also inspired the creation of professional leagues in Korea and Taiwan, and many players from these countries developed their skills in Japanese leagues. The Japanese also devoted themselves to friendship exchanges across Asia. However, baseball was first introduced to Korea not by the Japanese, but by an American missionary and former college baseball player from Colorado, Philip L. Gillett, in 1905.[42] The first Korean baseball game was played the following year. Some players wore leather boots and modern baseball uniforms, while others played in straw sandals and long, ornate Korean robes.

Far more important to Korean baseball, however, was the presence of the Japanese, who occupied Korea soon after Gillett introduced the game and remained there until the end of World War II. Some Koreans learned the game from the occupying Japanese, while others went to school in Japan, where they experienced the passion the Japanese people had for the game. By 1910, the game was so enthusiastically established in Korea that it was even played in the depths of winter.[43] Koreans also began to challenge Japanese teams with a dedication born of their determination to humble their political masters, but with few exceptions, the Japanese teams won. Koreans also rebelled against Japanese rule. During 1919, frequent anti-Japanese demonstrations provoked deadly retribution. Before calm was restored a year later, over 6,000 Koreans had been killed, 16,000 wounded, and nearly 50,000 arrested.[44]

Korean ballplayers exhibited such passion for the game that violence often broke out on the field and in the stands. Enthusiasm for the game faded in Korea from the mid-1930s until the end of World War II, but thanks in large measure to the presence of U.S. troops in South Korea after the war it once again became popular. In 1958, John R. Gilbert was assigned to Osan Air Force base in South Korea. He was horrified to find the country exhausted and without baseball. In response, he initiated Little League baseball. In 1997, the Korean Little League Baseball Federation invited Gilbert back to Seoul to honor him for his achievement.

With baseball once again in play in Korea, South Korea hosted and won the coveted Asian Amateur Baseball Championship in 1971 and 1975, placed third in the World Baseball Championship in Italy in 1978, and was co-champion with Japan in 1980. The following year Korea upset the U.S. team to win a gold medal at the World Youth Baseball tournament in Ohio, and in 1982 South Korea inaugurated its first professional league. Present at the league's first game were Baseball Commissioner Bowie Kuhn, Dodgers' president Walter O'Malley, and Japanese Baseball Commissioner Takeso Shimoda. Following pregame ceremonies that lasted two and a half hours, South Korean President Chun Doo Hwan threw out the first pitch. In 1987, the seven South Korean professional teams drew 10 million paying fans, and one star pitcher earned a salary of $125,000—in a country where the average annual income is less than $2,000. Three years later, a former major league pitcher, Marty DeMerritt, was paid $200,000 to coach the Samsung Lions pitching staff.[45]

At the same time, more and more Koreans played professional baseball in Japan, where they were even less popular than American "imports." To escape public scorn, many took Japanese names and tried to pass as natives. One who did so amazingly well was Masaichi Kaneda, a 6 foot, 2 inch hard-throwing left-handed pitcher. He is generally considered to be the greatest pitcher in Japanese history, known to the Japanese as the "Golden Arm" and the "God of Pitching" during his 20-year career, in which he won 400 games and struck out 4,490 batters. Few Japanese knew that he was a Korean who had been born in Japan and had adopted a Japanese name.[46]

It was widely known that Hokkaido-born star pitcher Victor Starfin was of Russian ancestry. A large man, 6 foot, 4 inches, weighing 230 pounds, Starfin won 42 games for the Yomiuri Giants in 1939, a year when the team won only 66 games all season.[47] He was the first foreign-born player to be inducted into Japan's Hall of Fame. At the age of 40, he was killed by a car as he crossed a street in Tokyo. Sadaharu Oh hit 868 home runs during his 22- year career in

Japanese baseball, 133 more than Hank Aaron's total. Oh was greatly respected by the Japanese, yet his popularity among them was not as great as one might expect. Although he was born in Tokyo and raised there by his Japanese mother, his father was a Chinese immigrant. Because of the ancestry of his father, Oh was not even allowed to play in the Japanese national high school championship.

South Korean baseball, with its star players, has created great fan interest. Its professional league, known as the Korean Baseball Organization, draws almost 5 million fans a season. But the most striking feature of Korean baseball is its propensity for violence. Japanese baseball often refers to "fighting spirit," by which is meant earnest dedication to the game. The Koreans emphasize actual fighting. In an attempt to limit fan violence, beer sales are now banned in Korean ball parks, but violence explodes during ball games nevertheless, just as it does elsewhere in Korean society. Serious physical injuries do occur as fans hurl broken bottles, trash cans, rocks, and even chairs. Fans often yell, "Tear' em to pieces," "slaughter' em," or "kill the umpire," and managers have been known to assault umpires. Riots are routine at ballparks, and physical violence takes place on the field, too. Many things about the game—strategy, cheerleaders, managing styles, practice drills and even scoreboards—reflect Japanese baseball culture, but the casual acceptance of violent outbursts is distinctive of the Korean game.[48] Despite Koreans' passion for the game, South Korea has only 45 high school baseball teams. Japan has 4,000.

Korean baseball culture is not only violent, it also has some unique traditions. Old women loudly taunt visiting pitchers while cheering sections are led by dozens of young women in very short red skirts, red halter tops, bare midriffs, white gloves and calf-high white leather boots. Their vigorous pelvic thrusts accompany an explosive cheer—"Eeee-Aye—Eeee-Aye-Oh" taken from "Old MacDonald Had a Farm." It is meant as an insult to the opposing players. Six umpires in powder blue silk polo shirts officiate the games with such firm authority that it borders on arrogance, but this attitude is praised by the press.[49] In

2003, the first Korean non-pitcher to reach the U.S. major leagues was 24 year-old, 6 foot, 5 inch, 240 pound, left-handed, power-hitting Hee Seop Choi. First signed in 1999, the Chicago Cubs expected him to be their starting first baseman for some years to come. He started for them in 2003 but was injured in a collision and sat out most of the season. Although he is as likeable as he is talented, Choi was traded to the Florida Marlins at the end of the 2003 season. In 2004, he was their starting first baseman before he was traded to the Los Angeles Dodgers, where he played well during the 2005 season.

Baseball was played in North Korea during Japan's rule over the peninsula. It re-emerged in 1990 when Pyongyang joined the International Baseball Association and built a modern stadium like the one in Seoul, with an electric scoreboard and comfortable seats for spectators. There are now at least four adult teams, and there are many secondary school teams in North Korea. The teams import baseball equipment from China. The International Baseball Association approved membership for North Korea in 1990.

As noted earlier, organized baseball was played by Americans in Shanghai in 1860, long before it was played in Japan. Chinese immigrants formed baseball teams in the United States in the 1880s, and one team successfully barnstormed through the South. Chinese students in Japan also learned the game, returning to China to create baseball leagues as early as 1913. In 1914, baseball was played at the second National Sports Games in Beijing, and the Far Eastern Games held in 1915 in Shanghai drew large crowds to its baseball games. Chinese communist revolutionaries were especially keen on baseball throughout the 1930s and 1940s. In the People's Liberation Army, the game was known as "army ball."[50] In 1949, the year of communist military victory, baseball was said to be one of the most loved sporting activities of the People's Liberation Army.[51] During World War II, nationalist soldiers also played baseball. An American Army major wrote that Chinese spectators at these games "roared at spectacular plays, laughed at errors, and were awed by long drives."[52]

China also has a national women's softball team. Although only some 1,000 Chinese women play this game, they are so rigorously trained in long, intense practices that since joining the International Softball Association in 1980, they have been able to compete successfully against the national women's teams from the United States and Japan. Their success has been achieved without much competition in China and with no fan support or material incentives. American Jonathan Kolatch studied these women and concluded: "They simply work harder than anyone else."[53] Some of these skilled players left China to play softball in Japan and Italy, where in the late 1980s each woman was able to earn the for-them hefty sum of $25,000 a year.[54]

In 1999, there were 100 baseball teams and 2,000 players in the People's Republic of China. However, the growing popularity of baseball in mainland China is dwarfed by the game's adoption as a national obsession in Taiwan, where, in that same year, there were 300 teams and 15,000 players.[55] Like Korea, Taiwan learned to treasure baseball while under Japanese occupation from the end of the Sino-Japanese War in 1895 until 1945. The Taiwanese eagerly accepted the Japanese model of respect for elders, whether coaches, managers, or older players. However, after the war, the American style of free swinging was adopted rather than the contact hitting and bunting that the Japanese favored. The year 1968 was pivotal in Taiwan's baseball history. A team of aboriginal boys of Malayo-Polynesian ancestry from a mountainous farming village in southeastern Taiwan, known as the "Red Leaf" team, defeated Japan's reigning Little League World Champions in a series of games. Until not long before their trip to Japan to play the world champions, the aboriginal boys of the Red Leaf team were so poor that they practiced barehanded with bamboo sticks for bats and stones for balls.[56]

Although the Han Chinese majority in Taiwan had previously scorned these aborigines, they now embraced them warmly. Victory over Japan was monumental, and baseball immediately became a national treasure. "The Taiwanese were ecstatic. The conquerors had been vanquished by a group of young players descended from the island's first inhabitants."[57] Emboldened, Taiwan promptly joined the worldwide Little League program. Their first team flew to Japan where it posted two shutouts versus a pair of Japanese teams, then crushed a U.S. team. Two weeks later, they won the World Little League Championship. The team of aboriginal children returned to an eight-hour victory parade through the streets of Taipei and an audience with exultant President Chiang Kai-shek.

This was only the first of 17 Little League world championships the Taiwanese boys would win over the next 27 years. All of these overseas games were broadcast by radio live to Taiwan where millions rose hours before dawn to listen. Many of Taiwan's victories were so one-sided that suspicions of cheating arose. However, no evidence of cheating was ever found. Instead, there were strong assertions by the Taiwanese that their boys were simply more diligent about practicing than boys of other countries.

For years, baseball ended as an organized sport for Taiwanese boys once they passed the age of 12, the maximum for Little League play. However, university teams slowly came into being, and in 1974 a Taiwanese pitcher was signed by the San Francisco Giants to a minor league contract. Two more players were signed by Cincinnati in 1975. As we saw earlier, outfielder Chin-Feng Chen is playing for the Los Angeles Dodgers' Triple-A Team. Several other Taiwanese have played well for Japanese professional teams. And in 1985, Taiwan initiated its own professional league, with new domed stadiums, and the four-team league began play in 1990. The league prospered with television revenue trickling down to the players, but in 1997 a massive gambling scandal exploded. Several star players were arrested for throwing games. One pitcher confessed that he was paid as much as $36,000 for each game he intentionally lost. Others confessed to receiving as much as $145,000 to lose a game.[58] However, both gangsterism and corrupt politics had long been commonplace in Taiwan. Baseball was so deeply embedded in Taiwanese culture that it survived these scandals.

Baseball in Asia was originally driven by the Japanese game, and it still is. Americans played baseball, in part at least, for pleasure, but for the Japanese it was deadly serious, it was work, it was their "national religion."[59] As we have noted, from the earliest days to the present, practices were so intense that players literally vomited and urinated blood. They also sweated so profusely during pregame practice that they had to change into clean uniforms for the game.[60] Spring training began on February 1, in the dead of winter. Consider their spring training schedule, which had to be exactly adhered to every day. The players were awakened exactly at 7:30. From 8:00 to 8:30, they participated in a so-called "speed walk" around their hotel. By then thoroughly awake, they ate a substantial breakfast from 8:30 to 9:30. From 9:30 to 9:50, they changed into their uniforms, then walked to the stadium. From 10:20 to 11:15, they ran ten laps around the field, a total of 2½ miles. They next did 200 situps, 200 back arches, ten wind sprints of 100 meters each, and ten "jumping" sprints of 50 meters each. From 11:15 to 11:25, they played catch; from 11:25 to 11:35, they played "pepper," then, until noon, they took infield and outfield fielding practice.

From noon to 1:30, the players divided themselves into three groups for batting practice against right- and left-handed pitchers and a pitching machine. For the next 20 minutes, they consumed a light lunch consisting of rice balls, then, from 1:50 to 2:00, they once again loosened up. From 2:00 to 3:15, they played an intrasquad game, then spent 30 minutes practicing fielding and 15 minutes practicing sliding. From 4:00 to 5:00, there was more batting practice, followed by 10 laps around the field, another 2 ½ miles. Dinner followed from 5:30 to 7:00, with a choice of Chinese buffet, Western buffet, or Japanese food. They rested from 7:00 to 7:30, then had an hour-long team meeting to review the day's practice. Finally, every player had a massage – by a male trainer – before going to bed. And lights had to be out by 11:00.[61]

Japanese major leaguers practiced every day during the season as well, from early morning until game time.[62] Practice was seen as so important that if rain cancelled practice but cleared up in time for the game to be played, the game was nonetheless cancelled.[63] Without practice on game day there could be no game. What is more, during the league season, starting pitchers were required to throw between innings as well as every day between starts. Some pitchers pitched two complete games on the same day, and several pitched the following day as well.   Korean pitchers learned to do the same. Not surprisingly, arm injuries were common, and pitchers' careers were brief. Japan had no history of sport for fun. Instead, it was *Bushido*, the way of the *samurai* calling for loyalty, self-control, discipline, piety, ceremonial propriety, and selflessness. Players ran ten miles every day, and one 38-year-old veteran took 900 ground balls before he collapsed.[64] *Wa*, the spirit of team unity, was all-important.[65] And a player was expected to apologize to all team members for any failure he might make.

All players, including the three foreign "imports" each team was allowed, had to bow deeply to their coaches and managers, then obey them no matter how incomprehensible or unpleasant their orders might be. As former Minnesota Twin player, "import" Charlie Manuel, put it, "I've never experienced anything like it in all my years in baseball. One manager I had used to call me up at night to make sure I was in bed. Then he'd call me in the morning to tell me what to eat for breakfast."[66] Players imported from the United States often found the Japanese practice regimen unbearable and many complained openly. A few who complained became so hated that they received written death threats. Black Americans were singled out for even more abuse than white ones with shouts of "nigger" heard in many ballparks.[67] Umpires openly favored Japanese pitchers over American batters, greatly expanding the strike zone when Americans were at the plate.[68] Despite these tensions and concerns, six Americans have somehow managed Japanese major league teams. The best known of these were Wally Yonamine (a Japanese-American from Hawaii), Don Blasingame, and Bobby Valentine.

Still, the game is played for the Japanese fans, and they attend in throngs. Ball parks, many of them modern and all of them sparkling clean, are usually filled by fans watching teams that bear the name of their corporate sponsors rather than the city in which they are located. Hence, the Chunichi (newspaper) Dragons, not the Nagoya Dragons, and the Yakult Swallows, rather than Tokyo Swallows.[69] And it is perhaps no surprise that the biggest winners in Japanese baseball history are the Yomiuri Giants owned by a media group with a highly popular television station and a newspaper with the largest circulation in the country. To approach any stadium, one must run a gauntlet of concession stands selling balls, caps, T-shirts, bats, and all manner of souvenirs. Once inside, fans may purchase *sushi* and *sake* from miniskirted cocktail waitresses, and a plush Chinese restaurant serves Mandarin duck along with other delicacies. However, most food is plain, especially the American-style hamburgers, hot dogs (*hotto dogu*), and french fries. And before each batter comes to the plate, his team's brass band blares a fight song.

Each batter is introduced by a female announcer. The fans, many of them also female, form themselves into cheering sections with scantily-dressed cheerleaders who make karate-chopping motions. They also rap brightly colored plastic bats together in a staccato rhythm. During the seventh-inning stretch, thousands of colored balloons are released. One girl likened the game to a rock concert, "We just have a lot of fun yelling."[70] Most fans sit quietly throughout the game, but the organized cheering groups are raucous. And fans love to open their umbrellas to signal to the opposing pitcher that it is time for him to take a shower.[71] Secondary school girls flock to games, where they regularly scream and fall down. Occasionally, hundreds of cheering-section fans storm the field to scream at the umpires. Players are taught to respect their managers, coaches, teammates, umpires, and even opponents, but cheering-section fans have no such scruples.

Imported American players almost unanimously disliked the Japanese game. As they saw it, their coaches and the press never stopped criticizing them for lacking proper form, fighting spirit and *wa*. In 1984, three Americans unceremoniously walked out on their rich contracts in mid season. Japanese baseball was simply too much for them. The press struck back. *Nikkan Sports* concluded, "All of these men are Anglo-Saxons, a class of people that has too much pride."[72] Despite this disdain, Japanese broadcasters, players, and sportswriters have adopted many English terms concerning the game. On television and radio broadcasts one hears *pitchā* (pitcher), *battā* (batter), *pinchā hittā* (pinch hitter), *batto* (bat), *erā* (error), *hōmuran* (home run), *pooray boru* (play ball), and scores of other such terms.[73] But Japanese stadium scoreboards differ from those in America. They keep track of the number of walks that batters receive because a base on balls is as valued as a base hit.

The Philippines also has a long history of baseball. The first baseball game there was played in May 1898 between marines and sailors from Commodore George Dewey's fleet only a few days after it defeated the Spanish fleet at the Battle of Manila Bay. Before the arrival of these military men and American missionaries and teachers, the Philippines had no history of team sports, but the baseball the Americans played and taught spread rapidly. It was not uncommon to see an Igorot boy, clad in only a loin-cloth, playing the game as a catcher with a mitt and mask.[74] Women and girls also took up the game zestfully, and played with such remarkable skill that they often actually outplayed males. Despite wealthy Filipinos' aversion to physical exertion as entertainment as well as exposure to the sun that would darken their skin, the game spread rapidly among poor Filipinos, with the first ballpark being built in 1902 to accommodate the already thriving Manila Baseball League. Fans flocked to ball games, often rushing onto the field to congratulate a player for a fine play, and interrupting the game as a result. In one game, 5,000 fans swarmed over the diamond, holding up the game for nearly an hour. Despite their zeal, fans never openly criticized an umpire, something they could not have learned from Americans.

In the 1920s and 1930s, Japanese teams toured the Philippines as did American major leaguers. In 1934, Ruth, Gehrig, and other American stars played before standing-room only crowds. During World War II, the Japanese military encouraged baseball and so did the Americans after the war ended. Baseball continued after the war with the Filipino Little League program achieving great success by winning the World Series, but that title was stripped after allegations that the Filipino players did not meet age and residency restrictions.[75] Over the years baseball gradually lost its popularity, being replaced in the public's affection by basketball. However, in 1992 a Filipino Little League team won the Little League championship in Williamsport, Pennsylvania. The manager of the U.S. team, former major leaguer Jeff Burroughs, said: "Those kids play at a different level than we do. They are five times better than any Little League team I've ever seen."[76]

One reason for the game's eventual loss of popularity was the difficulty that low-income Filipinos had in buying expensive baseball equipment. Once U.S. troops left the Philippines, their cast-off baseball equipment was no longer available. A single basketball, on the other hand, allowed ten people to play, and there were many backstops and hoops already available because the game had been widely played since 1910, when the YMCA had promoted it across the islands.

In the United States, Filipino-American baseball teams flourished in California in the 1920s and 1930s. And pride in Filipino identity continued among baseball players. In 1999, the New York Mets star outfielder, Hawaiian-born Benny Agbayani, told the press, "I'm Filipino, Samoan, Hawaiian, Portuguese, Spanish, Irish, and that's it. . . . I can't say I'm not Filipino because I'm from Hawaii. I carry a name that is Filipino, and I should represent all Filipinos."[77]

Although Chinese Americans usually stressed education and business over sports, they organized several teams in California, including one in Oakland in the 1930s managed by Lee Gum Hong. Hong had pitched for the Pacific Coast League Triple-A team, the Oakland Oaks, in 1932 under the name of Al Bower.[78] This team, known as the *Wa Sungs*, was very successful and had a large fan base. The Chinese University of Hawaii also fielded a successful baseball team. During 1914, it toured California, defeating teams from Stanford, St. Mary's, and Occidental. The *Los Angeles Times* wrote that "nine little Chinamen" had beaten Occidental and went on to praise them for "sensational base running and perfect fielding."[79] The Chinese players not only played well, they also took great pleasure in "aggressively and joyfully riding the umpire and the opposition."[80] How the targets of this abuse felt about it is not recorded.

First-generation Japanese immigrants, the *Issei*, brought the game with them from Japan, organizing their first team in California in 1903. By the 1920s, second-generation, or *Nisei,* teams traveled to California to play other second-generation Japanese-American. Teams from Hawaii and California several times traveled to Japan to play against Japanese university teams. For example, Kenichi Zenimura, who was born in Hiroshima in 1900, later moving to Hawaii as a child, organized teams in California whose all-stars several times traveled to Japan to compete against major Japanese university teams, compiling a record of 40 wins, only 8 losses and 2 ties. In 1927, Zenimura played on a team led by Lou Gehrig that defeated one led by Babe Ruth 13-3. A photo of Zenimura, Gehrig and Ruth together appeared in several newspapers in Japan.[81] In 1937, a *Nisei* team from California toured Japan, Korea, and Manchuria for six months winning 41 games and losing 20. Three years earlier, another Nisei team from California played in Kansas, where the local people were shocked to discover that people of Japanese ancestry spoke colloquial, accent-free English.[82]

If any people have adopted baseball more ardently than the Japanese, it is Japanese Americans. They seized upon the game not only as wholesome recreation, but also as a means of proving that despite rampant racism and discrimination by American whites, they were equal to anyone on the baseball field. The first wave of Japanese immigrants to the United States, the *Issei*, were poor immigrants who came originally to Hawaii in 1885, then later to California in search of income that would allow them to make a triumphant return to Japan. By about 1907, most of these same people had become farmers in California's central valley and had changed their minds about returning to Japan. They now hoped to stay in the United States permanently. All new immigrant populations to this country experienced difficulties adapting to the new ways Americans expected of them, but at least they were able to become naturalized citizens. The Japanese immigrants were denied that right until 1924, but their children who were born here were citizens, and these second-generation people, the *Nisei*, were determined to prove themselves. Baseball, the all-American pastime that had so fascinated their ancestors in Japan, seemed the ideal place to start.[83]

They truly loved the game and practiced fervently to improve their skills, but like the Japanese before them, they also devoted themselves to baseball because it demanded deference to authority, teamwork, discipline, honor, and determination. The first Japanese-American team —the "Excelsiors"—was formed in Hawaii in 1899, and by the early 1900s, Japanese-American baseball teams had sprung up throughout Hawaii, California, Washington, and across the Rocky Mountain states as far east as Nebraska. A Japanese-Canadian team, the Asahis (Rising Suns), was formed in Vancouver in 1914.[84] In 1921, 13 years before the first visit by a U.S. major league team, the Asahis toured Japan. They remained a popular team in Vancouver-area baseball, and they were heroes to the substantial British Columbia Nisei population for more than 20 years. However, although Nisei in nearby Washington's Yakima Valley played baseball with their usual gusto, for some reason they were not well accepted by white Americans. Several of their houses were actually dynamited and badly damaged. There were six separate cases of dynamiting and arson in 1933. After the Japanese-American prisoners were released from a World War II internment camp at Heart Mountain, only ten percent of those who were from Yakima Valley returned to their former homeland.[85]

United States Nisei teams played in church leagues, city and county leagues and soon were so skillful that they regularly defeated top U.S. college teams. And it was not only players who rejoiced in the game; large numbers of fans attended baseball games, laughing, betting, cheering and sharing a sense of pride and community. And this was "American" pride, because baseball was viewed as "America's game." Although these people worked very hard on their farms six days a week, Sundays brought them to a ball game to share victory or defeat with the players who were their "pride and joy."

The earliest teams were staffed by Issei who had learned the game in Japan, but by 1912 teams had all-Nisei players and, as early as 1914, two all-Nisei teams toured Japan, playing against Japanese university teams with success. Other Japanese-American teams from Hawaii and California followed in their footsteps. By the early 1920's, baseball had become so popular that every Japanese-American farming community in the San Joaquin Valley had its own team. One team was led by Kenichi Zenimura. He stood only 5 feet tall and weighed only 105 pounds, but he was a gifted athlete who played, coached, and managed for his championship team, one so talented that, as we noted earlier, it played against a barnstorming team led by Lou Gehrig and Babe Ruth in 1927. Kenichi's team also toured Japan, Korea, and Manchuria in 1924 and 1927. In 1937, it compiled a 40-8-2 record against Japan's "Big Six" universities.[86] By World War I, there were some 50 Nisei teams in California, and some Nisei women starred on these teams as well. Pitcher and hitter Alice Hinaga was a star on four different men's teams from 1934 to 1938, and other women starred as well. Interestingly, until 1949, women in Japan only played softball, not baseball, and they did not play on men's teams. In 2002, however, Chihiro Kobayashi, a young woman, pitched superbly for a Japanese men's university baseball team.

Early in 1942, President Franklin D. Roosevelt ordered that the 112,000 Japanese-American men, women, and children living on the West Coast be forcibly removed from their homes with nothing more than what they could carry, and relocated to one of ten internment camps in remote and desolate areas. They were said to represent a threat to the security of the West Coast states. Almost all of the Japanese Americans in Hawaii were not relocated, apparently because the government recognized that Hawaii's economy would collapse without them. Somehow, it seems, these Japanese Americans were not a threat to security. Those who were interned not only lost almost all of their possessions, they also faced a new life behind barbed wire, in primitive living conditions, standing in long lines for unfamiliar food, with virtually no privacy even in bathrooms, and surrounded by armed soldiers who saw them as the enemy. Their shock and humiliation were profound.

Some internees suffered in silence, but Kenichi Zenimura, who along with 5,000 others, was interned in horse stalls at the Fresno fairgrounds, took action. Appalled but determined, Zenimura supervised the construction of a baseball stadium complete with seats for fans. Within weeks, thanks to donations from the internees and some non-Japanese people in Fresno, a rudimentary field was ready for play. It helped greatly to restore morale as most of the internees came to the games. Only six months later, Zenimura and his family, along with many others, were moved to a desert site near the Gila River that held over 13,000 Japanese Americans on what was a portion of a Pima Indian reservation. Despite the desert heat and wasteland terrain, Zenimura set about building another ballpark, and this one proved to be a masterpiece, with dugouts, stands, bleachers, a grass infield, and an outfield fence adorned with castor beans, creating a sight similar to Wrigley Field in Chicago.

Games were played every day, and, thanks to generous donations by *Issei* internees, enough equipment was purchased to field 28 teams. Zenimura himself spent more than $2,000 on equipment and uniforms. More money was raised by passing a hat around to spectators at games. Internees also funded bus trips for Gila River teams to play other internment camp teams as far away as Heart Mountain, Wyoming, and rural Arkansas. These games not only entertained spectators, but they also instilled pride in the players and created a sense of self-esteem among detainees struggling to find meaning and respect in their lives. Women also played baseball, children practiced to develop baseball skills, and older people loved to cheer players and bet on games.

Japanese Americans continued to play baseball after the end of the war returned their lives to some semblance of normalcy. Although many families lost all of their possessions during internment, hard work led many of their children to universities and later to success in a variety of professional careers in law, medicine, the arts, business, engineering, and science. They also prospered in business. And some young men continued to excel in baseball. After playing football for the San Francisco Forty-Niners in the National Football League in 1947, Japanese-American Wally Yonamine signed with the Yomiuri Giants in 1951 and played for them until 1962, compiling a career batting average of .311 with excellent power. He then coached and managed in Japan until 1988. He was voted into the Japanese Hall of Fame in 1994, as was another Japanese American from Hawaii, Henry "Bozo" Wakabayashi. Before the war, 18 Japanese Americans played in Japan with several of them becoming famous for their skills. Twenty-two other Japanese Americans have played in the Japanese major leagues since the war. Because of their loyalty to the United States, some of them faced hostility soon after the war, but when two of the first Japanese-American players to play in Japan arrived in Hiroshima in 1956, they were greeted by 100,000 cheering fans.[87] Pitcher Ryan Kurosaki of the St. Louis Cardinals was the first Japanese American to play in the American major leagues. Len Sakata won a World Series ring with the Baltimore Orioles, and Don Wakamatsa played for the Dodgers and the Cincinnati Reds. Today, several others are in the minor leagues, and some are considered to be top prospects.[88]

In November 2002, the U.S. major league all-star team won its fifth consecutive seven-game exhibition series against the Japanese all-stars in Tokyo, but it was not easy. The major leaguers warmed up for the series by playing the Yomiuri Giants, winning 8-1 on two home runs by Barry Bonds. But when the all-star exhibition series began, the Americans lost the first three games, finding themselves just one more defeat away from losing the series. Bonds again saved them with a grand-slam home run that gave the Americans a 6-5 victory in game four. The major leaguers won the next three games as well, taking the final game by a score of 4-2. Ichiro Suzuki had four hits for the Americans, Bartolo Colon started and pitched well, and the Dodgers' star closer, Eric Gagne, recorded the last three outs.

In 2003, Hideki Matsui, Japan's star, power-hitting outfielder, signed a $21 million, three-year contract with the New York Yankees. On February 27, 2003, the Yankees' first spring training exhibition game was televised live to Japan, where it was 3:15 A.M. Nevertheless, millions are said to have watched. In his first at-bat, Matsui grounded out, but in his next at-bat, he crushed a long home run. In the Yankees' first home game of the regular season, as his parents and brother watched in Yankee Stadium, Matsui won the game with a bases-loaded home run. The fans literally screamed their approval.

106

NOTES

---

[1] Roosevelt (1900).

[2] Roden (1980a).

[3] Ibid., p. 513.

[4] Ibid., p. 515.

[5] Spalding (1911: 3-4).

[6] Whiting (1977: 3).

[7] Hughes (1899).

[8] Whiting (1990).

[9] LaFargue (1942: 53).

[10] Whiting (1990: 27).

[11] Quoted in Roden (1980a: 521).

[12] Whiting (1990: 32).

[13] Roden (1980a: 524).

[14] Ibid., p. 525.

[15] Ibid., pp. 529-530.

[16] Ibid., p. 529.

[17] Ibid., p. 534.

[18] Ibid.

[19] Ibid., p. 57.

[20] Obojski (1975: 25).

[21] Whiting (1990: 44-45).

[22] Maitland (1991: 22).

[23] Whiting (1990:244); Literary Digest, March 17, 1928.

[24] Gregorich (1998).

[25] Dawidoff (1994).

[26] Ibid.

[27] Guttman (1994).

[28] Reaves (2002:80); Light (1997: 386).

[29] Reaves (2002: 80).

[30] Ibid., p. 84.

[31] Ibid., p. 52.

[32] Ibid., p. 44.

[33] Kolatch (1992: 53).

[34] Ibid., p. 56.

[35] Fang, Ka-won, Deputy Secretary General, Hong Kong Baseball Association.

[36] Kolatch (1992:47); Daily News (New York), December 23, 2001.

[37] Derr (2002).

[38] Ibid., p.155.

[39] Baseball America, April 14-27, 2003.

[40] Whiting (2004: 24).

[41] Reaves (2002: xxvi).

[42] Ibid., p. 114.

[43] Ibid., p. 118.

[44] Wells (1990: 103).

[45] Fresno Bee, March 19, 1990.

[46] Whiting (1977: 71).

[47] Obojski (1975: 37).

[48] Whiting (1977); Reaves (2002); Los Angeles Times, August 28, 1990.

[49] Reaves (2002: 11-12, 128).

[50] Ibid., p. 43.

[51] Ibid.

[52] Doulens (1946: 13).

[53] Kolatch (1992: 9).

[54] Ibid., p. 258.

[55] World Baseball Magazine N.1/1999, p. 53.

[56] Butterfield (1969: 4).

[57] Dawidoff (1991: 64).

[58] Pomfret (1997).

[59] Maitland (1991: 7).

[60] Obojski (1975: 120).

[61] Whiting (1977: 43-44).

[62] Oh and Falkner (1984).

[63] Whiting (1990: 25).

[64] Whiting (1990: 65).

[65] Ibid., p. 50.

[66] Asian Week, 4, p. 19.

[67] Whiting (1990: 190).

[68] Ibid., pp. 17-18.

[69] Maitland (1991:11).

[70] Ibid., p. 113.

[71] Ibid., p. 56.

[72] Whiting (1990: 100).

[73] Ibid., p. 105ff.

[74] Forbes (1928: 454-455).

[75] Long Beach Press Telegram, August 30, 1992.

[76] New York Times, August 30, 1992; Reaves (2002: 110); Van Bottenburg (2001: 181).

[77] Filipino Reporter, July 15, 1999.

[78] Franks (2001: 230).

[79] Los Angeles Times, March 10, 1914.

[80] Franks (2001:237).

[81] Nakagawa (2001: 126).

[82] Ibid.

[83] Ibid.

[84] Prentice and Clifton (1995: 570).

[85] Ibid.; Mullan (1999).

[86] Ibid., p. 125.

[87] Ibid., p. 128.

[88] Ibid., pp. 131-132.

Chapter Four: Baseball in Latin America, South America, and the Caribbean

Baseball has long been a revered national sport in Venezuela, the Dominican Republic and Puerto Rico, in part because all three countries have highly regarded winter leagues that have attracted star players from throughout Latin America and the United States. The game has also become popular in Panama, Bolivia, Chile, Colombia, Jamaica, El Salvador, Costa Rica, Mexico, Honduras, Guatemala, Nicaragua, Belize, the Bahamas, the Virgin Islands, and the Netherlands Antilles, not to mention Brazil, Peru, and Argentina. In Bolivia, the Urura team plays at 15,000 feet above sea level. Needless to say, a batted ball travels long distances at three-miles of altitude. And despite Fidel Castro's decision to outlaw professional baseball in Cuba in 1961, the amateur game of baseball remains Cuba's national passion.

Since 1871, more than 600 Latin-born players have joined American major league teams, although only two did so before 1911. American fans did not always know that these players were Latin American. For example, outfielder Chili Davis played in the major leagues for over a decade, but few fans knew he was from Jamaica. In 2000, left-handed pitcher Juan Mendoza became the first person from Ecuador to play professional baseball in the United States. However, six Latin American players have received the U.S. major league Most Valuable Player Award, 17 have been Rookie of the Year, three have won the Cy Young Award, and 17 more have won major league batting championships. Five are in the Cooperstown Baseball Hall of Fame: Luis Aparicio, Rod Carew, Roberto Clemente, Juan Marichal, and Martín Dihigo.[1]

With the exception of Paraguay, Uruguay, Guyana, Suriname, and French Guiana, every country in Latin America and the Caribbean is devoted to playing baseball. So are most South American countries. Although Nicaragua has sent only five men to the major leagues, it has played baseball since 1939, and in 25 World Cup competitions it has won five silver medals and three bronze. In 1939, the second Baseball World Cup included the United Sates, Nicaragua and the host country, Cuba, which proved to be the winner. Despite the outbreak of World War II, in 1940 seven Latin American teams took part in the third. Baseball World Cup in Havana where World Cups were also played in 1941 and 1942. During the eleventh World Cup in 1950, a record 12 countries competed, with Cuba being declared the winner after Puerto Rico was disqualified for using professional players. While soccer, or *futebol* as it is known there, is Brazil's passion, baseball is also played so skillfully that during the twelfth World Cup, Brazil defeated Taiwan's highly rated team, and its under-16 team won the gold medal in 1993 in an international tournament played in Brazil. It is little known, but the Argentineans also play baseball well. For example, in the 1998 World Cup held in Italy, Argentina crushed favored Mexico 11-0.

American fans can be very enthusiastic, as the thunder-stick-clacking, rally-monkey-waving, wildly cheering Anaheim Angels' fans showed during the 2002 World Series, but Latin American fans make them seem morose. Wherever the Latin American game is played, their fans are seemingly electrified. Salsa music blares, Merengue and Mariachi bands play and, throughout the game, from its first inning to its last, fans dance in the aisles, many of them thoroughly drunk. Gambling at games has long been commonplace, too, especially in Cuba, where, before Castro's takeover, bookmakers used to stalk up and down the aisles in zoot-suit pants and two-tone shoes, their long keychains jangling, seemingly willing to take bets on anything.[2] All manner of wonderfully aromatic food is served in the stands. Local beauty queens often serve as team mascots, sometimes sitting primly on the bench next to the players and sometimes stepping onto the field to flaunt their curvaceous beauty to the crowd's loud delight. And in some places such as the Dominican Republic, drunken fans often confront one another angrily, even though, unlike Korean fans, they usually stop short of violence.

The first Latin American country to play baseball was Cuba, a 750-mile-long island populated by some 12 million people, many of them of African slave ancestry. But many Spaniards also came to the island in search of high wages, and most Cubans of middle and upper class status were white. Some of them played baseball. Many Chinese laborers came to Cuba as well, and a few of them also played baseball.[3] As a Cuban reporter wrote in the mid-1980s for Fidel Castro's official government newspaper, "In Cuba, baseball is more than a sport. It is part of the culture; it is part of our national pride....It is part of being Cuban. Baseball is one of the roots of Cuban reality."[4]

Baseball came to Cuba in the 1860s. It is possible that the game was first played there in 1866 by U.S. sailors docked in Havana, but it was not truly introduced until the brothers Nemesio and Ernesto Guillót, along with their friend Enrique Porto, who had been students at Alabama's Spring Hill College, returned to their homeland in 1864 with a bat and ball.[5] Another Cuban student who had played baseball in America, Fordham-educated Éstéban Bellán, also taught the game to Cubans. Bellán, who was partially of African descent, played in the U.S. major leagues in 1868-1870. The game also took root among other Afro-Cubans, the *mambises*, guerillas who led the fight for independence from Spain from their forest camps.[6]

In 1869, Spanish authorities attempted to outlaw the game because of their alarm over the spread of bats, which they saw as potential weapons that could be used against them, but they did not succeed. During the Ten Years War of 1868-1878, as Cubans rebelled against slavery and Spanish rule, many slave-owning Cubans fled to the Dominican Republic taking baseball with them. In 1889, others took the game to Nicaragua where nearly every small town soon had a team of its own.[7] It quickly became the national passion, played by Nicaraguans from six to sixty. Still other Cubans took the game to Mexico, to Puerto Rico, and then to Venezuela, where in the mid-1890s a wealthy Cuban cigar manufacturer put together a five-team league. A Venezuelan all-star team played exhibition games to raise money in support of the Cuban revolution. At the same time, other Cubans fled to Yucatán in Mexico, again taking baseball with them. The earliest teams to play in Yucatán had names such as "Cuba" and "Havana," and to this day Yucatán remains the most baseball-enthused region in Mexico.[8]

The first Cuban professional teams were organized in 1878, more than 20 years before Cuba gained its independence from Spain, and professional baseball was played there until Castro abolished it in 1961. During U.S. military rule in Cuba from 1906 to 1909, many United States players played in Cuban winter leagues, several major league teams visited, and a U.S. all-star team also toured the country. In 1911, the Cincinnati Reds signed Cubans Rafael Almeida and Armando Marsans, both of whom, although relatively light skinned, had some African ancestry. Marsans played in the majors for eight years and was so highly regarded that major league scouts began to recruit actively in Cuba. In the years that followed, some Americans played as so-called "imports" on Cuban teams, among them pitcher Jim Bunning, later a U.S. senator, and Bill Virdon, who played there in 1954 before going on to become Rookie of the Year in the National League in 1955. John McGraw, Leo Durocher, and Dick Sisler also played in Cuba.

Although Cuban baseball was played by all of the same rules followed in the United States, in one custom, Cuban baseball was unique: when each batter first came up to bat, he had to shake the hand of both the catcher and the umpire.[9] Beginning in 1946, Havana fielded a team in the U.S. Florida International League, winning the pennant for five years in a row. And from 1956 to 1960, Havana fielded a team in the U.S. Triple-A International League. Cubans also played in the U.S. major leagues, 135 of them from 1947 to 1960.[10]

Baseball in Havana's *Gran Stadium* was an impressive social event.

Except for the Sunday doubleheaders, baseball was not a spectacle for children, but part of the nightly entertainment of a very cosmopolitan city. This does not mean that children did not go to the stadium, but it was not in shorts, with a glove in one hand and a soda in the other. A visit to the stadium as a child, was a serious outing, and one dressed in the better clothes reserved for wear after the daily afternoon bath. Moreover, night games began at nine o'clock, to allow for the Cuban family dinner hour, which was at about eight o'clock. Because it was winter, people, particularly women, dressed well, and it was not unusual to see furs in the more expensive box seats. In fact, it was quite common for people to go to the game and later catch the second show at one of the nightclubs, such as Montmartre, Tropicana, or Sans Souci. . . . The Gran Stadium was a place to be seen if you were in show business or politics. Social chronicles would be written about who among the rich and famous was at the stadium, underscoring their affiliations to the various social clubs. Ballplayers were celebrities with whom to mingle. The popular Sonora Matancera, one of the better popular orchestras in the forties and fifties, would do a live radio show at eight and then go see the game. Cab Calloway and his Cavaliers, in town to play at the Montmartre, would show up regularly at the stadium during the 1949-50 season.[11]

Many of the men who stayed in Cuba to play were enormously talented. Silvio Garciá starred from 1931 through 1954. No player who ever lived could have been more versatile than Cuba's 6 foot, 3 inch, 225-pound Martín Dihigo. His African ancestry barred him from playing in the U.S. major leagues, but playing first in Cuba, then in the American Negro League, and later in Mexico, he was not only a pitcher who threw several no-hit games, he also played every position on the field, including catcher, hitting with great power and for a high average while fielding brilliantly. Negro League great, Buck Leonard said of

Dihigo: "He was the greatest all-around player I know. I'd say he was the best ball player of all time, black or white.... If he's not the greatest I don't know who is. You take your Ruths, Cobbs, and DiMaggios. Give me Dihigo. I bet I would beat you almost every time."[12]

Blessed with a fast ball that might have been the equal of Satchel Paige's, Dihigo also had legendary homerun power. After a long career in the Negro and Caribbean winter leagues, he played in Mexico until he was over 40 and also managed teams in Cuba, Mexico and Venezuela. A cheerful man with an excellent command of English, he was very popular everywhere he went in the game. The white Cuban pitcher, Adolfo Luque, was the exact opposite, a man who spoke poor English, possessed a terrible temper, and was disliked by everyone. He carried a gun and often threatened to use it. Former Dodgers' manager, Tommy Lasorda, who once played for Luque in Cuba, called him "The worst human being I have ever known."[13] Yet, although he was only 5 foot, 7 inches tall, he was a superb pitcher with a great curveball, winning 194 games in the U.S. National League. In 1923, he had 27 wins and an earned run average of only 1.93. Although Dihigo had never played in the United States, he was inducted into the American Baseball Hall of Fame. Luque was not.

Baseball flourished in Cuba. In addition to Cuba's professional leagues, there were hundreds of semiprofessional teams, sugar mill teams and amateur clubs. There were also various leagues for boys aged seven to eighteen.[14] No one was a greater fan than Fidel Castro, though he was by no means a gifted player. After he took power in 1959, professional baseball briefly continued to flourish in Cuba. In fact, most Cubans were joyous when Castro's guerillas took power. A carnival atmosphere prevailed, but the mobs did little damage. Order was soon regained, and only five games of the baseball season were lost.[15] However, attendance rapidly declined as baseball fans were increasingly distracted by politics. In 1961, after Castro publicly announced his conversion to Marxist-Leninism, he ordered that the professional game be ended in Cuba. He insisted that professional baseball was evil because teams "owned" players and "exploited" them by selling or trading them like merchandise.[16] From that time on, Cuban players would demonstrate the superiority of socialism by playing what Castro called "revolutionary baseball" as amateurs. They would no longer be permitted to play in the United States, either. They would play in Cuba, earning just enough to live, and admission to their games would be free. To maintain the public illusion of the players' amateur standing, Castro's government paid them for jobs they never performed—one man who was paid to be a typographer did not even know what typography was. His monthly salary was $7.45.[17] Most Cuban men, including baseball players, worked in factories, sugar cane fields, or the newly developed mining and tourism industries.

Castro's "revolutionary" baseball grew to an unprecedented level. By 1964, there were 5,000 teams with 60,000 players, and eight Cuban baseball instructors had been sent to China, Vietnam, and Algeria to teach the game. Over 600 playing fields had been built, and Cuba produced about 1 million baseballs and 50,000 bats annually.[18] From November through February, 18 teams competed in a 48-game national tournament to select eastern and western champions. These teams met in a final national championship game. Somehow regional pride and socialist ideals of sportsmanship overcame the absence of rich salaries, and play was spirited and skillful. After this national championship was decided, another league representing Cuba's eight provinces took up play. This league play led to the selection of the 24 best players for Cuba's national team, which has competed in Pan American, World Tournament, and Olympic play. Cuba has won 12 of the 15 World Amateur Baseball competitions held since 1969. In 1963, a power-hitting Cuban team beat a U.S. team 13-1 in the fourth Pan American Games in São Paulo, Brazil, while pro-Cuban students elatedly pounded bongo drums in the stands.[19] And from the time of Cuba's victory in the 1987 Pan American Games in Indianapolis, to its victory in the 1992 Olympic

Games in Barcelona, the Cuban national team won an incredible 72 of the 73 games it played against international competition.[20]

Despite this extraordinary record of success, playing conditions in Cuba were often appalling, especially after the collapse of the Soviet Union left Cuba impoverished. Before long, night games had to be canceled to save electricity. The players traveled in ramshackle, Soviet-made school buses, numbing themselves with rum and sleeping inside the stadiums, or in dorm rooms that were like barracks. "Imagine traveling from Havana to Guantánamo on a bus with no air-conditioning," said one player referring to the eastern city some 15 hours by road from Havana. "Sometimes the bus would break down at dawn in the middle of nowhere. You waited hours in the heat for another bus. Then you finally get to Guantánamo and there's no running water. Then, after the game, you have thirty players staying in the same room in their sweaty, dirty clothes. A lot of the time we slept in the stands. We dragged our sleeping mats into the stands and laid them on top of the dugout. The mosquitoes were the size of portable radios, but you didn't have any choice."[21] Under conditions like these, it is not surprising that alcoholism was widespread among players, that gambling was rampant, and that players were accused of throwing games for payoffs from gamblers.[22]

Faced with conditions like these and almost no income, the temptation to defect to the United States where large contracts were known to be waiting for star players was tremendous. Surprisingly, all but a few Cuban players refused to defect. Great Boston Red Sox pitcher, Luis Tiant, followed his father's advice and left Cuba in 1961 before Castro forbade players to leave. He did not see his family for the next 14 years. Probably the best player in Cuba, home run king Omar Linares, turned down a $1.5 million offer from the New York Yankees, saying that to defect would be "An act of treason," and adding, "Money doesn't interest me."[23]

Money did interest pitcher René Arocha, who was also disgusted by the playing conditions in Cuba, and he did defect in 1991, followed by pitcher Livan

Hernández. After he was denied the right to play baseball in Cuba because he was Livan's half-brother, Orlando Hernandez defected in a small boat and was signed by the New York Yankees. He started his first game for them, after some minor league outings, on June 3, 1998, and won, 7-1.[24] Since Arocha defected, 12 Cubans have pitched in the major leagues, but only the Hernandez brothers had great success, Livan with the San Francisco Giants, and Orlando, known as "El Duque," with the New York Yankees. In 2003, both Livan and Orlando were traded to the Montreal Expos. Several other players have defected as well, sadly leaving their families behind.[25] Cuban Rafael Palmeiro has starred as a power-hitting first baseman for the Texas Rangers for over a decade. A few Cubans also play in Italy and Japan. Since 1991, 30 Cuban players have defected.

After a long negotiation that was initiated by the Clinton administration and included Henry Kissinger, the U.S. Department of State allowed the Baltimore Orioles to play two games against the Cuban national team, known as *seleccíon Cuba*. One game would be played in Havana in March 1999, the second in Baltimore two months later. Profits from the sale of tickets and television rights would be shared between the two countries to support baseball, although why United States baseball needed such financial support is unclear. A few minutes before the first pitch in Havana, Castro walked across the field to the Orioles dugout. Dressed in his traditional military fatigues and cap, Castro was applauded wildly by the fans, who chanted "Fí-del, Fí-del." He spoke briefly to the Oriole players before he marched over to the Cuban dugout to greet them enthusiastically. He then sat in a front-row box seat with major league Baseball Commissioner "Bud" Selig on one side and Orioles owner Peter Angelos on the other. When "The Star Spangled Banner" was played, he stood at attention. Unlike a typical game in Cuba, there were no drums, air horns, dancing in the aisles, or loud music. By Castro's order, admission to the game was by invitation to Communist Party faithful, "exemplary workers," and a few others, all of whom behaved with great restraint.[26]

Omar Linares carried the Cuban flag in pregame ceremonies, and his RBI single in the eighth inning tied the score at 2-2, but the Orioles won in extra innings, 3-2. The fans and a large television audience were dazzled by Cuban pitcher José Ariel Contreras, a 6 foot, 3 inch, 225-pound, 27 year old who came on in relief in the second inning to pitch eight scoreless innings while giving up only two hits and striking out ten! As noted in chapter one, Contreras defected late in 2002 and was signed to a lucrative, long-term contract by the New York Yankees. He lived in New York without his wife and two daughters until late June 2004, when, along with 18 other Cubans, his family escaped to south Florida in a small boat. The family's reunion was joyful, as photographs taken at the time and published in many U.S. newspapers made clear.

When the Cuban team visited Baltimore on May 3, 1999, the Orioles were deep in last place in the American League East and the game against Cuba was not only meaningless to them, it was also annoying, because it came on what would otherwise have been a day off. They played without any sign of enthusiasm and lost, 12-6. When the Cuban team's chartered plane landed in Havana, Castro was there to embrace physically team captain Omar Linares, then he delivered a passionate three-hour speech in which he lashed out at U.S. baseball for trying to recruit Cuban baseball players like Linares with "Yankee dollars." He pointed out repeatedly that no Cuban player had defected while his team was in Baltimore, and he gloried in their victory, insisting that the game the Cubans had lost in Havana meant nothing but the game in Baltimore before American fans had meant everything. He gleefully gloated, declaring that Cuba had won the game that mattered![27]

The future of baseball in Cuba is unknowable, but in December 2002, the University of Tennessee baseball team won the three games it played against Cuban junior teams, two by shutouts and the third, 10-1. Two Tennessee players, Catcher Javi Herrara and outfielder Alex Suarez, are the sons of Cuban parents who years earlier had emigrated to Miami. Both played well against the Cuban teams, and they greatly enjoyed the hospitality shown them by ordinary people in Havana. They were also delighted when members of Cuba's elite national team traded jerseys, bats, and batting helmets with them.[28]

Baseball in Mexico has taken a very different course from Cuba. Although soccer is the most popular sport in the rest of Mexico, in Yucatán baseball is king. When Yucátan's Merida's *Leones* (Lions) team in the Mexican League won its first championship in 1984, people in the modern city of Mérida and surrounding towns celebrated so wildly that all businesses were shut down for two whole days. Yucatecos called baseball "the king of sport."[29] As noted earlier, Cubans took baseball to Yucatán in the 1890s. Kids in Mérida played "street ball" bare-handed and bare-footed, but the game soon became the sport of Mérida's elite, and its most popular team, *El Sporting Club*, was made up of well-to-do young men who had learned the game while attending school in the United States. It has also been played by Mayan Indians in Yucatán since 1929. They prefer baseball to either basketball or soccer.[30]

Fans across Mexico are exuberant, chanting "MAY-hee-co, cha, cha, cha" and dancing atop the home team's dugout. Fans are not allowed to bring bottles to the stadium, so they fill supermarket plastic bags with tequila, and they drink from the bag. Boys rush onto the field between innings to collect autographs, and when an opposing player makes a crucial error, the public address announcer will sometimes derisively thank him by name.

During the dictatorship of Porfirio Diaz from 1876 to 1911, Mexico underwent dramatic modernization. The army eliminated the long-standing Apache Indian threat to northern Mexico, the constabulary crushed banditry, railroads financed by British and American investment spread across the countryside, telegraph wires followed, and foreigners rushed to Mexico to make their fortune.[31] Sports came with them. German beer brewers favored bowling and billiards, Spaniards loved *Jai-alai* and bull-fighting, Englishmen introduced cricket, soccer and rugby, Scotsmen enjoyed competition with lances and broadswords, and Americans built tennis courts, golf courses, and baseball fields. By 1875, there was even a roller-skating fad like the one seen earlier in Europe and the United States, as rinks were opened in several cities, and both men and women skated, hoping to improve their health and morality.

Baseball was played in Guaymas as early as 1877 by U.S. marines, and it first appeared in Mexico City in the early 1880s. It had spread widely across Mexico by the early 1890s. In 1886, teams of unskilled Frenchmen and Spaniards played a bungled game of baseball against one another before an audience of fashionable spectators in Mexico City who actually paid to watch this improbable contest.[32] American employees of Mexican railroad lines and telephone companies played baseball during these years, too, and in 1888, Mexican workers on the national railroad played their first game against American workers, losing 9-8. In that same year, A. G. Spalding opened a sporting goods store in Mexico City, where he sold baseballs, bats, gloves, and other baseball gear. Athletic clubs in the city quickly took up the game. Elsewhere in Mexico, miners joined railroad workers in organizing baseball teams. The game received its greatest boost when the Chicago White Sox visited Mexico City in 1907, with large and enthusiastic crowds turning out to watch them play against Mexican teams. It was spring training for the White Sox, and Comiskey hoped to find good weather and to make money. He also found a warm welcome.

In an odd quirk of history, the first Mexican to become a baseball hero was a pitcher named Valenzuela.[33] His first name is unknown, but in the 1980s his namesake, Los Angeles Dodgers pitcher Fernando Valenzuela, would become the most famous Mexican player of all time and one of the most famous players from any country. The youngest of 11 siblings, Fernando Valenzuela was raised in poverty in the tiny 20-homestead pueblo of Etchohuaquila on the west coast of Mexico. The pueblo was so poor that it had no electricity until 1970. When Dodgers scouts first saw him, he was pitching for the *Leones* in Mérida. In 1981, at the age of only twenty, this left-hander came to the Dodgers, where he won his first ten games. He had a dazzling array of pitches, including a nearly unhittable screwball. He not only won the Rookie of the Year Award in 1981, but he was also the Cy Young winner, the only man ever to win both in the same year.[34] Mexican and Mexican-American households burst with such pride that it came to be known as "Fernando-mania." At that time, there were 23 million Latinos in the United States, many of them of Mexican origin. When Valenzuela was scheduled to pitch, many families lighted religious candles. Valenzuela's games were described in Spanish by a Dodgers announcer and broadcast by 31 stations. A Mexican television station beamed all of his games to Mexico City.[35] In his second year, Valenzuela earned $350,000, and the following year, at the age of only 22, he signed for a whopping $1 million.[36] In 2003, Valenzuela's son, a power-hitting outfielder, signed a minor league contract, and Valenzuela himself, after years of distancing himself from the Dodgers, became one of their Spanish-language broadcasters.

Thanks to the railroad, baseball also entered Mexico through Laredo, Texas, spreading to its sister city, Nuevo Laredo, just across the border in Mexico. Baseball in these two cities, whether played by Mexicans or "Anglos" from Texas, was known as "borderland ball." Mexico's first professional league, the Mexican League, began play in 1940 with Nuevo Laredo as one of its teams, and several of its players were Cubans.[37] Soon after the league began play, the flashy, cosmopolitan, Mexican multi-millionaire businessman Jorge Pasquel began a campaign to sign U.S. players for the league. Pasquel, who kept a loaded .45 automatic pistol in plain view on his desk for dramatic effect, loved to hand large sums of cash to prospective players. American Tom Gorman, a pitcher with a bad arm, was given $20,000 in a paper bag to sign a contract. Newly married, injured and penniless, Gorman was ecstatic: "And there it was, right there before me on the desk, waiting for me to pick it up. Jorge put all that money into a paper sack, a little grocery bag, and handed it to me. So I had twenty grand and I hadn't thrown a ball."[38]

One of the first star players to sign was Ray Dandridge, the brilliant Negro League player, who was already playing in Mexico but had threatened to resign if he did not receive a handsome raise. Pasquel happily agreed. The Mexican League was making a profit, and in 1944 Hall of Famer Rogers Hornsby agreed to play for and manage the Vera Cruz team. Other Negro League players signed as well. Satchel Paige was among those who signed, saying, "I went to Mexico when Jorge Pasquel was giving all that money away. I jumped and went too."[39] And many enjoyed the experience. As black American Willie Wells put it, "In the United States everything I did was regulated by color. Well, here in Mexico I am a man."[40]

In 1946, Pasquel made the biggest news yet when he signed Mickey Owens, catcher for the Brooklyn Dodgers, and Vern Stephens, the St. Louis Brown's shortstop who had led the American League in home runs in 1945, to three-year contracts. But after only a week in Mexico, Stephens returned to the United States, complaining to the *New York Times* that Mexico was like a concentration camp, no one spoke English, the ball parks were inferior, there were no showers in the dressing rooms, and the over-7,000 foot altitude in Mexico City bothered him.[41] Mickey Owens, however, remained in Mexico, saying "I'm perfectly happy here. My wife likes Mexico and we moved into this super-modern apartment today and everything is just dandy."[42] Pasquel went on to sign another 15 major leaguers, including Sal Maglie and Max Lanier, and he sent a signed blank check to Bob Feller, telling him to fill in any amount he wanted. Feller declined. Pasquel bragged to horrified American baseball owners that he would soon sign Hank Greenberg, Ted Williams, Phil Rizzuto, Stan Musial, and Jackie Robinson. His brother told the press that Pasquel had offered Commissioner "Happy" Chandler $50,000 a year plus living expenses to become the commissioner of the Mexican League. The story was untrue, but it was good publicity.[43]

The U.S. press blasted Pasquel: "Pancho Villa's raids over the border looked like pale stuff Thursday night compared to the antics of a peso-happy caballero who is promoting big-time baseball in Mexico and using Brooklyn Dodgers for bait."[44] After Pasquel's business partner and boyhood friend, Miguel Aleman, was elected president in 1946, Pasquel showed far less interest in buying American players, and even failed to meet some of his previous contractual promises. Many believed that his interest in Mexican baseball had been solely a means of helping to elect Aleman, but it may have been the case that his resentment against America drove him into open competition against major league baseball.[45]

Sparked by controversy over Pasquel's signings and the determination of major league owners to control their players' salaries, in 1946, a players union, known as the American Baseball Guild, was created in the United States. Thanks to the efforts of Boston lawyer, Robert Murphy, baseball's first pension fund was created, a minimum salary was agreed upon, spring training expense money was provided, and the ten-day severance clause in players' contracts was increased to 30 days. To the surprise of everyone, especially Pasquel, Mickey Owens left Mexico to return to the United States and the Dodgers in August, 1946. There were other problems with Mexican baseball. Many wondered how Nuevo Laredo, a town of only 10,000 people, could possibly support a "major league" team as Pasquel intended. Nevertheless, Pasquel lobbied hard to have his league accepted as part of U.S. major league baseball. The best he could get was a Double-A rating, and attendance was so poor that by 1948 the league was reduced to four teams, all of them in Mexico City, the only Mexican city with an adequate fan base.

Still, some Mexican players achieved greatness. Although he spoke no English when he came to the Cleveland Indians in 1951, Roberto Avila was taken under the wing of a Californian of Mexican descent, pitcher Mike Garciá, who quickly taught him English. Avila won the American League 1954 batting championship over Ted Williams with an average of .341, and that same year, Garcia won 19 games. Although Héctor Espino never played in the U.S. major leagues, he is Mexico's most famous and popular player, whose home run power caused fans to label him "Mexico's Babe Ruth." He dominated Mexican baseball from 1962 to 1984.

Teams continued to play in Nuevo Laredo and Laredo, Texas, with various degrees of success and fan enthusiasm until 1985 when the two teams were formed into a single, bi-national team, the *Tecolotes*. It was the first bi-national team in any sport in the world.[46] Two-thirds of the team's games would be played in Neuvo Laredo, one-third in Laredo. The players, several of whom were American, were struck by the difference between fans in the two small cities. American fans were quiet, seemingly disinterested, while their Mexican counterparts were rowdy, unruly, and often drunk.[47] Women shouted obscenities, and cherry bombs were sometimes thrown onto the field. And Mexican players also expressed their emotions, their pains as well as their joys, much more freely than their American teammates.

It was plain to the Americans that the Mexicans were every bit as "macho" as advertised, but they could also be kind, gentle, and sympathetic. Unlike Americans, who were reluctant to hug a teammate in public for fear of being thought homosexual, Mexicans often embraced one another, slapped one another on the behind, or kissed each other on top of the head. American players can be uninhibited in the privacy of their clubhouses, as Jim Bouton illustrated in his book *Ball Four*, with an episode of playful kissing among some players.[48] But they are quite restrained on the field. At the same time, Mexican players were truly devoted to the game. Andrés Mora, an older player nearing the end of his career, said about the possibility of retiring, "You know, I'm thinking of quitting after this year. My bat slowed down and I have aches and pains everywhere. I can't move my leg back any further than this [he shows me]. It's just that I don't know what to do. Baseball has been my life. I'm lost without it. It's very sad."[49]

American sportswriters were often unsympathetic to Latin American players. Instead of reporting their dreams, fears, or their efforts to adapt to American life, the writers delighted in quoting their broken English, and if an offended player then refused to be interviewed, he was described as temperamental and uncooperative. The press also garbled Spanish names. Cuban Saturnino Orestes Arrieta Armas Miñoso's name was always written as Minoso, and pronounced without the "ny" sound called for by the *tilde* over the n. He was soon nicknamed "Minnie," to rhyme with Minoso. Sports writers also wrote about Latin players' flamboyance on the field and their antics off it. When the Philadelphia A's exuberant black star outfielder, Puerto Rican Vic Power—whose real name was Victor Pellot—drove his flashy convertible to nightclubs, he was sometimes followed by reporters. And when he dated blondes, as he often did, writers disparagingly described that as well. Willie Mays and Roberto Clemente also dated blondes, although not so openly. When a player spent money lavishly—Miñoso's multiple cars, or Rico Carty's expensive clothes and shoes— they were derided as spendthrifts.[50]

The press also made much of the violent tendencies of some Latin players. Giants Star pitcher Rubén Goméz was a famous brushback pitcher. Once, after he hit huge Joe Adcock on the wrist, Adcock charged the mound. Gómez fled to the dugout, where he armed himself with a switchblade knife, then rushed back onto the field.[51] Some of these men did not deserve their bellicose reputations, but Dominican Republic pitcher Juan Marichal certainly did. Often hostile, he was not at all reluctant to throw his blazing fastball at the heads of batters. In 1965, Los Angeles Dodger catcher, John Roseboro, an African-American, was sufficiently annoyed by one such pitch that when Marichal came to bat the following inning his return throw of a pitch intentionally nicked Marichal on the ear. Marichal responded by clubbing Roseboro over the head with his bat, a blow that could have been lethal. Marichal was fined $1,750, suspended for nine games, and reviled by the press. Nevertheless, he was such a successful pitcher that he was elected to the Hall of Fame. Late in his career, he actually joined the Dodgers. The gracious Roseboro not only accepted him, he urged fans to support Marichal..

Although Cuba and the Dominican Republic are usually seen as the premier Caribbean centers of baseball, Puerto Rico is not far behind. This island colony, annexed by the United States in 1898, has long been plagued by poverty and limited by its lack of political autonomy. But thanks to its baseball winter league, which has attracted star players from the United States and across the Caribbean, it became a mecca for young players on the verge of stardom and a winter haven for many of the world's best talents. Puerto Ricans Orlando Cepeda, Francisco Coimbre, Roberto Clemente, Juan Pizarro, and Vic Power all played in Puerto Rico's winter league, and so did many Americans, including Willie Mays, Bob Thurman, Wes Covington, Hank Aaron, Luke Easter, Bob Cerv, and Bobo Holloman.

The first game of baseball to be played on the island was in 1897, one year before the United States invaded Puerto Rico and took possession of it from Spain. Amateur baseball spread around the island, especially in cities like San Juan and Mayaguez, but it was not until 1938 that professional baseball began with the inauguration of the winter league. The same seven teams that made up that original league still compete, although recent economic woes have weakened fan attendance while high player salaries in the United States have kept most star major leaguers from competing there during the winter. The league was at its peak in the 1950s when Puerto Rican stars were joined by illustrious Americans. Puerto Rico won four of the first seven championships during the newly-formed Caribbean World Series. By 2005, it had won ten such championships, second only to the Dominican Republic's 13 wins.

During the early years of Puerto Rican baseball, its most remarkable stars were Francisco "Pancho" Coimbre and Pedro "Perucho" Cepeda, the father of famed home-run hitter Orlando Cepeda. Both men were brilliant hitters, each one logging a batting average over .400 for a winter season. Major league pitching star, Puerto Rican Juan Pizarro, also dominated the winter league, leading it in strikeouts for five straight seasons. And Luís "Tito" Arroyo learned to pitch in Puerto Rico before signing with the New York Yankees, where he became one of baseball's best relief pitchers during the 1960s. During the past decade, several Puerto Rican players have achieved major league all-star status.

Few players anywhere were more talented than Pittsburgh's Puerto Rican Roberto Walker Clemente. A great hitter and brilliant outfielder with a rifle arm, he starred for the Pirates for 18 seasons. He was the most valuable player in the National League in 1966 and the most valuable player in the 1971 World Series. In 1970, he hit .352. The son of a poor sugarcane worker, Clemente was extremely active in charities in Puerto Rico during his off-seasons, and after a deadly earthquake killed thousands and left many more homeless in Managua, Nicaragua, in December 1972, he led a Puerto Rican relief effort that produced a large fund of relief supplies for the survivors. After Clemente was told that local officials, perhaps including Nicaraguan dictator Somoza, had stolen most of the $30 million worth of blankets, food, and clothing earlier sent by the United States to the survivors, he decided to fly with the supplies he had collected and watch over their distribution.

The supplies had been loaded into an old rented DC-7 that had been retired from service by a Florida airline a year earlier because it was known to have mechanical problems. Nevertheless, on New Year's Eve it left San Juan only to crash into the sea soon after take off. Clemente's body was never recovered. Clemente had long dreamed of building a "Sports City" in San Juan where many impoverished children could both go to school and learn to play baseball. The government did not produce the necessary money until after Clemente's death, when donations from U.S. baseball fans also poured in. The Sports City now stands in San Juan, where it serves as many as 1,200 poor youngsters at a time. And a major bridge near Pittsburgh's baseball stadium has been named the Roberto Clemente Bridge.[52]   Clemente was posthumously inducted into the Baseball Hall of Fame, the first Latin American player to be so honored. On opening day of the 1973 season, almost 52,000 Pirates fans watched tearfully as Clemente's uniform number 21 was retired. It was the first time that a Latin American player had his uniform retired by a U.S. major league team.

Clemente was not the only star player to come from Puerto Rico. Today, two of major league baseball's best catchers are Puerto Ricans Benito Santiago and Ivan Rodríguez; Roberto Alomar is a star second baseman, and Rubén Sierra and Juan González are outstanding power hitters. Many young Puerto Rican players have great promise, too. Despite the economic hard times that continue to plague the island, fans cherish the game. Since 1989, however, when major league baseball made Puerto Ricans subject to the draft, the export of star players has dropped off dramatically. Today, none of *Baseball America's* top 100 prospects comes from Puerto Rico. Scouts blame this decline in talent on the fact that since the draft, players who used to be able to sign at age 16 must now wait until they are 18, just as their U.S. counterparts do. However, because there is no high school baseball in Puerto Rico, youngsters who used to receive professional coaching at 16, instead spend two long formative years more or less on their own with their skills suffering as a result. In 2003, the Montreal Expos chose to play 22 of their home games in Hiram Bithorn Stadium in San Juan, and crowd support was enthusiastic. The Expos played another 22 games there in 2004. Whether this approach will help to rejuvenate baseball in Puerto Rico remains to be seen.

The United States Virgin Islands of St. Croix and St. Thomas, located just off Puerto Rico's east coast, have also been home to baseball. Despite their small population of only 115,000 people, the islands have sent 12 men to play in the major leagues. The best-known of these are Pittsburg relief pitcher Alvin O'Neal McBean and Baltimore catcher Elrod Hendricks from St. Thomas, and the New York Yankees catcher Horace Clark from St. Croix. The islands were initially a colony of Denmark, but the United States took control in 1917, and the U.S. Navy administered them until 1930, popularizing the sport of baseball that Puerto Rican immigrants had brought there many years earlier. Baseball's heyday in the Virgin Islands was from the 1950s to the early 1970s. After that time, a host of social, political, and economic problems caused many Virgin Islanders to emigrate to the mainland, and budget woes crushed the economy to such an extent that the government could not pay its water or electricity bills.

Games are still played at festive Lionel Roberts Stadium, and youth baseball remains popular with food and drink for sale and various strains of Caribbean music in the air. Yet the islands have stopped producing major league players. Instead, the Virgin Islands' most famous recent athletic export is National Basketball Association star Tim Duncan. Elsewhere in the Caribbean, baseball was introduced to Trinidad and Tobago in 1993, thanks to a visit by Georgia Southern University coach Jack Stallings and the entrepreneurial spirit of Trinidadian Michael Legerton. Little leagues have sprung up in St. Vincent and the Grenadines. And the five-foot-tall San Blas Indians who worked in U.S. soldiers' mess halls in the Panama Canal Zone took up baseball with exceptional zest. And other Panamanians have taken up the game eagerly as well.[53]

The brilliant pitching of 20-year-old Francisco Rodriguez of the Anaheim Angels during the 2002 American League championship series and the World Series led several sportswriters to look into his baseball boyhood in an urban slum of Caracas, Venezuela. Abandoned by both parents, he had grown up using a broomstick and a bottle cap for a bat and ball. In the furor over Rodriguez, fans and sportswriters alike had seemingly forgotten that Venezuela has sent players to the major leagues since 1939, starting with pitcher Alex Carrasquel. He was followed by Hall of Fame shortstop Luís Aparicio and three other star shortstops, Alfonso "Chico" Carrasquel, "Ozzie" Guillen and "Davey" Concepción. Venezuelan "Bo" Díaz was an all-star catcher, "Vic" Davalillo was a major league outfielder for 17 seasons, Tony Armas was an American League home run champion, and Andrés Galarraga led the National League in hitting in 1993, creating a sensation among Venezuelan fans.

Cubans brought baseball to Venezuela in 1895, but the sport was slow to develop. Amateur teams competed within the country, but Venezuela did not play in the World Amateur Tournament until 1940. However, in 1941 they defeated Cuba to win the tournament and they also won in 1944 and 1945. In 1946, Venezuela inaugurated a professional winter league, with four teams featuring players primarily from Cuba and the United States. Over the ensuing years, this winter league has had economic success and has inspired many Venezuelan boys to play the game. By 1990, Venezuela had 29 men in the major leagues, the third largest number from any Latin country behind only Puerto Rico and the Dominican Republic.[54] Venezuelan fans support the game with a passion equal to that of fans anywhere in the Caribbean.

Nowhere in Latin America are fans more devoted to the game of baseball and to its players than the people of the Dominican Republic, who began to play the game in 1871. When a baby girl is born in San Pedro de Macorís, she is given a pink ribbon; a boy receives a toy baseball glove.[55] The achievements of Dominican Sammy Sosa, the long-time Chicago Cubs' great home-run hitting outfielder who was traded to Baltimore in 2005, have done much to dramatize the poverty of his homeland, the country with the lowest per capita income in Latin America.[56] To make themselves seem more attractive to major league scouts, many Dominican youngsters gave themselves false names and lowered their ages by several years. In 2002, 180 Dominicans playing in the U.S. minor leagues were found to have done so.

For many Dominican youngsters without shoes or schoolbooks, using paper milk cartons for baseball gloves, baseball is their only hope of escaping life-long poverty. Whether in the dusty seaport of San Pedro de Macorís or the nearby city of Santo Domingo, for many Dominicans, baseball is life itself. The modern era of Dominican baseball began in 1955 when Quisqueya Stadium opened as the ballpark for the country's two premier teams, Escogido and Licey. Over the years, the stadium has become more and more run down, with its paint peeling, its concrete cracking, its bathrooms and its loudspeakers out of order. Its 16,000 seats are creaky, too, but spirited music blares between innings, and fans roar even when nothing exciting is happening in the game. Advertisements on the outfield walls attempt to sell everything from Dominican beer and rum to Johnnie Walker Scotch and Coca-Cola.[57]

Fans arrive late, sometimes not until the third inning.[58] In the parking lot outside the stadium, attendants park fans' cars for a fee and others can be hired to wash them. Scalpers are everywhere trying to sell tickets that are lent to them by the ticket office. Closer to the stadium, women sell oranges, grapefruits, local candy, M&M's, and cheese. Baseball caps and other souvenirs are for sale as well. Police at the turnstiles carry M-16 rifles and search fans for weapons. Once inside, fans are led to their seats, not by ushers, but by street urchins who wipe their seats clean for a small fee. Inside the stadium, vendors serve all manner of food from peanuts and fried chicken to pizza. After an interesting play, vendors imitate what occurred as a kind of "instant replay," and the fans either shout their approval or argue in protest.[59]

There are bookies throughout the stands, and although taking bets is illegal, the police ignore the practice. Almost all of the fans are black, dressed in T-shirts with various logos or in imitations of Lacoste shirts. Women color their hair, some wear cowboy boots, and few have expensive clothing. Yet they wear skirts, not jeans, and they carry themselves gracefully. The most remarkable thing about the crowd is that many of them, often as many as half, root for the visiting team, not surprisingly because the two Santo Domingo teams, Escogido and Licey, often play each other in the stadium. The two sets of fans devote themselves to cheering their team and razzing the other one. When Licey is retired, the Escogido fans shout with joy, the band begins to play, and people dance.[60] Perfect strangers not only talk animatedly to one another, they laugh so hard that they fall into one another's arms. Men jump up and down like children and cry openly. But tempers flare, too, and fans sometimes shout obscenities at one another. Nonetheless, violence is rare, even though many fans fill themselves with potent beer and rum sold at the stadiums, and many others carry hip flasks filled with rum.

In his ethnographic account of Dominican fan behavior, Alan M. Klein stresses Dominican nonviolence. He notes that during a Caribbean Series game played in Miami, more than 1,000 Dominican fans attended the game, freely displaying their typical jubilant and raucous behavior. Shocked by such seemingly threatening behavior, Miami police rushed into the crowd and arrested people. Klein commented, "At home no one would have batted an eye at the merry-makers; in Miami, they were seen as a menace."[61] He continued to say, "The juxtaposition of passion, alcohol, and a hotly contested game should make anyone wary of attending a Dominican ballgame. But Dominican culture fashions a terrain on which verbal and body language are the weapons of confrontation: the ego is bloodied, but the opponent is left physically intact. Dominicans have ample opportunity to come to blows, but they do not…one can learn a lot about culture from watching a baseball game."[62]

How did baseball come to play such a vital role in the Dominican Republic? As former Los Angeles Dodger Dominican outfielder Manny Mota put it, "If you ask any Dominican what he is proudest of, he will read you a list of ballplayers. This country doesn't have much, but we know we are the best in the world at one thing [baseball]. That's not bragging, because it's true. And we plan to continue being the best in the world at it."[63] Former major leaguer Winston Llenas, then a Dominican Winter League general manager, added, "It's more than a game, it's our passion. It's almost our way of life."[64] As evidence of how this passion can lead to stardom, the most valuable player in the American League in 2002 was Dominican Miguel Tejada, former shortstop of the Oakland Athletics, who was traded to the Baltimore Orioles in December 2003. Third in the voting was another Dominican, Alfonso Soriano, the star second baseman of the New York Yankees who was traded to Texas for Alfonso Rodriguez early in 2004. Today, 361 Dominicans have played in the major leagues. Puerto Rico is second among Latin countries with 211.[65]

Baseball had a strange beginning in the Dominican Republic. Under Spanish rule, the country's economy was based on sugarcane, as was the case in Cuba. During Cuba's bloody war for independence from Spain in 1868 to 1878, many wealthy Cubans fled to the Dominican Republic where they put their knowledge of steam-powered sugar production to use just as the sugar markets in Europe and the United States were exploding. The United States attempted to annex the Dominican Republic, just as it had earlier done with Puerto Rico, but the bill failed to pass in the Senate by one vote.[66]

The population of the Dominican Republic today is about 7 million, but in 1870 it was only about 250,000 people, so in search of a much larger labor pool, the wealthy Cuban immigrants lured large numbers of workers from the Netherlands Indies and the British Caribbean. These people were slaves or former slaves of African ancestry. Most had been raised on British cricket and when their Cuban hosts and employers introduced the game of baseball, they took to it enthusiastically. The names of Dominican players who later became major leaguers clearly reflect their ancestry: for example, Jorge Bell, Rico Carty, Mariano Duncan, Alfredo Griffin, Manuel Lee, Nelson Norman, José Offerman, and Juan Samuel. However, perhaps the most famous Dominican ever to play did not have an English or Dutch name. Sammy Sosa rose from great poverty, shining shoes and selling oranges as a child to help his family survive. Although still malnourished, he was signed by the Chicago Cubs, and his game exploded. After hitting 66 home runs in the 1998 season, he rushed home to his hurricane-ravaged homeland with supplies for the needy.[67]

Baseball soon replaced cricket in the affection of these former slaves, whose employers urged them to play as a means of keeping them happy and willing to continue working in the Dominican. Amateur teams representing sugar companies competed for years. By the 1920s, Cuban mercenaries had been imported to play for the newly formed Santo Domingo teams of Licey and Escogido. When strongman Raphael "Papa" Trujillo seized power in 1930, he not only recruited star Cubans, but he also brought in star American Negro League players, including Josh Gibson and Satchel Paige. He hoped that baseball's popularity would deter revolution. The game flourished for a while, but it was not until the mid-1950s, when the Dominican winter league was established, that Dominican baseball became a magnet to local and foreign stars alike. Escogido, owned by dictator Trujillo's brother, played Dominicans Matty, Felipe and Jesús Alou, Juan Marichal and Ossie Virgil, as well as American stars Frank Howard, Stan Williams, Bill White, Willie Kirkland, André Rogers and Willie McCovey.[68] In 1962, one year after Trujillo's dictatorship ended with his assassination, the Dominican Republic sent the oldest rookie in major league history to play for the St. Louis Cardinals. Left-handed pitcher Guayubin Olivo was 43 years old.

The talent of Dominican players was so highly regarded by major league teams that several built so-called "academies," where they housed, fed and tried out young players. Toronto was the first team to do so, but the Los Angeles Dodgers soon followed, building a fifty-acre camp with beautifully manicured grounds, three baseball fields, and a modern dormitory and dining room. For the first time in their lives, the young prospects slept in beds with sheets and ate three healthy, well-balanced meals each day. Medical care was available, and there were weight rooms, television rooms, and locker rooms where the players changed into freshly laundered Dodger uniforms. Outstanding instructors were sent to the camp, which was managed by former major league player Ralph Avila, a Cuban-born, naturalized U.S. citizen. Each day began at 7:00 a.m. and ended at 10:00 p.m. after all manner of drills, instruction, and competitive games. The English language was taught as well, because it was understood that a Spanish-speaking player was greatly handicapped in adjusting to American baseball if he could not speak English reasonably well. Catchers and pitchers especially required English-language skills.

The Chicago Cubs also ran an academy in the Dominican Republic, but it was so horrible in every respect that it was called "Vietnam." Nineteen players lived in a ramshackle house without running water, fans, or ventilation. The players had to walk to a river a mile away to bathe or drink water. Their food consisted of rice and plaintains day after day. The house had no toilet, so the players had to urinate and defecate outside. Perpetually hungry and thirsty, the players had to use their own money to buy food and bottled water.[69]

Despite the excellence of academies like the one managed by the Dodgers, only 3 percent of the players trained in their academy have made it to the major leagues. Nevertheless, beginning with the Hiroshima Carp a decade ago, Japanese teams are investing in their own academies in the Dominican Republic.[70] However, Dominican players familiar with Japanese baseball are quick to say that they would much rather play in the United States because practices are too long and hard in Japan.[71] Nevertheless, some Latin players have signed with Japanese teams. In 2002, Latin import and former Arizona Diamondback, Alex Cabrera, tied the Japanese single-season home run record of 55 set in 1964 by Sadaharu Oh and tied in 2001 by black American import, Tuffy Rhodes. Cabrera went without a home run in the final five games of the season even though pitchers sometimes threw strikes to him.

Panama produced a number of exceptional players, including Rod Carew, who batted over .300 for fifteen straight season in the major leagues. No mention has been made of teams from Colombia, Honduras, Curaçao, Belize, or the Canal Zone, although all have played baseball well in international tournaments. So have teams from Brazil and Argentina, countries where most foreigners believe that soccer is the only sport played. For example, in 1990, an under-15 Brazilian team won a silver medal in an international tournament, then came in third in 1991 before winning gold the following year. Buenos Aires, Argentina, has six baseball fields and a modern baseball stadium. In the Italian World Cup competition of 1998, Argentina also played extremely well. Both Brazil and Argentina have seen their teams compete successfully in other international baseball tournaments as well.

Sailors from the U.S. battleship Nevada introduced baseball to the Brazilians in Rio de Janeiro in 1922, and Rio newspapers soon after demonstrated that Brazilians possessed a remarkable grasp of the game, including its many American slang terms. However, it was the large Japanese immigrant community centered in Sâo Paulo that came to dominate baseball in Brazil, and these so-called "Nippo-Brazilians" still play a large role in the game in that country. The same thing is true in Pero, where players of Japanese ancestry dominate the game. Many of Brazil's best players have names such as Diego Ito, Gabriel Asakura, Carlos Nakamura, Guilherme Morimoto, and Leandro Kirihara. There are three million Brazilians of Japanese descent. But Brazilian baseball fans come from all ethnic groups and social classes.

During spring training in 2002, more than 200 players on major league rosters lived in Latin America. Ninety-eight were from the Dominican Republic, 47 from Venezuela, 45 from Puerto Rico, and 12 from Mexico. Three players lived in Aruba in the Netherlands Antilles with another three in Panama, two in Curacao, two in the Netherlands Antilles and one in Nicaragua. Even though only one Nicaraguan now plays in the major leagues, baseball has been played there avidly ever since it was introduced by the U.S. Marines, who occupied the country in the 1920s and 1930s. Nicaraguan teams have competed well in Pan-American Games, and fans in Managua love the game. There were nearly twenty more players in the majors who learned the game in Latin America but now live in the United States.

And if any doubt exists about the vitality of baseball in Latin America, it need only be noted that proportional to their population, the Dominican Republic,

Puerto Rico, Venezuela, and Cuba have sent far more players to the major leagues than the United States has.

140

NOTES

[1] Regalado (1998:4).

[2] Fainaru and Sánchez (2001:18).

[3] González Echevarría (1999).

[4] Jamail (2000:1).

[5] Pettavino and Pye (1994:26); Bjarkman (2005: 2).

[6] Joseph (1988:33).

[7] Wagner (1988:130).

[8] Joseph (1988).

[9] Jamail (2000:4).

[10] Ibid., p.11.

[11] González Echevarría (1999:63).

[12] Bjarkman (1994:219).

[13] Fainaru and Sánchez (2001:20).

[14] Jamail (2000:36).

[15] González Echevarría (1999:332).

[16] Ibid., p.361.

[17] Ibid., p.51.

[18] New York Times, December 13, 1964.

[19] New York Times, April 22, 1963.

[20] Bjarkman (1994:246).

[21] Ibid. p.50.

[22] González Echevarría (1999:363).

[23] Ibid., p.47.

[24] Fainaru and Sánchez (2001).

[25] Baseball America, No. 1, February 3-16, 2003, pp.10-11.

[26] Jamail (2000:144).

[27] Ibid., p.149.

[28] Baseball America, No.1, January 6-19, 2003.

[29] Joseph (1988:29-30).

[30] Redfield (1950); Press (1975).

[31] Beezley (1985).

[32] Ibid.

[33] Ibid.

[34] Regalado (1998:183).

[35] Ibid., p.182.

[36] Ibid., p.185.

[37] Klein (1997:73).

[38] Ibid., p.66.

[39] Holway (1991:81).

[40] Klein (1997:74).

[41] New York Times, April 13, 1946.

[42] Laredo Times, April 17, 1946.

[43] Klein (1997:99).

[44] Laredo Times, February 2, 1946.

[45] Bjarkman (1994:276); Klein (1997:76).

[46] Klein (1997:111).

[47] Ibid., p.113.

[48] Bouton and Shecter (1970).

[49] Klein (1997:163).

[50] Regalado (1998:61).

[51] Bjarkman (1994:25).

[52] Ibid., p.80; International Baseball Rundown, October 1998.

[53] Perez Medina (1992).

[54] Regalado (1998:171).

[55] Klein (1991:1).

[56] Ibid., p.9.

[57] Klein (1991).

[58] Ibid., p.147.

[59] Ibid., p.140.

[60] Ibid., p.144.

[61] Ibid., p.147.

[62] Ibid., pp.147-148.

[63] Ibid., p.1.

[64] Ruck (1995).

[65] Bjarkman (2005: 161).

[66] Klein (1991:108).

[67] Dreier (2001:75).

[68] Bjarkman (1994:255).

[69] Marcono and Fidler (2002: 69-78).

[70] Ibid., p. 51.

[71] Ibid., p.52.

Chapter Five: Baseball in Australia, New Zealand, and Oceania

In his popular book about sport and Australian culture, anthropologist Jim McKay approvingly cited an earlier book that had insisted, "Australia is the most sport-drunk country in the world...sport participation and spectatorship and conversation is [sic] more pervasive in this culture than, apparently, in all others."[1] British writer Richard Twopenny agreed, calling Australia "The most sporting country in the world."[2] Many others have reached the same conclusion. One wrote, "Sport is as available to Australians – and as necessary – as meat pies, kangaroos, and Holden cars."[3] Australian sport features cricket, "Australian rules" football, rugby, boxing, golf, horse-racing, lawn "bowls," track and field, soccer, rowing, sculling, surfing, swimming, and, for over a century, baseball.

Although baseball is still seen by many Australians as a minor sport compared to cricket, it has been played avidly for many years, and today hundreds of thousands of Australian boys and men play baseball for clubs and professional teams in a variety of leagues. Some women play the game as well. During World War II and the early post-war period, Australian women played baseball enthusiastically, but during the 1960s and 1970s, when softball became seen as more "feminine," most switched to that game. But in the 1990s women in the state of Victoria again took up baseball, and there are now 500 women on 35 baseball teams. Women in other Australian states are following suit.[4] "Tee-ball" for boys, or "T-ball" as it is often written, began in earnest in Western Australia in 1974. Today 400,000 young Australian boys play the game all over the country.[5]

Native peoples have lived in Australia for perhaps 60,000 years, and the first European Australians came from Britain when a ship bearing some 1,000 men, women, and children landed in Sydney Cove in 1788. Many of the men were convicts taken to Australia to be exiled in that distant, seemingly barren land, but some free settlers soon joined them, including some who would serve as magistrates, police, and soldiers. By 1851, the European population of Australia had risen to almost 438,000, only a small minority of whom had ever been convicts.[6] There were even a few aristocrats among the new immigrants. During the eighteenth century, when this large immigration began, cricket was very popular in England, with teams of gentlemen playing matches against other gentlemen, and tradesmen playing against one another. But from 1750 to 1820, brutal bare knuckle prize-fighting was the British national sport.[7] Ale houses were enormously popular too. Both men and women gathered there to drink, play cards and skittles, dance, and watch prize fights and spirited horse races. There was excitement in such places, and no small amount of sexual tension. After 1800, the gentry avoided these rowdy and dangerous ale houses.

Still, there was much gambling, drinking and violence continuing throughout Britain, and the British authorities did their best to limit these activities in Australia. At first, they did not bring sports to Australia, because the convicts were being sent there for punishment, not to enjoy themselves. Many of the convicts were Irish, known to the British for their drunken violence. Many others were urban women, described as disorderly, dishonest and whorish: "the refuse of London," as they were known. But these women were not so wretched that crews of the convict ships found them repellent. A good many of these women were seduced aboard the ships that carried them to Australia, and others were raped.[8] After arrival, some were forced to become the mistresses of ex-convict settlers or of military officers. Despite British efforts to control the convicts who often refused to work except on their own terms, violence, drinking and gambling soon became widespread in newly settled Australia. There was a major armed rebellion in 1804 and again in 1834. Before long, despite this unrest, sports took hold with the first cricket match taking place in 1803. Horse racing, boxing, and cock fighting soon becoming popular as well.[9] By 1850, bare-knuckle boxing had become so brutal and disreputable that it was no longer a popular sport.

The first man to bring baseball to Australia was an American merchant, Samuel Perkins Lord, who arrived in Melbourne aboard his ship, *The City of Norfolk*, in September, 1853. He and his crew demonstrated the game, then tried, without success, to interest people in Melbourne in organizing their own teams. After Lord left, other visiting Americans played baseball against teams of Australian cricketers in Melbourne. In February, 1857, one club defeated another by the astonishing score of 350-230. How this score was arrived at is not known, but it is likely that each base that was reached was counted as a run, a practice that was sometimes followed at that time. Some historians believe that American gold miners in the small city of Ballarat played baseball during their free time in that same year.

By 1878, baseball was played in Sydney, and the following year, a touring black American music troupe, the Georgia Minstrels, played baseball against an Australian cricket club. Other American minstrel groups, as well as sailors from U.S. ships, played baseball against Australian cricket clubs as well. In 1882, Americans and Canadians who were living in Australia formed their own baseball club which competed against visiting minstrels and local cricketers alike. In 1886, several Australian clubs joined together to form what was called the New South Wales Baseball Association (NSWBA). Several games, or "matches" as they were called, were played, but attendance was sparse. These same teams played more games in 1887, but there was little enthusiasm from fans or players, and the NSWBA collapsed. It was then that news was received that American Albert G. Spalding, the former major league pitcher, manager, team owner, and, recently, the millionaire owner of a sporting goods business, intended to bring two American teams made up of professional baseball players to tour Australia.

In 1874, when he was the manager of the Boston Red Stockings major league team, Spalding had taken his team on a tour of Britain, where the Red

Stockings had played a series of games against the touring Philadelphia Athletics. The English were polite but doubted that baseball could ever become popular with them. Spalding insisted that he was not trying to replace cricket in the hearts of the English. He offered his two- to three-hour-long baseball game to the "masses," leaving the sometimes five-day-long matches of cricket for the enjoyment of the "leisure classes." His players had also contested top British sides in cricket matches, amazing the cricket players with their skill in hitting and catching the cricket ball. The Americans did not lose a single match.[10] Some British journalists were favorably impressed by baseball, but teams would not be formed until 1903, when some British miners and factory workers took up the game.[11]

In 1876, Spalding left the Red Stockings to become manager and president of the Chicago White Stockings. Spalding hired a detective, who soon reported the players' drunkenness and debauchery. When Spalding confronted the players, Mike Kelly made this response, "I have to offer only one amendment. In that place where the detective reports me taking a lemonade at 3 a.m., he's off. It was a straight whisky. I never drank a lemonade at that hour in my life."[12] In that same year, Spalding founded the A. G. Spalding and Brothers sporting goods company. By 1888, this company had made him so wealthy that he did not give a second thought to the expenses involved in shipping two teams of players to Australia and back, paying for their salaries and all their expenses. One of these two teams was the Chicago White Stockings, starring first baseman Cap Anson. The other was a team of all-stars called the All-Americans, originally featuring outfielder "Slide Kelly Slide" Kelly. At the last moment, Kelly decided not to participate.[13] The purpose of Spalding's tour was to create a market for sporting goods, especially the baseball gear he hoped to sell in Australia.

Spalding took young Harry H. Simpson, a skilled baseball player and cricketer from New Jersey, as his assistant. Spalding also took his white-haired mother, some of the players' wives, and a highly popular daredevil entertainer known as "Professor" or "Proff" Bartholomew who delighted audiences by going aloft in a hot air balloon and parachuting to earth. During his parachuting career, Bartholomew suffered several broken bones and a gouged-out eye. There was also Clarence Duval, the tour "mascot." Duval was a slender, imp-faced African American with a talent for all sorts of "hoe-down" plantation dancing and for twirling a silver-tipped baton. Dressed in a red coat, gold lace, tight-fitting white trousers and high-topped patent leather boots, he led the teams onto the field, deftly twirling his glistening baton to the enthusiastic applause of the crowd. Journalists joined Spalding's tour as well.

After the last game of the White Stockings' major league season, the tour members met with President Grover Cleveland at the White House, then left Chicago in late October, 1888, travelling to San Francisco in two lavishly appointed rail carriages with luxurious dining and sleeping coaches. The carriages were adorned with white linen, with the words "Spalding's Australian Baseball Tour" inscribed in red. The two teams played against each other in a different city almost every day. As they traveled west across the United States, the crowds that paid to see them play were so large that Spalding nearly made enough money to finance the entire tour by the time the teams reached San Francisco.[14] The tour spent two full weeks in California, playing games from San Francisco to Los Angeles and back. Leaving San Francisco, the tour sailed to Hawaii aboard the U.S.S. *Alameda*, a ship with a well-stocked library and saloon. Despite rough seas that caused most players to suffer painful sea-sickness before they reached Honolulu, where the teams played more games before the group sailed on to New Zealand. This time, the sea was calm, and the ship's captain set up a cricket pitch on deck with a canvas roof and sides. The teams played cricket every day.

The first game in New Zealand was played in Auckland on December 10, 1888, in front of a crowd of 4,500, a huge gathering for New Zealand at that time. However, the New Zealand press criticized the "blow-out" game because Chicago blasted the All-Star team 19-4. Baseball did not catch on with the public. The mayor of Auckland attended the game and later did all he could to support baseball, which he saw as a valuable outdoor amusement for the summer months. The tour sailed on to Australia aboard the *Alameda*, entering Sydney harbor, where they were greeted first by two steam tugs crowded with people waving American flags, then by hundreds of small boats carrying red, white, and blue bunting and American flags. Brass bands played, steam whistles blew, and on nearby rooftops and hills thousands of people cheered and waved flags and handkerchiefs. The tour disembarked at Wooloomooloo wharf. The players were driven to their hotel, the Oxford, in elegant, four-horse coaches. The hotel was decorated with an American flag. The Americans were greeted by the U.S. consul, and after dinner they were taken to a theater performance starring two popular American actors. After the show, the tour members gathered on the stage, where they were welcomed by Sydney political figures. In response, Spalding expressed his gratitude, adding that baseball was already known in Sydney, a remark that drew a roar of "hear, hear" from the audience.[15]

While the tour was still in New Zealand, Spalding's public relations expert, Leigh Lynch, had gone ahead to Australia to publicize American baseball. The Australian press and public were so eager to see the Americans play that Lynch had no difficulty encouraging their great interest. All the major newspapers in Australia covered the tour extensively and praised the players' skills. The Sydney newspapers gave Spalding's baseball tour enthusiastic coverage, and the first game in Sydney drew 6,000 people. Surprisingly, the majority of them were elegantly dressed women. The tour then took a train to Melbourne, where the first game drew 10,000 spectators, and the second drew 6,000. When the two teams moved on to Adelaide, three more games drew well, and, for another game played in the mining town of Ballarat, some 60 miles northwest of Melbourne, a remarkable crowd of 4,500 turned out, nearly the entire population of that small city. Games were also well attended in Sydney, again by women as well as men, and the final game in Melbourne drew 11,000 people who warmly welcomed the Americans. A major reason for this crowd interest was the spectacular daring-do of "Professor" Bartholomew, the parachute jumber. However, during the tour's stopover in Ballarat, he landed on a zinc cornice on the roof of a shed near the Buck's Head Hotel where he had hoped to land, cutting his legs so badly that he was forced to abandon his crowd-pleasing routine for the rest of the tour.

The Australian spectators did not understand the game of baseball, but they were greatly impressed by the Americans' fielding, throwing, and powerful hitting. After a game in Adelaide, Governor Sir William Robinson shook hands with the players, then warmly welcomed them to Australia, stressing the common heritage and friendship between America and Australia and looking forward to a day in the near future when an Australian baseball team would tour the United States. The American teams were also fêted as they traveled about, lavishly fed and shown the sights. After an elegant lunch on New Year's Day 1889, they were treated to a demonstration of boomerang throwing and rope skipping by Australian Aborigines. The last game in Australia was a double-header. The first game was played between the All Stars and Australian cricketers, and the Americans won easily. The second game was closely fought, but Chicago nipped the All Stars. The afternoon ended with a long-distance throwing contest with a cricket ball. After a running start, an All Star pitcher won with an impressive throw of 384 feet.

The Americans' last evening in Melbourne was spent in various forms of entertainment including visits to theaters, boxing matches, and music halls. Although the men drank alcohol freely, there do not appear to have been any untoward incidents. The next day, after a rousing farewell, the tour sailed out of Melbourne on a German steam-ship. Its first stop was Colombo, Ceylon, followed by a visit to Cairo. The tour's stopover in Cairo did little to increase the popularity of baseball in Egypt, but it was assuredly memorable. The game was to be played at the foot of the Great Pyramid of Gizeh for the edification of the Khedive of Egypt. Although the Khedive was unexpectedly called away on official business, the game went ahead. Cap Anson's Chicago White Sox and Johnny Ward's All Stars had to choose between camels and donkeys as their mode of transportation from their hotel to the pyramid, a distance of about eight miles. As little bootblacks followed the two teams hoping for work, and beggars cried for "baksheesh," Anson, his teammates, and their wives chose donkeys, while Ward's people mounted camels, a decision they soon came to regret. These animals were not only uncomfortable mounts, they were unruly. After four miles, Ward's team dismounted and somehow convinced Anson's people to ride camels, while they switched to donkeys. Ward's group arrived at the pyramid well ahead of Anson's by-then cranky teammates and their wives.

Once at the foot of the pyramid, both teams consumed a hearty lunch they had carried from their hotel. Refreshed, they discovered that a diamond had been laid out on a green-grass field. As the players' wives and crowds of Arabs clad in long gowns looked on, A. G. Spalding served as the umpire, and Ward's All-Stars defeated Anson's White Sox, 10-6. Anson later remarked that he apologized to the Sphinx for his team's performance. It's not known how the players and their consorts made their way back to the *Hôtel d'Orient*, but there was much grousing about camels for the rest of the tour.[16]

Visits to Naples, Rome, Florence, Paris, London, Bristol, Birmingham, Sheffield, Bradford, Glasgow, Manchester, Liverpool, Belfast, and Dublin followed. Although tour members were treated in a kindly manner everywhere they went, unlike Australians, the people of these cities showed little interest in baseball, although a total of 60,000 spectators watched the games played in the United Kingdom. In Italy and France, the tour had great difficulty even finding a place to play, but the players greatly enjoyed being tourists in Paris and Rome. The Prince of Wales (later King Edward) was an exception to this pattern of indifference. He watched the game played in London with considerable interest, posing many intelligent questions to A. G. Spalding. After the game, he said, "I consider Base Ball an excellent game: but cricket a better one."[17]

In late April 1889, the tour members enjoyed a welcome-home banquet at Delmonico's, the most expensive and best restaurant in New York, attended by Theodore Roosevelt, Mark Twain, and 300 other dignitaries. Twain exuberantly told them that baseball was "the very symbol, the outward and visible expression of the drive and push and rush and struggle of the raging, tearing, booming nineteenth century."[18] The tour pressed on to Chicago, where they finally completed their "around-the-world to the west" journey.

Harry Simpson remained behind in Australia to promote the development of baseball. He was well respected and succeeded in helping several Australian cities to develop baseball and set up a league. But in 1891 he contracted typhoid and died alone at the age of only 27. Simpson was without family and, seemingly, forgotten by Spalding, but a number of his friends attended his interment. For some reason, Simpson was buried in an unmarked grave.[19] Before his death, Simpson was often asked about the feasibility of an Australian baseball tour of America. He urged everyone to wait several years until the skills of Australian players improved.

After Simpson's death, plans for a tour were put on hold until 1896, when Harry Musgrove, a cricketer who had managed the Australian cricket team on a recent tour of England, took an interest. Musgrove's cricket tour had visited America on its return home, and Musgrove, who had recently begun to play baseball himself, became interested in leading an Australian baseball tour to America. He selected a team of fourteen men, all of whom were cricketers who also played some baseball. With help from Albert Spalding, he tried to schedule a coast-to-coast tour, but finances were lacking and opponents hard to identify. Musgrove was so discouraged that he recommended postponing the tour. At that point, an Adelaide cricket patron, A. J. Roberts, promised to cover all expenses.

The tour members, calling themselves the "Kangaroos," joyfully set sail on March 15, 1897, on what would soon become known as the "Disaster Tour."

After a brief but pleasant stopover in American Samoa, they landed in Honolulu where they had no games scheduled. They did meet some local baseball players and were able to practice on a "real" baseball field that, compared to their own converted cricket fields, delighted them. They stayed in an elegant hotel and were amazed to learn that every house in the city apparently had both a telephone and electric lights. When they sailed away, they gave three cheers for Honolulu. They practiced again when they arrived in San Francisco, then went sightseeing and partying. They watched several college teams play and were duly impressed. Not surprisingly, they lost the first game they played, 20-9. Newspaper accounts wrote that they played baseball like it was cricket, but they won their third game, 13-10. After losing their next game, 23-18, against a team they accused of using professionals, they won the next one, 26-25. The Australians justifiably complained about unfair umpires and partisan crowds, but after giving serious thought to abandoning the tour, the Australians decided to press on, in no small measure because they wanted to see the country. Their train trip over the Sierra Nevada mountains in California allowed them to see snow for the first time, and they were delighted by the spectacle. Arriving in Salt Lake City, they won several games, but after travelling farther east to Omaha they lost two games badly to Omaha University. Moving on, they played an appallingly bad game against a Council Bluffs team, losing 24-4.

The team next traveled to Chicago, where Musgrove had been able to arrange for only one game during their ten-day stay in the city. They lost this one game to the Illinois Bicycle Club. However, they were warmly welcomed by Chicagoans and enjoyed meeting Australian Joe Quinn, who was there playing for the Baltimore Orioles against the Chicago White Sox of the American League. Quinn had been born and raised in New South Wales, but his family had moved to Iowa when he was a boy. He had learned the game so well that he played in the major leagues from 1884 to 1901. He managed and played for St. Louis in 1895 and Cleveland in 1899.[20]

The Kangaroos made up for poor play in their one game in Chicago by devoting themselves to drinking, partying, and feasting with Chicagoans. The Chicago press treated them hospitably as well, complimenting them for playing well, behaving as gentlemen, and never complaining about an umpire's decision, a conclusion based on witnessing a single game in which the Kangaroos were on their best behavior. They next played well but lost in Pittsburgh, then moved on to New York City, where they were welcomed by Cap Anson, who had greatly enjoyed his tour of Australia. He spared no expense making the Australians comfortable and showing them the town. He also arranged for them to work out at the fabled New York Polo Grounds, something they enjoyed enormously. Albert G. Spalding then met the team, took them to a major league game between the New York Yankees and the Cleveland Indians, showed them the New York sights, and gave them a sumptuous dinner party at his grand Manhattan home.

After New York, the Kangaroos played in Boston, Providence, Atlantic City, and Philadelphia, before taking a four-day sightseeing trip to Niagara Falls. They then sailed for London. During the trip, Musgrove confessed to several players that he had misappropriated some of their money and mismanaged many of their other resources. He promised to pay back the money after he arrived in London. In fact, he did nothing of the sort. Instead, he disappeared. Most of the players had to cable home for enough funds to return to Australia. Two players were even reduced to working ignominiously as stokers in the ship's boiler room to pay for their trip. Although the tour ended on this sad note, in general it gave the Australian game a major boost by showing the Americans and themselves that they could master the complexities of baseball. New baseball teams arose in Australia, and the tour team members continued to play both cricket and baseball.

Not everyone in Australia was pleased with the American game. A Sydney magazine wrote scornfully soon after the Spalding tour, "Americans think baseball the only game worth playing, abuse and revile football, and ridicule cricket. They think their players the only people on earth, and that the world should bow down and worship them."[21] But as Joe Clark has shown in his book *A History of Australian Baseball*, many Australian newsmen wrote very favorable opinions about baseball. In 1889, one newsman observed that baseball had obtained a very strong foothold in Australia.[22] Many cricketers continued to play "their" game during the dry summer months, but some also played baseball during the rainy winters to "keep fit for cricket," as they said.

Thanks in part to the publicity generated by the American tour, the game continued to grow in popularity in Australia, with 16 club teams competing in Melbourne by 1907 and twenty in Sydney by 1908. In that same year, the 16 battleships of the American Pacific Fleet, known as the "Great White Fleet," visited Australia, and their crew members played several baseball games against Australian teams in Sydney and Melbourne, winning all but one. Baseball's popularity continued to grow. In 1912, Melbourne had 33 club teams in competition with one another. By 1913 there were 36 club or church-based teams in Sydney and another 16 school-based teams. In January, 1914, baseball received another boost when the New York Giants and Chicago White Sox played games against each other in both Sydney and Melbourne before large and enthusiastic crowds. John J. McGraw, who managed the Giants, wrote:

> The brand of baseball which the Australian boys showed us during our visit there surprised every member of the party. . . . Being naturally athletic, some of them have become quite proficient and they tell me that the game is growing very popular here. They marveled as much over our work as we were surprised over theirs, as it was the first chance they had to see major leaguers in action.[23]

Australian baseball suffered from a lack of manpower during World War I, but in 1918, Australian soldiers played baseball against Americans during lulls in combat along the Somme. As soon as the war ended, baseball quickly regained its popularity, with games scheduled during the summer to compete with cricket matches. Interest in baseball was heightened by the tours of Japanese teams in 1919 and 1924, and by American teams in 1923, 1928, and 1929. In 1925, a 43-ship United States fleet, said to carry 525 baseball players among their crews, docked in Australia. They played three games against Australian teams and, to the delight of spectators, lost all three.[24] Australian girls and women began to play baseball in the 1920s as well, and women's teams flourished during the 1930s. In 1933, Norrie Claxton, one of Australia's leading sportsmen, donated a shield for an annual competition between state teams. For over half a century, winning the Claxton Shield was the ultimate annual award on Australia's baseball calendar. The award did not end until 1988.

Baseball suffered again during World War II when so many Australian troops served overseas, but the presence of American servicemen in Australia kept interest alive, as more than one million Americans served there before the war ended. Among them were thousands of African Americans, some of whom played baseball on racially segregated teams. When peace was restored, Australian baseball resumed, and, by 1953, there were 700 teams throughout the country and 10,000 players. By this time, most women had shifted their play from baseball to softball but some continued to play baseball on men's teams.[25] After a 33-year hiatus, women's baseball was reestablished in 1990, and women's teams now play in four states: Victoria, New South Wales, Queensland, and Western Australia. There is also a national women's baseball tournament.

A Japanese team visited in 1954, but protests by World War II Australian Army veterans forced the Japanese tour to be cancelled after a few games had been played. The game was no longer played only during the winter months. By the 1970s, it was played year-round, and youth baseball had become very popular.

In 1978, Australia played in the World Series in Italy, and a team of 18-year-olds toured the United States and Canada. By the 1960s, American major league scouts had flocked to Australia, and in 1986 shortstop Craig Shipley became the first Australian to play in the major leagues since Joe Quinn. By the 1990s, several Australians were playing in the American major leagues. Catcher Dave Nilsson, relief pitcher Graeme Lloyd, and pitchers Mark Hutton and Mark Ettles, among others, played very well, and so did infielder Trent Durrington. In all, about 180 Australians have been signed by major league teams, and in 2004, some 100 Australians were playing for the minor league clubs of U.S. major league teams. Another 50 Australians play baseball for U.S. colleges or universities. By 1992, two dozen American minor league players had been assigned to teams in the eight-team semipro Australian Baseball League, where they were able to gain valuable experience in a so-called "winter league" that was more suitable for their talent level than the more competitive Latin American winter leagues. They were also very well treated, traveling by air and staying in five-star hotels.[26]

By that time, each of Australia's six states and two territories had its own central baseball program which controlled the game. The Australian Baseball Federation (ABF) coordinated these programs, but each state directed its own leagues and competitions, including competitions between states, such as the Commonwealth Cup and the International Baseball League of Australia (IBLA). Unlike America and several other countries that play baseball, there are no Australian college baseball teams, and there is very little high school baseball, with its cheerleaders, parents, and other zealous fans. However, in addition to state baseball clubs, there are many local baseball clubs, 100 in Sydney alone.

And thanks to a major initiative from U.S. Major League Baseball, an Australian Academy Program has been established in which the most promising 17- to 20-year-olds from throughout Australia and Oceania receive professional

U.S. and Australian coaching. An Australian associated with this academy described it as follows:

> It allows us to get sixty to seventy of the top Australian kids and Oceania kids in a very intensive six-week training program, which is fast tracking the development of these kids so we can give them a taste of what it's like in professional baseball. The direct aims of the program are to develop professional baseball players. The program is also educational because the kids go to school while they're at the Academy and there's a strong component of sports medicine. We're telling the kids, 'This is what it takes to play professionally,' but there are other things in their life that are important too. . . . Each player gets their personal development program so they go away with their own course of off-field stuff they should work on. It's not visual – you have to tell people what's going on – but if you're an athlete you appreciate it. It may look like we're signing a lot of kids, but the feedback from the States is that they like what we're doing in development. . . . They know the kids are coming in with the best knowledge possible.[27]

Australian children often play ball games in their back yards, school yards, streets or local parks, but the game they play is cricket, not baseball. Baseball is rarely played spontaneously, because it is a club sport requiring transportation to a ballfield, as well as coaches and managers to oversee both practice and competitive games. Nevertheless, almost all ages play. Boys and girls aged 7-10 play "T-ball" as well as baseball, and from ages 11-16, "junior" baseball is played. There are other leagues for youngsters 17-19, and many leagues for older adults as well, from the top level, or "First Grade," down through other leagues made up of less skilled players. Some of these lesser leagues play middle-aged or even older men, and women play in others.[28] By 1990, 300,000 Australian boys played junior ball and 150,000 adult players were registered as well.[29]

Australian players, like those of other foreign countries, are not subject to America's major league draft. They are free to negotiate with American teams as they see fit. Since the 1960s, more than 100 young Australian players have been signed by major league clubs. During the 1990s, many of these players had previously played in the Australian Baseball League, Australia's highest national league. Unfortunately, the ABL was always on the verge of financial collapse; players demanded higher salaries and owners refused to pay, equipment was too costly, and so were stadium rentals and travelling expenses. Attendance was poor, with an average per-game of only 1,600, and media coverage was lacking.[30]

In 1999, Australian star player and former U.S. major leaguer, Dave Nilsson, invested $5 million of his own money in a new International Baseball League that would replace the struggling ABL. Buoyed by Australia's victory in the 1999 Intercontinental Cup, the new league was welcomed by baseball fans. But despite initial enthusiasm, the new league quickly collapsed as ABL owners refused to cooperate, attendance was only in the hundreds, and media coverage was virtually non-existent. Despite all of Nilsson's efforts, the league closed after its initial year. Nilsson described this calamity as "a shattering blow."[31]

In the 1956 Melbourne Olympics, baseball was played for the first time as a "demonstration sport." The Australian team lost to the United States team, 11-5 before 100,000 people. Baseball was still a "demonstration sport" during the 1988 Seoul Olympics, and Australia was thought to have an excellent team, but they were eliminated when they embarrassingly lost to a supposedly weak team from Guam. However, Cuba was eliminated from the Olympics due to a political boycott, and Australia was reinstated. They finished a disappointing fifth. In the 1996 Atlanta Olympics, the Australians were again highly regarded, but again they finished fifth.[32]

The Intercontinental Cup, which is held every two years, was played in Sydney in 1999. It was a trial event for the 2000 Olympics. Among the teams that competed were Australia, Cuba, Italy, Japan, Netherlands, South Korea,

Taiwan and the United States. Cuba was favored to win. In their first Intercontinental Cup in 1981, Australia had finished last. But at Barcelona in 1997 they were second, and at Sydney in 1999 the Australians won by defeating Cuba 4-3 in an exciting 11-inning game. The crowd was ecstatic.

As the Olympics approached, Australia asked the commissioner of American Major League Baseball to allow the 18 Australians on American major league rosters to compete for Australia. The commissioner agreed, but several major league teams refused to allow their Australian players to participate, and the Australian Olympic team was significantly weakened as a result. Tommy Lasorda, former Los Angeles Dodger manager, and then the U.S. Olympic baseball team manager, was highly critical of those teams, including the Dodgers, that would not allow these players to compete, saying publicly that the Australians should be allowed to represent their country, as players from several other countries did.

Despite the fans' enthusiastic rallying cry of "Aussie! Aussie! Aussie! Oi! Oi! Oi!," and some sparkling play, the Australians won only two of seven games, losing to Italy among others. Their loss to the U.S was a dazzling three-hit shutout by pitcher Ben Sheets. Sheets went on to star for the Milwaukee Brewers in the American League, striking out 18 Atlanta Braves during a game in May 2004. Despite Australia's disappointing play, 400,000 fans attended Olympic baseball games during the Sydney games. The game continues to be popular, but a key problem for Australian baseball has always been the lack of baseball diamonds and stadiums. Club teams have had to improvise, playing games on cricket pitches or football fields. Even professional teams have lacked adequate stadiums and clubhouse facilities.

Although the game played by the Spalding Tour in Auckland in December, 1888, stimulated some interest in the game among New Zealand cricketers, it soon faded. No team was actually formed for 100 years. There are several reasons for this. Even more so than Australians, New Zealanders sought to earn the respect of men in Britain by competing with them in the ultimately genteel sport of cricket, and even more importantly by defeating them in the "manly" sport of rugby, a game that was literally brutal as the New Zealanders played it. There were some 18,000 rugby injuries during the 1967 season, and in 1991 a New Zealand player bit off an opponent's ear.[33]

It was not until 1989 that the first New Zealand baseball team was formed. It was followed two years later by the formation of the nonprofit New Zealand Baseball Foundation. The game was soon embraced because it was seen as embodying teamwork, sportsmanship, and fair play. Baseball diamonds with an atmosphere for spectator enjoyment were developed, coaching and umpiring clinics were organized, and parents were encouraged to become involved by coaching, fund raising, organizing playing fields, or simply offering support as players advanced through different age levels. In 1992, a New Zealand team participated in the Merit Cup held in the United States, losing all six games but coming away enthused. They played hard and learned a great deal about the game. Soon after, New Zealand players joined others from New Caledonia, Papua New Guinea, Palau, Pohnpei, Northern Marianas, Marshall Islands, and American Samoa in a baseball training course in Guam sponsored by Olympic Solidarity and the International Baseball Federation. Other training camps followed, including a six- to eight-week camp in 2003, held in Brisbane, Australia, and sponsored by both U.S. major leagues.

Today, there are numerous teams for New Zealand adults and youths, most of them in the greater Auckland area. Since 2000, New Zealand Under-14 and Under-16 squads have played in Australia and New Caledonia, competing well. In 2001, the first New Zealand Little League team competed in the Pacific Regional Championships in Hong Kong. They did so again in 2002 in Manila. In 1993, a strapping 18-year-old named Gus Leger was signed by the Anaheim Angels. Leger was presented to the media at Anaheim Stadium, where he happily admitted that he had never played baseball. He lasted two seasons in the Angels' minor league system, did not hit a single home run, and was released.[34] In 1996, another New Zealand softball player, Travis Wilson, who had grown up in Christchurch, a city on the South Island where baseball is not played, signed a major league contract. He had seen baseball played on subscription Sky TV but had never played it himself until he reported to the Atlanta Braves for spring training camp in Florida. Several other young New Zealand men have also played baseball on U.S. college teams.

Families have become involved in baseball not only as excited spectators, but also as sponsors of youth programs, including T-ball. They raise money, organize leagues, coach, and provide baseball gear. New Zealand is also developing more media attention, with increased newspaper and television coverage of the sport. Unlike Australia, international-standard baseball diamonds have been built, and New Zealand hopes soon to host international tournaments. Bill Clark, former international scouting supervisor for the Atlanta Braves and most recently the San Diego Padres, has visited New Zealand for the last eight years. He praises the country for its development of youth programs in which youngsters learn to play the game well. He predicts that New Zealand will become a regional power in five years.[35] He also notes that most countries that have adopted baseball recently have not given sufficient attention to youth baseball. An example can be taken from the 1998 Youth Championships played in Illinois. The U.S. team won, and the next six places were taken by countries with long histories of baseball competition.

In addition to New Zealand, baseball has been played across much of the Pacific. In the eastern portion of Polynesia, it is played in the Cook Islands. To the west, the game appears in American Samoa, Fiji, and the French island of New Caledonia, positioned between New Zealand and Australia. Farther east, baseball is played in parts of Papua New Guinea where Australians introduced it. To the north in Micronesia, it is played enthusiastically in Palau, where the game is known as *Yakiu*. It is the number one sport on Pohnpei (also known as

Ponape). Still farther north in the Marianas, the game is played on Saipan by Palauans. There is also a Palauan team on Hawaii. The Thais have played baseball avidly for the past twenty years, with twenty teams for adults and an equal number for youth of various ages. In 1993, Thailand held its first baseball tournament for ten teams. A team from Kasetsart University won.[36] In 1998, Bangkok hosted the All-Asia Games.

Introduced by U.S. Navy officers and men, baseball was played on Guam early in the 1900s after the formerly Spanish-held island was taken over by the United States in the Spanish-American war of 1898. Guam was used as a U.S. Navy coaling and communications station, and baseball was popular there with naval personnel. By the 1920s, several baseball fields were kept busy, seemingly all the time. During World War II, the Japanese played baseball on Guam. After the war, the island continued to be a U.S. naval base, but its civilian population grew, and the game spread widely with eight adult teams eventually coming into being along with more than 50 Babe Ruth, high school and Little League teams. Today, there are four major league-size fields and nine youth fields. There is also a municipal stadium with a 2,500 seating capacity. The Guam Little League championship team won the Pacific Regional Tournament in 2001 and 2002, and this team also advanced to the 2001 and 2002 Little League World Series in Williamsport, Pennsylvania.[37] In 2004, the Guam adult national team competed in the Oceania Championship in Australia for the right to face South Africa for a spot in the Athens Olympics. Australia won easily.

Before German conquest in the early 20th century compelled the men of the Chuuk (formerly known as Truk) Islands in the Eastern Caroline Islands of Micronesia to surrender their firearms and give up warfare, these Trukese men were as ferociously warlike as any people on earth. Foreigners who visited Truk quickly and painfully learned how brave and vicious armed Trukese men were. Most foreigners learned to stay away from Truk. But the Germans eventually conquered the island. When Trukese men were forced to give up warfare, they replaced it with drunken brawling. Everyone but children and the elderly was a target for drunken assault, although, in reality, women were seldom attacked.[38]

After the Japanese introduced baseball to the islands during World War II, Chuukese men adopted the game as a substitute for warfare. In an article called "Waging Baseball in Truk," George Peter Murdock argued that baseball was seized upon as a new form of warfare, a practice that continued after the war when Chuuk became a U.S. Trust Territory. He described preparations for baseball games in the late 1940s that followed almost exactly their former traditional preparations for battle. He noted that women don't play the game "because baseball, like war, is men's business."[39] And the games themselves were played with nothing less than ferocity. Although there are photographs taken in Chuuk in recent years showing young women in dresses posing with bats, there are apparently no women's teams on Chuuk.

Organized baseball was introduced to American Samoa in 1979 when a Little League Program was begun under the tutelage of Tolia "Tony" Solaita, the first major leaguer of Samoan ancestry. Solaita's father was a U.S. marine. When Tony was nine, the family moved to Hawaii, where he learned to play baseball. He went to high school in San Francisco. In 1968, he hit 51 home runs in the California League before being called up to the New York Yankees as a 21-year-old rookie. He returned to Samoa after his American playing career ended. There are two baseball stadiums where youth league teams compete. One is named after Solaita who was tragically killed in 1995. Samoan teams have competed in tournaments in Australia, New Zealand, Taiwan, Guam, Hawaii, and California and have done well. But in 2003 they lost 6-0 to Palau in the South Pacific Games. The game is very popular with Samoan parents, who go to games to watch their children play, but there are as yet no adult teams. Only adult softball is played.[40]

Baseball was introduced to Indonesia by the Dutch early in the twentieth century. It was called Honkball, "honk" meaning base. The Japanese military also played baseball there during World War II, and the game became popular with high school and university students in the 1950s. In 1967, the Indonesian Amateur Baseball and Softball Federation (PERBASASI) was founded, but, in that same year, baseball was ended. Only softball was played until 1993 when PERBASASI reactivated baseball. Today, there are at least 100 adult baseball teams, with a similar number of youth teams. There are numerous baseball fields throughout the country. Since 1993, both youth and adult teams have played in tournaments throughout Asia and Oceania, competing well. PERBASASI is now soliciting international aid to provide baseball equipment, train coaches, create clinics, and construct baseball fields. Although Indonesia was admitted to the IBAF, at present, the Indonesian government does not provide government funding for baseball.[41] Even so, in 2001 Indonesia hosted the Fourth Asian Cup Championship in Jakarta. The competing teams were from Hong Kong, Pakistan, Malaysia, Thailand, Uzbekistan, and Indonesia.[42]

In August, 2002, a Little League team from Saipan won the Asia-Pacific Little League championship by beating the Filipino team, 10-5 in their home ballpark. Philippine president Gloria Macapagal-Arroyo attended the game, but she left after the first inning when the boys from Saipan had scored three runs and the Filipinos were scoreless.[43]

NOTES

---

[1] McKay (1991:1); Rowse (1978: 257).

[2] Twopenny (1973:204).

[3] Mossop (1989: 165); Stoddart (1986).

[4] Dabscheck (1995); International Baseball Rundown, June 1997.

[5] Clark (2003:156).

[6] Waterhouse (1995: 3).

[7] Ibid., p.7.

[8] Ibid., p.11.

[9] Ibid., pp.35-37.

[10] Spalding (1911:184).

[11] Ibid., p.383.

[12] Spalding (1911: 525).

[13] Appel (1996:134-135).

[14] Clark (2003:5).

[15] Sydney Morning Herald, December 15, 1888.

[16] Kiernan, J. "In the Shadow of the Pyramids." New York Times, March 14, 1932.

[17] Spalding (1911:263).

[18] Zoss and Bowman (1989:67).

[19] Clark (2003:53); Palmer (1889).

[20] Bjarkman (1994).

[21] Clark (2003: 16).

[22] Ibid.

[23] New York Times, January 6, 1914.

[24] Clark (2003: 108).

[25] Vamplew et al. (1992:52).

[26] Dabscheck (1995).

[27] Clark (2003:132).

[28] Ibid.

[29] Vamplew et al. (1992:52).

[30] Clark (2003:232).

[31] Ibid., p.248.

[32] Ibid., p.179.

[33] Belich (2001).

[34] Los Angeles Times, July 30, 1999.

[35] New Zealand Baseball Federation Website, February 27, 2003.

[36] World Baseball Magazine, Fall 1993.

[37] Dennis M. Zermeno, Guam Baseball Federation.

[38] Marshall (1979).

[39] Murdock (1948: 69).

[40] Robert Coulter, American Samoa Baseball Association.

[41] Harry A. Trisnadi, Vice-President, PERBASASI.

[42] The Jakarta Post, February 23, 2001.

[43] Filipino Reporter, August 8, 2002.

Chapter Six: Baseball in Europe

We have now looked at various aspects of baseball among countries in Asia, Latin America, Australia, New Zealand and Oceania, but as was noted in the introduction, a great many other countries have recently joined the International Baseball Federation to play the game against all sorts of international competition. There are teams throughout Southeast Asia, India, Pakistan and even Iran. The game is also played in Africa, the Middle East, and throughout Eastern and Western Europe.

Baseball was first seen in the United Kingdom in 1874 when Albert G. Spalding took the Boston Red Stockings major league team he then managed on a tour of Great Britain. Despite a pronounced lack of enthusiasm for the game in some parts of the United Kingdom, the game spread from city to city rapidly enough that by 1890, the National Baseball League of Great Britain was founded, followed by the British Baseball Federation in 1892.[1] A team from Preston North End was named national champion after it defeated teams from three other cities. Derby was accused of using experienced American players, but despite this controversy, attendance was good. However, over the years, public interest waned and newspaper coverage was uninformed and sometimes downright hostile, declaring baseball a threat to cricket and an American insult to British good taste.[2]

However, World War I revived interest in the game. In 1917, Princess Victoria joined 2,000 other British spectators to watch a game between a British and an American team. And on U.S. Independence Day, July 4, 1918, Britain showed its support for its military ally and former colony by the attendance of 38,000 British spectators at a baseball game played in London between a team from the U.S. Navy and one from the U.S. Army. Among those in attendance were King George V, his wife, Queen Mary, his daughter, Princess Mary, Prime Minister David Lloyd George, and his two predecessors A. J. Balfour and H. H. Asquith. Also in attendance were two future prime ministers, Arthur Bonar Law and Winston Spencer Churchill, along with many members of the cabinet and leading statesmen from South Africa, Australia, New Zealand, and Canada. Finally, three senior army officers were at the game, including Field Marshal Sir William Robertson, the only man to begin his British military service as a private soldier and rise to the rank of field marshal. What any of these luminaries thought about the game (won by the Navy team) or the occasion itself is not recorded. But the Illustrated London News praised the players: "They display wonderful agility in running from one base to the other, whilst they are brilliant catchers and return the ball with extraordinary smartness."[3]

By the 1930s, the game had become so popular that a professional league was formed in the north of England in 1933. Baseball was also played in Scotland, and in 1934, a team of Scottish college students beat an English team, 24-3. Despite this embarrassing defeat, English baseball continued to grow in popularity. In 1937, a game at Hull drew 11,000 spirited fans. And in 1938, the British made baseball headlines when they defeated an American team in what was billed as the first World Amateur Baseball Championship. The American team was preparing for the 1940 Olympic Games, which they did not then know would be cancelled due to World War II. At the time, however, there was little thought of war, and the U.S. team, led by a former major league player, Leslie Mann, and featuring a formidable hitter in Mike Schemer, who would go on to play for the New York Giants, came to Britain filled with confidence. They were unaware that the British team was made up largely of extremely skilled Canadians, led by star pitcher, Ross Kendrick. Before a crowd of 10,000 in Liverpool, the brilliant Kendrick shut out the Americans, 3-0, allowing only two hits and striking out sixteen. Two days later, the British won again, 8-6 before 5,000 loudly enthusiastic spectators in Hull. The star of this game was England's shortstop Sam Hanna who hit a two-run home run as the spectators roared their approval. The Americans won the third game in Rochdale, but Kendrick pitched the fourth game in Halifax, shutting out the Americans once again, this time by a score of 4-0. England won the final game in Leeds, 5-3. Following this surprising result, the newly formed International Baseball Federation decided to designate this series of games as the first Baseball World Cup Championship and named Britain the first World Amateur Champion.

The presence in the United Kingdom of 1.5 million American military service men during the second World War reinforced British interest in baseball. After World War II, national championship baseball resumed in Britain, and it has continued every year to the present time. The winning teams have nicknames such as Greys, Bees, Mills, Royals, Aces, Tigers, Trojans, Green Sox, Warriors, Spartans, Mets, Lions, Saints, Patriots, and Buccaneers, but, strange to say, some winners were the Liverpool Yankees, the Cobham Yankees, and the Burtonwood Yanks. In 1997, a commercial television channel began to telecast two U.S. major league games a week in Britain.

In 2001, the Rawlings National League was established as the highest standard of baseball in Britain. For the first time in Britain, all six teams in this league used wooden bats. This rule change was so positively received that teams from the United States, American Samoa, and Europe were attracted to play in Britain. The Rawlings National League teams are the Bracknell Blazers, Brighton Buccaneers, Croydon Pirates, London Warriors, Menwith Hill Patriots, and Windsor Bears. Brighton has already seen one of its players, John Foster, signed by the major league Atlanta Braves organization. Today, the British national team is ranked tenth in Europe. Despite these successes, British players must buy their own equipment, pay for their own travel, and no players are paid a salary.

Although baseball has not yet become a sport for international competition in Wales, since early in the twentieth century it has been the most popular summer sport for working-class Welshmen and women in the southern, industrialized port cities of Cardiff and Newport. Known as "poor man's cricket," baseball spread in these cities even though playing fields were in short supply. A former Cardiff glassworker fondly remembered the game and the social contact it brought to him: "I really enjoyed playing baseball. The comradeship and the getting together in the night times practising like and then on Saturday afternoons playing. . . . It used to be great fun." After a match he and other players would go with their girlfriends (who had watched the game) to the cinema and make a night of it.[4] Working-class women also played the game avidly in a women's league with teams representing factories, chapels, churches, and districts set up in Cardiff in 1922. Men greatly enjoyed watching women play. In 1926, a Welsh women's team played an English women's team. For many men and women alike, baseball in South Wales was the highlight of their week.

More affluent Welshmen continued to favor the leisurely, several-days-long cricket match, but the working-class men and women in Cardiff and Newport, many of whom were Irish Catholics, only had time for a brief game on Saturday. As early as 1906, the game was played widely by 36 teams. In that year, a newspaper reporter wrote, "the majority of players belong to the artisan class – fellows who toil hard all week and like to spend their Saturday afternoons playing this grand old American pastime."[5] By 1921, there were 60 baseball teams and 1,400 registered players in the Welsh Baseball Union located in Cardiff and Newport. The game was also played in schools by children of all ages. By 1951, schoolgirls' baseball became a part of the Welsh school system. Many women continued to play the game after leaving school, saying that baseball was their social life. Women's games were eagerly watched by friends, family, boyfriends, and husbands who cheered the players on. By 1924, a Welsh men's team competed against an English team before 10,000 fans, and in 1948, a similar game was attended by 16,000 cheering fans. Baseball was lauded in Wales for its remarkable ability to provide wholesome exercise, to shape clear thinking, and to instill respect for the rights of others.

In 1923, the Honorary Secretary of the Welsh Baseball Union wrote the following:

> Baseball . . . combines all other forms of athletic exercises – running, jumping, throwing, and adds to them "Batting," one of the greatest of many delights. It affords an unlimited opportunity for the boy to give vent to his youthful energies. It brings him into the open air and provides action for his muscles, lungs, and brain. Baseball stimulates the player's mind and serves to fill the vacancy when leisure time would have no occupation to divert him from the many pitfalls that present themselves. For that reason, Baseball is greatly favored as being of immense value in shaping the lives of young men. It teaches quick thinking, self control, a regard for the rights of others, and the ability to look after one's own interests.[6]

In 1953, the European Baseball Federation was founded under the presidency of Prince Steno Borghese of Italy. The first member countries were Belgium, France, Germany, Italy and Spain. Three years later, the Netherlands was added, followed by Sweden, Great Britain, San Marino, Denmark, Finland, Malta, Yugoslavia, Austria, the USSR, Czechoslovakia, and Romania. After the political breakup of the Soviet Union, Czechoslovakia, and Yugoslavia in 1992, the federation has accepted eight new members: Croatia, Estonia, Georgia, Lithuania, Russia, Slovenia, Ukraine, and Bulgaria. In subsequent years, the Federation added the Czech Republic, Hungary, Romania, Moldova, Norway, Slovakia, Armenia, Belarus, Ireland, Portugal, Israel, Yugoslavia, Greece, Cyprus, Turkey, and, in 2003, Luxembourg. Despite its title, the "European Baseball Federation," some of its member countries such as Turkey, Cyprus, Armenia, and Israel would not ordinarily be considered part of Europe.

In the same year that the European Baseball Federation came into being, the Asian Baseball Federation was formed at a conference in the Philippines. And in 1955, the United States Baseball Congress held what was called the "Global

World Series," featuring teams from Colombia, Japan, the United States, Venezuela, and one European team from Spain. The American team won, but in the following year when the second Global World Series was played, Japan won. The sixteenth World Baseball Cup was held in 1966 in Colombia where the newly communist Cuban team was refused entry visas. Four years later, in 1969, the seventeenth World Baseball Cup was held in the Dominican Republic where Cuba was welcomed and the United States participated for the first time in 26 years. The Cuban team won the cup, beating the Americans, 2-1. The following year, the World Baseball Cup was again held in Colombia. Twelve teams took part including two from Europe—Italy and the Netherlands. The Cubans again won the cup, defeating the U.S. team in a best-of-three-games final series.

In 1971, 18 countries competed for the World Cup in Havana, and in 1972 at Managua, Nicaragua, Asian teams took part for the first time, with Japan finishing fourth and Taiwan coming in sixth. Once again, Cuba won, as they did again in 1973. For the first time, a second baseball World Cup was played in 1973, this one also in Nicaragua. This time, the United States team won the Cup. The following year, the Cup was held for the first time in the United States. Playing in St. Petersburg, Florida, the U.S. team defeated the Nicaraguans to win the Cup. In 1975, the Cup was played in Canada, and in 1978, it was played in Italy. It was the first time the World Cup had been held in Europe, even though it was 25 years since the European Baseball Federation had been created. Cuba won, the United States finished second, Australia competed for the first time, and the European teams did not play well. The next World Cup was played in Japan in 1980, the first time an Asian country had been its host.

In 1986, at the International Olympic Committee meeting in Lausanne, Switzerland (also the home of the IBAF), baseball was included in the official program of the 1992 Olympics in Barcelona. While world teams prepared for the Barcelona Games, the 1988 Baseball World Cup was again held in Italy, and Cuba once again won. Cuba also won the next World Cup in Edmonton, Canada, then went on to win the gold medal at the 1992 Barcelona Olympics. The Olympic silver medal went to Taiwan and the bronze to Japan. During the 1996 Olympic Games in Atlanta, an extraordinary 1,134,203 spectators purchased tickets to baseball games. In that same year, the IBAF met in Lausanne where it voted to allow professional players to take part in its international competitions. In 1998, the Baseball World Cup was hosted by Italy for the third time. After qualifying tournaments including teams from 50 countries, 16 countries competed. The 2000 Sydney Olympic Baseball Tournament consisted of 32 games with an attendance at 97.44 percent of capacity. For the first time, a team from Africa competed. The gold medal went to the United States.

As we saw in Chapter One, bat-and-ball games have been played for centuries over much of Europe. Today, every European country sends junior and adult teams to compete in tournaments organized by the European Baseball Confederation. In youth baseball, teams from Israel also compete. Belgium began to play in 1927, and today it has 3,000 baseball players at six levels, including a professional league. During the 1953 Helsinki Olympics, a U.S. team played *pesäpallo*, a game somewhat similar to baseball that was Finland's national sport. It was originally intended to toughen Finnish troops and was played violently, with an "out" referred to as a "kill." The Finns beat the Americans in a game of *pesäpallo*, 14-6. In recent years, Finns have become enthusiastic about modern baseball and have developed skilled national teams, but they have only five adult teams, and their favorite sport continues to be *pesäpallo*. In Sweden, baseball is now played widely by children and adults alike. The Swedish Elite (Major) League has 12 teams in two divisions, and the game is also played in Lithuania and Estonia but not in Latvia.

Baseball was initially played in Berlin in 1884 between two teams of American students attending German schools. The New York Times reported, "The game itself created a great sensation among the German spectators, who looked upon it as something altogether novel and unique."[7] Another game was played in Berlin in 1909 between a team from the United States residential colony and the American Medical Post-Graduate Club. One of the most distinguished spectators was Count Von Bernsdorf, the German Ambassador to the United States. He said the game would soon catch on in Germany. It was slow to do so, although it received a boost after World War II when U.S. troops stationed there played the game, among them the future major league star Ernie Banks.[8] Although Germany is one of the five original members of the European Baseball Federation, most German sports fans idolize soccer players, and until recently some did not even know that German baseball or softball existed. In 1987, only about 1,000 Germans played the game. Today, however, there are over 25,000 active baseball and softball players in Germany on some 450 teams. Germany leads all European countries, with 11,000 adults playing baseball. Italy is second with 7,901.

Part of the reason for this interest was the desire of many young Germans to experiment with American sports, a desire that was fueled by the return to Germany of foreign exchange students who had learned to play softball or baseball while studying in the United States. As early as 1990, many young Germans followed U.S. baseball on television, and others devoured tapes, films, and books about the game.[9] The game is still in its formative years in Germany, and most youngsters take to the game between the ages of 12 and 15 and then play only some 20 games a year. However, since 2001, two German baseball players have been signed by the U.S. minor league farm teams of the Milwaukee Brewers and Minnesota Twins.[10] The German Bundesliga, or "First League," uses wooden bats and attracts quite a few foreign players from the United States, Canada, South Africa, Australia, and even the Dominican Republic. There are also nine baseball fields and 2,000 players in neighboring Austria, where the game is growing in popularity.

The French have played baseball skillfully for many years, as well. Thanks to the spirited play of American soldiers in France during World War I, the French took to the game eagerly, although clumsily at first. French soldiers entertained the Americans with their stiff-armed throwing and suffered many injuries from reckless slides and broken fingers from bad catches. By 1918, the Paris Baseball Association of 26 teams was formed. These teams played every Sunday during the warm months, and crowds as large as 6,000, many of them women, have watched their games. Children immediately played eagerly. At the end of World War I, French Army commanders were ordered to invite Americans to teach the game to their men. General Cottes of the French Ministry of War explained this order as follows: "I consider this game constitutes excellent exercise, develops precision and quickness of eye, and is an attractive pastime."[11] To the surprise of the Americans, the French eagerly took to the game, especially after the Chicago White Sox and the New York Giants toured France in 1924, playing before large crowds. By 1930, French teams played so well that at the Barcelona Exhibition held that year, a French team defeated Spain's best team before a crowd of 65,000 stunned spectators.[12]

Shortly after the end of World War II, a team of American GIs agreed to play a French baseball team. When they arrived for the game, they were startled to see the French players limbering up. The second and third basemen wore blue shorts, aviation goggles, and coal miners' caps. The pitcher wore the uniform of an ice-hockey goal keeper, complete with heavily padded shin guards. The shortstop and left fielder wore military steel helmets, while the right fielder wore a one-piece bathing suit and a straw hat. The umpire wore a World War I gas mask, while the wire mask meant to protect his face was strapped across his groin. As bizarre and comic as their "uniforms" seemed to the Americans, the Frenchmen played so skillfully that they won the game, 5-3.[13]

The French have continued to play baseball well ever since. For example, in 1995, a French team hosted a highly rated South African team in Paris, winning two out of three games. The South African players, who had expected to win easily, were shocked. French schools and universities do not play baseball, and there are as yet no professional teams, but there are 230 baseball and softball clubs for all ages. Because no ball players are paid, all adults must be gainfully employed, and finding time away from work to play the game, much less to practice, is difficult. Boys practice all year to play perhaps eight games. There is media attention for these games, and about 400 spectators attend games, but money for equipment is scarce, as sponsors and qualified umpires are hard to locate.

Denmark has four adult teams that participate in Nordic and European baseball championships, but fast-pitch softball is more popular than baseball with boys and men alike among the Danes. Although Switzerland is not a member of the European Baseball Federation, it is a member of the International Baseball Federation. The game was not introduced in Switzerland until 1981, but there are now 24 Swiss adult teams and 23 youth teams for different ages. However, there is only one regulation baseball field in all of Switzerland. Except for this regulation field in Berne, teams play on soccer fields. There is no baseball stadium, and few spectators watch games. Even playoff tournament championship games draw only 50 to 100 spectators. Still, Switzerland hopes to develop more competitive teams. Plans to build a modern baseball stadium are being discussed as well.

Unlike the Swiss, the Dutch have played baseball since Dutch physical education teacher, J. C. G. Grace, returned from a visit to the United States in 1901. Grace set up a Dutch baseball federation. By 1996, the Netherlands had 1,050 teams and 26,000 players at all age and skill levels.[14] They have also dominated play in the European Baseball Federation, winning 14 championships. Italy has won seven times, the second best record in the European Baseball Federation. One Dutch player, Wilhelmus "Win" Remmerswaal, pitched for the Boston Red Sox in 1979, and in 1993 center fielder Rikkert Faneyte played successfully in the major leagues with the San Francisco Giants and later with the

Texas Rangers. The most famous Dutch player was pitcher Bert Blyleven, who won 287 major league games and became an all star.

Dutch baseball has been dominated by the Neptunus team of Rotterdam, led by outfielder Dirk Van't Klooster who led the Dutch Major League with a .376 average in 2002. In 2003, Neptunus became the first team to capture four consecutive European Cup titles, outscoring its opponents by a startling 48 runs to 2 in the three-game series.[15] During the 2003 Baseball World Cup, played in Santiago, Cuba, outfielder Sharnol Adriana hit three home runs in the Netherlands' 12-0 win over France. In 2003, former major league player and manager, Davey Johnson, began to coach the Dutch national team in its bid for a spot at the Athens Olympic games. Johnson took this position after the previous manager, his friend Ryan Eenhorn, stepped down to be with his terminally ill son. Although Spain has been dominated by the Netherlands' teams in European baseball, Spaniards played the game spiritedly as early as 1913 and have surprisingly sent three players to the U.S. major leagues -- Alfredo A. Cabrera, Brian Alois Oelkers, and Alberto J. Pardo.[16] Baseball is also played in Portugal, where it was introduced by Venezuelans living there in 1990. However, the game has yet to become very popular or widely played in Portugal.

Although the Spalding tour played baseball games in Naples, Rome, and Florence after leaving Australia in 1889, the Italians showed little interest in these games. Their first club teams were not organized until 1919. However, in 1931, 43 would-be instructors were sent to America to learn the game.[17] The Italians appear not to have organized any more teams until after World War II, when, inspired by the play of American soldiers serving in Italy, Italians took to baseball with great enthusiasm, just as Italian immigrants to the United States had done earlier. Today, Italian baseball is played at various levels, always with aluminum bats. The pitcher is *lanciatorre*, the catcher is *ricevitore*, and the batter's box is *boxedebutta*. Scoreboards list the innings in Roman numerals, vendors sell pizza, and fans shout nonstop.

Each team is allowed two foreign players, known as "imports." Several imports were former U.S. Major League pitchers who dominated Italian batters. The A/1 division is comparable to professional AA League teams in the United States, and many of the American "imports" who have played for Italian A/1 teams have had previous major league experience. Rimini, its championship team, is led by Australian "import" pitcher Shane Tonkin and Venezuelan outfielder José Malave, who formerly played for the Boston Red Sox. In 1990, Richard Olsen, a former minor league pitcher for Milwaukee, pitched a no-hitter, striking out 18 to lead Grosseto to a win over Turin. These teams play in stadiums designed solely for baseball, complete with floodlights for night games. Beginning in April, each of the ten teams in this A/1 division plays 54 games, on Fridays, Saturdays, and Sundays only. The stadiums are full, and the fans are rabid, singing raucously, chanting, and pounding olive oil cans as drums. They arrive carrying baskets of fruit, cheese, bread, and wine along with brightly colored pennants. Young Italian women dressed like Dallas Cowboy cheerleaders kick their legs high in the air.

A/2-series games are played among 24 teams in three divisions. The quality of play varies greatly, but most teams are on approximately the same talent level as small colleges in the U.S. Series B has 51 teams in eight divisions. No foreign players are allowed. The level of play is similar to that of good high schools in the U.S. Series C/1 is played by 72 teams. Again, no foreign players are allowed, and the level of play is somewhat below that of Series B. Series C/2 is similar to U.S. high school junior varsity teams. *Primavera* is played by youngsters aged 16 to 18 while *cadetti* is played by 13- to 15-year-old boys and is equivalent to Babe Ruth League play in the U.S. *Ragazzi* is the equivalent of "Little League," played by children aged 9 to 12 on a smaller-sized diamond. Among European players, the talent level in Italian baseball is second only to that of the Dutch. Pitcher Craig Minetto became the first Italian professional league player to play in the U.S. major leagues.

Russians have long played a bat-and-ball game called *lapta*, in which, like earlier American versions of baseball, the batter was out if a fielder could catch his batted ball and hit him with a thrown ball before he could run to first base. During the 1930s, many Americans went to the Soviet Union to experience socialism, and they taught baseball to Russians, who took to the game so eagerly that there soon were dozens of teams in the country. They even published rule books in Russian. But baseball in the Soviet Union came to an end in 1938 when Stalin declared baseball "a bourgeois influence" and arrested many players who had been "corrupted" by it. Some of those arrested were actually executed.[18]

The Soviet Union became interested in baseball once again in 1986 when it first became an Olympic sport. The Soviet Sport Committee made baseball an official Soviet sport, and in early October 1986, two Soviet university teams gave baseball its Soviet premiere on a near-freezing day before only about 200 spectators, who later declared the game "boring," "incomprehensible," and "not interesting."[19] Soviet officials then recruited the most talented athletes from other sports such as tennis and track and field, and some of these new recruits for baseball were sent to Florida to learn the game. They learned enough about playing the game that, in April 1987, Soviet players went to Japan to compete in their first international game.

Following the collapse of the Soviet Union in 1990, Russia took up baseball so seriously that it sent a team of young players to train in Florida for three weeks. The youngsters visited major league teams' spring training camps where they ate and slept baseball before returning home to join leagues that were being formed, and competition began. In 1992, the Moscow Red Devils team went to Alaska to play against local teams, and they were grandly fêted. While there, they bought chewing tobacco and imitated the American players' practice of spitting. Three of their players were signed to minor league contracts by the California Angels, but all three were released after two years. In 1993, the Red

Devils played games against U.S. college teams in Florida, and later that year Russia once again played an international game in Japan.

The following year, on a tour to Chicago to play against local Little League teams, the Russians were amazed to discover seven ball fields, all in use. Moscow has only one baseball stadium for its 10 million residents. Funded by a wealthy Japanese fan who wanted his countrymen to play on an excellent field when they played in Russia, it has artificial turf, two club houses, training rooms, a lounge and snack bar. It seats 2,000 and cost $3.2 million to build. By 1996, Russian players had learned the game so well that they finished second in the European Cup. Thanks to an international oil consortium, including Marathon Oil, McDermott International, Mitsui, Mitsubishi, and Royal Dutch/Shell, the game took hold ten years ago on oil-rich Sakhalin Island, where a Little League team called the "Locomotives" became one of the best in Russia. The game also took root in the million-person city of Krasnoyarsk in central Siberia. Their youth team was accepted by the Little League. Krasnoyarsk also has an adult team in Russia's ten-team, so-called "major league."

By 1998, Russians were sufficiently skilled to compete in the World Cup, where they lost all of their games but cherished the honor of playing against experienced and talented teams from Australia, Canada, Nicaragua, Taiwan, and South Korea. In 2002, a team from Moscow won the European Senior League World Series, earning the right to compete against the U.S. champion in Bangor, Maine. During a visit to a local Bangor mall, the Russians were thrilled to see a host of publications about baseball that were for sale. Saying that little about baseball is written in Russia, they enthusiastically referred to the Bangor mall as a "museum."[20] And in July 2003, Russia played host to the European Juvenile Baseball Championship for boys, 10 to 12, with nine countries represented. It was the first time Russia had hosted a major international competition. More and more Russians are becoming devoted to the game, and boys practice all year round, indoors during the winter. The standard of play improves every year. In

October, 2003, Russia shocked the international baseball world by defeating Chinese Taipei 4-1 in the 25th Baseball World Cup, only Russia's second World Cup victory in history.

Russian players realize that they are not yet ready to compete successfully with leading European teams like the Dutch or Italians, but they now have perhaps 4,000 men and boys playing the game, and some have shown themselves to be so talented that U.S. baseball scouts have signed at least six Russians to play for U.S. minor league teams. The Russian teams are happy that U.S. scouts recognize the skill of their players, but they are concerned that these young players may not return home. When the Cold War ended in 1991, many Americans took the opportunity to work with Russians to develop baseball. Some donated equipment, others coached, and the Texas-Louisiana Independent Baseball League hosted a tournament that the Russians participated in. Baseball has come to attract the attention of many Russians, and it seems to be flourishing.[21]

The Romanian national sport, *Oina*, is similar to baseball, and Romanians avidly took to baseball as well. Cristian Costescu is president of the Romanian Baseball Federation. He saw his first game of baseball in 1988 in Italy, and, for the next two years, he and some physical education teachers studied the game, translated the rules into Romanian, scouted potential playing fields, and published articles in sports newspapers. A few trial games were played as well, but when Costescu approached sports officials with a request to endow a baseball federation eligible for government funding, he was told that baseball was an "American capitalist sport" that could not be countenanced. Costescu argued to no avail that baseball was very popular in communist Cuba and that Romanians already played two American sports, volleyball and basketball. In 1989, however, a popular revolution overthrew the communist government. The dictator, Nicolae Ceausescu, was executed. On February 4, 1990, Costescu founded the Romanian Baseball Federation. He visited the United States, then took 13 Romanians to

Italy for a two-week coaching clinic. After equipment was donated by various American sources, the game became popular.[22] Today, there are over 50 teams for men and boys in Romania.

The game also became popular in the Czech Republic, which has quickly built four modern baseball facilities in Prague.[23] Despite the ravages of war, Czech youth love baseball so much that many have given up soccer and other sports in order to play baseball. The Czech Republic national junior team played in the eighth International Baseball Festival in the United States in 1993, losing only one game. Czech fans, including teen-age boys, are not only spirited but are also famous for the amount of beer they drink while watching a game.

Slovenia, a small country of some 2 million people located between Croatia and Austria, first played baseball in 1974. During the first year of play, the batter was called out if he was hit by a pitch. During the following year, that rule was eliminated. There are now six Slovenian adult teams and 11 youth league teams playing on four regulation size fields. Both adult and youth teams compete in European Championship games. Baseball has become a popular spectator sport, and Slovenian officials are actively seeking to improve their baseball equipment. They hope to visit the United States with their national team in the near future.[24] The game is also played in an outdoor theater complex in Vilnius, Lithuania, where the pitcher's mound is made of plywood with rubber on top.[25] And, Armenian youngsters in Turkey, Russia, and Iran have long played the game. However, Slovakian boys have shown little interest in baseball.

Baseball was first seen in Bulgaria in 1913, but the game did not achieve popularity until 1987 when a group of university students established a baseball team called the "Academics." Several other teams were created soon after, and by 1989 Bulgaria was a member of the International Baseball Federation as well as the European Baseball Federation. In 1992, Dale Parker, 67, a retired baseball coach and major league scout, was sent by his Seattle-based United Presbyterian Church, along with several college-aged instructors, to Sofia, Bulgaria to teach the game. He found what he called "baseball fever" among the Bulgarians, who wanted to make the game their national sport. They now have 10 adult teams and 22 youth teams (age groups 16-18, 13-15, and 9-12). Bulgaria has four regulation baseball fields, with two others under construction. Bulgarian fans are enormously enthusiastic, and their numbers grow each year. Baseball is being promoted in schools in several cities, existing stadiums are being improved, more baseball equipment is being made available in schools, more baseball literature is being published, and more training courses are being offered to coaches, umpires, and school teachers. And in 2003, Bulgaria held its first National School Tournament.[26]

The nearby country of Ukraine has also taken to baseball with a remarkable passion. When the Cold War and the Soviet Union came to an end, Basil P. Tarasco, an American baseball coach of Ukrainian ancestry, made his first of what would be more than a score of extended visits to the newly independent country of Ukraine. Many young men were brought together in the capital city of Kyiv (formerly spelled Kiev), and many showed great promise in the game, but funds could not readily be located to send them to tournaments in Europe, much less overseas. Soon after, however, U.S. equipment was donated, and funds were located to enable junior teams to begin to compete in European tournaments. In a junior league tournament in France, Ukraine finished second, earning the right to face a more experienced team from Italy, which won that game, 15-4. Surprisingly, the Ukrainian team defeated the French team 7-6 to win the bronze medal. At the closing ceremonies, all the teams marched onto the field, and the Ukrainian boys were proud to see their country's flag flying in the evening breeze. In 1997, Ukraine's 16-18 year olds flew to London for the European Junior B- pool Baseball Championship. They won their first game against Georgia and then routed Israel, 17-2, and Poland, 9-3. They next played for the championship against Israel, eager to avenge their earlier defeat. Darkness forced the game to be called in the sixth inning with the score tied, and the closing ceremonies had to be held without a winner being declared.

In 1998, Ukraine's 16 and under National Baseball Team qualified to compete in the Youth World Baseball Championships held in the United States near St. Louis. This was the first ever trip by a Ukrainian national baseball team to the United States, and the players felt deeply honored. Surprisingly, Ukraine won two of three exhibition games before losing in the tournament to South Korea, Taipei, South Africa, Brazil, and Italy. Still, they were able to attend two games at Busch Stadium where they saw Mark McGwire hit two towering home runs, and they marveled at McGwire, the stadium, and the sell-out crowd.[27] After the tournament, two Americans of Ukrainian descent invited the team to their home for a traditional Ukrainian meal of borsch, sour cream, dark bread, and dozens of *varenky*. The Ukrainians loved the food and the attention.

Later that year, the Ukrainian team of 16- to 18-year-olds competed in the Junior European Baseball Championships in the Czech Republic. They lost badly to Italy, but they beat Russia in a game in which Alexander Trofimenko struck out 11 Russians. A major league scout who attended the game declared him to be a promising professional pitching prospect. Ukraine next defeated Croatia before losing to the Netherlands and the Czech Republic, even though Trofimenko pitched nine innings, striking out fifteen Czechs and walking none.[28] Despite this loss, baseball has continued to flourish in Ukraine, where a two-tiered stadium with lights, dugouts, and dressing rooms was built in 1997.

Baseball has also grown in popularity in Poland where the game was first played by American "Doughboys" in 1919 but was not taken up by Poles until 1986. The game came to the Poles from their southern neighbor, the Czech Republic, and from Castro's Cuba, which sent instructors. Warsaw had no baseball fields at that time, and the first games were played on soccer fields and a field used for speed skating in the winter. By the end of 1986, there were 300 registered players, 60 percent of them coal miners. Games often drew as many as

3,000 enthusiastic spectators. In 1987, the legendary Polish American player, Stan Musial, and star pitcher, Moe Drabowsky, visited Poland with enough bats, balls, gloves, and catchers' equipment for twelve men's and six women's teams. The equipment was donated by Major League Baseball. Polish players were talented, and they could be quite zany. In 1988, before the end of the Soviet Union, a Polish-American visitor described Polish baseball as one part opera, one part circus, and one part "pretty good baseball." One player was seen crossing the plate in a jubilant handstand, while a catcher turned somersaults after making a spectacular catch.[29]

That baseball was so late in coming to Poland is curious when one considers that Polish Americans played an early version of baseball in the early 17th century at the Jamestown colony. Polish Americans played in the major leagues as early as 1903. By the 1920s, there were several Polish American major league stars, such as Harry Coveleski, "Big Ed" Konetchy, "Whitey" Witkowski, "Bunny" Bratzki, Stan Coveleski, Al Simmons (born Szymanski), and John Grabowski. In the post-World War II era, players like Richie Zisk, Whitey Kurowski, Eddie Lopat, Moe Drabowsky, Ron Perranowski, Frank Tanana, Carl Yastrzemski, Ted Kluszewski, Bill Mazerowski, Phil Niekro, and Stan "The Man" Musial all starred in major league baseball.

Despite the fame of these Polish American players, baseball is still not that popular in Poland, where the main sport continues to be soccer. In 2001, thanks to a Polish American, Al Koproski of Stamford Connecticut, a Little League baseball field was constructed in Poland. Little League programs and school systems in Connecticut donated over 3,000 pounds of bats, balls, uniforms, bases, gloves, and other equipment to Polish Little Leaguers. The dedication of the new baseball field was attended by over 1,000 people. The American flag was raised while a band played the American national anthem, followed by the raising of a Polish flag and the playing of the Polish national anthem.[30] The spectators were deeply moved.

A Little League baseball field in Brzeg, Poland, was named after former president George H. W. Bush, who had played baseball at Yale. He visited Brzeg in 1997 and played catch with some local boys. This was Bush's second visit to Poland. In 1989, he invited some Polish Little Leaguers to the American ambassador's residence and gave them a pep talk about baseball. He also handed out some bats, balls, and baseball uniforms. In Kutno, Poland, there are two youth fields, three adult fields, and two enclosed stadiums. The 35-acre baseball complex also has dormitories large enough to house sixteen teams. There are dining facilities, a training center, tennis courts, a basketball court, swimming pool, and a conference center. The 4,000-seat stadium is named after Musial, the best known U.S. athlete in Poland. He was in Kutno for its dedication on August 5, 2000. Eighty years old and walking with the aid of a cane, Musial stood beside Walter O'Malley, long a patron of international baseball.

In 2000, Bill Mathews, head baseball coach at Eckerd College in St. Petersburg, Florida, was chosen by the Major League Baseball International Envoy Program to coach Polish 11- to 17-year-old players. For four weeks, he ate and slept with 22 youngsters in a makeshift loft in Kutno. Mathews found the Polish youngsters so eager to learn that they practiced 12 hours a day. Their dedication paid off when the team went to Switzerland to play an Italian team that had won 45 consecutive games. With the game in the eighth inning, Mathews brought in his right fielder to pitch. Mathews had been teaching the boy to pitch, and he struck out the side on ten pitches, giving Poland a one-run win. The Polish fans exploded in cheers, hugs, and tears. Mathews said, "I'll never forget their faces and what a great feeling I had as they all came running up to hug the team, telling them it was the greatest day in Polish Little League history."[31]

Baseball came to other European countries in a variety of ways. Japanese merchant ships brought the game to Belgium in the 1920s, with crew members first demonstrating the game for Belgian onlookers, then instructing them. In 1992, the Austrians requested coaching from the IBAF, and the head baseball coach at San Francisco State University, Michael J. Simpson, was sent to instruct them. After some time spent coaching among the Austrians, Simpson wrote this: "To observe the Austrian players' insatiable thirst for knowledge of the game and their undying enthusiasm for playing was refreshing and rejuvenating."[32]

The Irish recently became interested in baseball after watching U.S. major league teams play on television. They created a baseball federation in 1989, at a time when there were no infields or pitchers' mounds anywhere in Ireland. By 1993, a team of 11-to-13 year olds had traveled to the United States to play against a Little League team from New Jersey. Thanks to a $140,000 donation by Walter O'Malley, a baseball facility was then built in Clondalkin, West Dublin, with a regulation adult field and an international-standard Little League field. In 1997, a team of 11-to-13 year olds played in the European championships in Italy, and in 2001, a Youth All Star team played in the Development Tour in the United States. In 1996, an Irish adult team played in its first international competition, and it has continued to do so every year since. The Irish finished a promising fourth after losing to Sweden and Poland but defeated Lithuania 8-7 in the European Championships in Stockholm in 2002. Today, about 200 men and 300 boys play baseball, but Ireland's adult league plays only a twenty-game season. Few spectators attend these games, but those who do attend are very enthusiastic.[33]

Thanks to Peter Angelos, the Greek-American owner of the Baltimore Orioles, Greece had at least one baseball team eligible to compete for a spot in the 2004 Athens Olympic Games. Before Angelos stepped in late in 1999, baseball was not played in Greece. But with the help of the Boston Red Sox, Angelos began to recruit and train a Greek national baseball team, and he provided all the necessary equipment. He also encouraged ball players among the nearly 1 million families of Greek ancestry in Canada, the United States, and Australia to volunteer their services to the Greek national team.[34] It will be interesting to see if baseball catches on in Greece as so many other sports have. That it might well do so can be seen in Greece's shocking July 2003 11-0 victory over Germany in the 2003 European Baseball Championships. Greece took second place in these games, losing only to the host team, Holland.

NOTES

[1] Bloyce (1997).

[2] SABRUK, May 14, 2002, www.sabruk.org .

[3] SABRUK Examiner no. 11:1918: Illustrious turnout for Baseball in Britain.

[4] Johnes (2000:162).

[5] Ibid., p. 157.

[6] Johnes (2000:160).

[7] New York Times, July 20, 1884.

[8] New York Times, September 19, 1909; International Baseball Rundown, late winter, 1999.

[9] World Baseball Magazine, Fall 1990.

[10] Sutton (2002).

[11] Los Angeles Times, September 26, 1918.

[12] New York Times, March 30, 1919; New York Times, August 26, 1919; New York Times, April 15, 1934.

[13] Reader's Digest, August 1946, pp. 26-27.

[14] World Baseball Magazine No. 3 1996.

[15] Baseball America, July 21-August 3, 2003.

[16] Bjarkman (1994:383); International Baseball Rundown, October, 1998.

[17] Light (1997:384).

[18] Chicago Tribune, April 5, 1993.

[19] Los Angeles Times, October 7, 1986.

[20] Bangor Daily News, August 13, 2002.

[21] Ibid.

[22] Wall Street Journal, April 8, 1991.

[23] World Baseball Magazine No. 3 1996.

[24] Igor Veselinovic, Pres. Slovenian Baseball and Softball Association, March 7, 2003.

[25] The Associated Press, July 18, 1993.

[26] Simon Vasileva, bfbaseball@dir.bg.

[27] Tarasco (1998)

[28] Igor Veselinovic, Pres., Slovenian Baseball and Softball Association, March 7, 2003.

[29] Gildner (1990).

[30] Ibid; International Baseball Rundown, August 5, 2000.

[31] St. Petersburg Times, September 9, 1998.

[32] World Baseball Magazine Fall, 1992, p.24.

[33] Mitchell, S (sean@baseballireland.com).

[34] Wall Street Journal, January 4, 2000.

Chapter Seven: Baseball in Africa, the Middle East, and Elsewhere

Baseball was slow to take hold in Africa, but today 18 countries in Sub-Saharan Africa field baseball teams despite tropical heat, humidity, and heavy rainfall in some areas. Most of these teams of men and boys play the game enthusiastically, and many of them play it very well. The first African country to take up the game of baseball was the Union of South Africa. Today, there are over 6,000 teams in South Africa, with 370,000 adult and juvenile players in various leagues in that sports-mad nation of over 40 million people. The origin of baseball in South Africa goes back to 1896 when American and Canadian immigrant gold miners working in the country introduced the game just before the outbreak of the bloody second Boer War in 1900. There are photographs of these heavily mustachioed and side-whiskered, nattily uniformed players posing in 1899 with crossed bats and grim expressions. Until the Boer War temporarily put an end to sports in South Africa, these men played the game on enormous open fields ordinarily used for cricket, soccer, and field hockey as good-sized crowds looked on, often in wonderment.

Surprisingly, despite the game's popularity throughout South Africa, there are no baseball stadiums in the country even today. Instead, baseball is still played on open soccer or cricket fields, where batters' and catchers' boxes are precisely delineated by green matting that is fastened to the ground by nails driven through the caps of soft-drink bottles. Players often complain that sliding over these caps can be painful and that their spikes – or "cleats," as they call them – sometimes catch in the matting. Foul lines are carefully laid down in chalk, and regulation-sized bases and a home plate are installed at the standard international distances. Strangely enough, however, there are no pitchers' mounds, and when South African teams play in foreign countries where there are mounds, South

African pitchers often find it difficult to adjust their delivery. Similarly, when teams from other countries play in South Africa, the absence of pitchers' mounds is a distinct disadvantage for them. Although South African women do not play baseball and only occasionally play softball, baseball games in South Africa are officially scored by women, who are carefully trained to carry out this complex task. First aid for fans and players alike is made available at games through the presence of well-trained ambulance corpsmen, who attend baseball games nattily attired in khaki uniforms and black berets. Despite these and many other differences between baseball in South Africa and the United States, baseball in the two countries has at least one thing in common. The spectators in both countries love hot dogs and mustard.[1]

During 1954 and 1955, an American amateur team toured the Union of South Africa, playing 32 games and winning them all, many by huge margins. The manager of the American team pointed out that because baseball was not a sport played in South African schools, South Africans of that era typically did not begin to play baseball until they were 15 or older. As a result, they not only lacked experience in the sport, they had too little time to develop fully their baseball skills. The largest crowd to watch the all-white American team was 10,000 for a game in Johannesburg, but most crowds were 5,000 or less, all of whom had to sit in rudimentary bleachers set well back from the field.[2] Even so, these were large crowds considering the lopsided scores and the lack of playing ability on the part of the South African players.

Since the end of South Africa's apartheid government in 1994, South African boys have begun to play baseball at a much younger age. Better skilled, racially integrated South African teams have played well in international competition. South Africa first sent a team to the World Cup in 1974, but they were banned from further participation in the World Cup until the end of apartheid 20 years later. However, in 1992, although apartheid was still in place, the South African team was allowed to play in the First African Baseball

Tournament in Harare, Zimbabwe, where it defeated Zimbabwe, Namibia, and Nigeria by huge scores. In 1995, an apartheid-free South African team played well in the Twelfth World Cup. Later that year, it won the Third African Cup. During the Seventh All-Africa Games in Johannesburg, South Africa crushed a team from the Kingdom of Lesotho by the astonishing score of 43-0, but the Lesotho players somehow rebounded to beat a previously highly regarded team from Ghana, 18-14.

Because the South Africans won the gold medal in the All-Africa Games where they trounced Nigeria, 19-1, they qualified for the 2000 Sydney Olympics where they impressively defeated a powerful team from the Netherlands, 3-2, in their opening game. They lost all of their remaining games, however, being soundly defeated by Australia, 10-4; Cuba 16-0; Italy 13-0; Japan 8-0; Korea, 13-3; and the gold-medal winning United States team 11-1. The U.S. team featured 6 foot, 11 inch, right-handed pitcher Jon Rauch, who struck out 13 South Africans in seven innings. Rauch's professional career was slowed by arm surgery in 2001, but he came up to the Chicago White Sox in 2004. In August, 2003, a Little League team from Cape Town, South Africa, became the first team from Africa to qualify for the Little League World Series. To do so, Cape Town had to beat Ukraine, which it did handily, 10-0. It was the tenth team to qualify for that World Series, which was played in South Carolina. The other Little League teams in that competition represented California, Florida, Illinois, Pennsylvania, South Carolina, and Texas as well as Canada, Guam, and Mexico.

Despite their poor play during the Sydney Olympics, South African baseball players increasingly attracted serious attention from American major league scouts. Earlier, a white South African slugger, 6' 8", 240-pound, Nick Dempsey, played several major league seasons for the Los Angeles Dodgers. Today, white South African pitcher Tim Harrell is playing in the Dodgers' farm system. After the 2000 Sydney Olympics, major league scouts not only scoured South African leagues for prospects, they signed several, including black players like Paul Bell, who starred at shortstop for South Africa's Olympic team. They also signed his white teammate, pitcher Wesley Botha, and the Kansas City Royals signed Konrad Weitz in 2001. The American major leagues have also provided hundreds of thousands of dollars to elementary schools in South Africa to develop the game as a school sport. As Raymond Tew, head coach of South Africa's national team, acknowledged, the main reason why baseball did not take off earlier in that country was that it was not a "school sport." Today, the game is taught and played in more than 1,000 schools. Schoolboys interested in baseball had to watch American films of the game until a few years ago, when satellite television brought ESPN and baseball games directly to South African viewers.[3]

The following description of the introduction of a baseball to a young Zulu chief in South Africa appeared in a Saturday Evening Post article written by Allen Sangree in 1905:

> The sport itself is a primitive instinct: a mystery in ethnology that I do not attempt to explain. All I know is that in Zululand a couple of years ago, we handed a new baseball to a young *induna*, or chief, and the first thing he did was to 'play catch' with it. After that, he threw as far as he could and then proceeded to soak [hit] it with his war club. He felt the seams, hooked his fingers around it like McGinnity or Chesbro [American major league pitchers], rubbed it over his cheek, and finally offered an *ingenue* from his harem in exchange.[4]

Whether this Zulu chief was the first black South African to become fascinated with a baseball is not known.

In more recent times, there has also been spirited baseball competition between African teams representing Kenya, Uganda, and Tanzania in East Africa, Cameroon, Ghana, Ivory Coast, Liberia, Mali, Namibia, Nigeria, and Togo in West Africa; the Congo Republic and Zaire in central Africa; and Lesotho,

Zambia, Madagascar, Botswana, and Zimbabwe in southern Africa. Americans have done much to encourage Africans to play baseball. For example, in 1989, International Baseball Association Executive Director David Osinski went to Zimbabwe, while Georgia Southern College baseball coach Jack Stallings went to Nigeria. Both men coached the game at clinics, distributed baseball equipment, and watched happily as the players improved and the game took hold. Other American coaches have held clinics elsewhere in Africa, and fan and player interest alike have continued to grow.

In 1990, five youngsters from Zimbabwe joined more than 200 12- and 13-year-olds from 23 countries, many of them in Africa, at Jackie Robinson Stadium at the University of California, Los Angeles (UCLA) as part of the World Children's Baseball Fair, a week-long baseball coaching event. The fair was organized by the famous Japanese home-run slugger Sadaharu Oh, who received funding from Hitachi, Mizuno, and American Airlines to put on the event. Oh succeeded in bringing legendary African-American major league stars Hank Aaron, Ernie Banks, and Willie Mays to the fair to encourage the youngsters in their enjoyment of baseball and to teach them baseball skills. The five young Zimbabweans greatly enjoyed the fair but admitted that they had never heard of Aaron, Banks, or Mays.[5] They also enjoyed living in student dormitories at UCLA for that week.

The first African Cup was played in 1993, and African Cup play has continued every year since. Although South Africa continues to dominate African Cup play, other countries are improving. With financial support from the Los Angeles Dodgers and a Japanese group known as The Friends of African Baseball, Zimbabwe now has 12 adult baseball teams, nearly 100 high school teams, and more than 150 junior school teams. Despite the fact that 50 percent of Zimbabwe's citizens are unemployed, the country's annual inflation rate is 70 percent, AIDS is rampant, the government is corrupt and brutal, and that baseball suffers from a lack of funds, Zimbabwean boys and men have shown great enthusiasm for the game and have played it skillfully.[6] And Zimbabwean fans love to watch them play, cheering and shouting all the while.

A former Japanese baseball player, Naohiko Tsutsumi, was sent to Zimbabwe by a Japanese sports-management company to coach baseball there from 1995 to 1998. He arrived with a huge backpack stuffed with baseball equipment for the young boys he had been sent to coach at several elementary schools. Delighted to see him, local people rushed to his aid. An auto repair shop melted down car engines to make bats from the metal. A shoemaker made leather gloves, and a carpet shop made home plates and bases. The children loved baseball, and Tsutsumi enjoyed coaching them so much that he hoped to return in the future.[7]

Kansas State University history professor Robert Linder, a former professional minor league baseball player, had spent the previous 15 summers in Australia, where he earned the nickname "Crocodile Bob." In the summer of 2000, his old friend and Kansas State University graduate Fred Sorrells, who was serving as Zimbabwe's national development officer for baseball, invited Linder to come to the country to help coach high school baseball and softball. Linder accepted and arrived in the city of Epworth to take up his coaching role, only to find that the place had virtually no electricity or utilities, almost no running water, or accessible roads. It did, however, have many boys and girls who loved baseball and softball. And many of them had baseball equipment donated by professional baseball players from the United States. They also saw American baseball on one of the country's two television channels once Zimbabwean television was up and running. Linder greatly enjoyed coaching baseball to Zimbabwean youngsters, and he also produced 12 television programs about the sport for them to watch.

Baseball began in Nigeria in the early 1960s when young men from the American Peace Corps volunteers played the game against Nigerian students from the University of Ibadan. The explosive Nigerian civil war of 1967 to 1970 ended baseball in that country until the late 1980s, when it was reintroduced. It has now spread widely. Today, there are 23 baseball clubs in 19 of the country's 36 states, but there is only one international-standard field that is in playable condition. It is located in the city of Abuja. Elsewhere, the game is played on soccer fields. Fortunately for Nigerian players and fans, three Nigerian benefactors who are also officers of the Nigerian Olympic Committee (NOC) have dedicated themselves to developing the sport in that country of more than 100 million people. Dr. William Boyd, Dr. (Mrs.) Ndi Okereke-Onyiuke and Major General Ishola Williams have not only encouraged the development of the game, but they have also made major financial contributions to the sport out of their own pockets. They have even paid the expenses of Nigerian teams competing overseas. In 2002, the Nigerian Baseball and Softball Association also received a grant of $70,000 from the International Olympic Committee to help train Nigeria's adult baseball team for the Eighth All-Africa games in 2003.[8]

Thus far, Nigeria's teams have not done well in international competition, but thanks to the spread of the game on local and international television channels, the game has grown in popularity, and a new baseball stadium has been built. In 2002, fans in Nigeria were treated to a new cell phone service, available through AT&T wireless at a cost of U.S. $19.95 per season, plus a modest charge for each minute used. The service allows fans to monitor games from a distance. It has become very popular despite its cost. In 2003, Abuja, Nigeria, hosted the Eighth Annual All-Africa Games, supported by Major League Baseball's Envoy Program, which has sent coaches on more than 600 assignments to more than 50 countries. Nigeria advanced all the way to the gold-medal game of the tournament before losing to South Africa by the embarrassing score of 15-0.

Baseball was first played in Kenya in 1934, but it did not become popular until 1967, when workers at the American Embassy began to play the game in Kenya's capital city of Nairobi. Inspired by these American players, many Kenyans took up the game, and leagues were quickly formed. In 2000, Kenya hosted the Africa Under-12 Championship, played by teams from South Africa, Zambia, Nigeria, and Uganda. Today, Kenya has 20 adult teams and about 100 youth teams. Baseball is also played in primary schools all over the country, although the sport is not as popular as soccer.

American Peace Corps volunteers introduced baseball to neighboring Tanzania (then known as Tanganyika) in 1961, playing games in the town of Arusha at the foot of majestic Mt. Kilimanjaro, the tallest peak in Africa. Bare-footed Tanzanian youngsters followed suit as soon as the volunteers could provide them with baseball equipment. They loved the game, and it caught on, although Tanzanian teams have not done well in international competition. Baseball wasn't introduced to Kenya's northern neighbor, Uganda, until 1998, but only five years later, in August 2003, the Ugandan under-12 team surprisingly qualified for the World Junior Baseball Championships to be played in Holland and Germany by resoundingly upsetting South Africa, 12-8, and Kenya, 24-8. The youth game is not only very skillfully played in Uganda, it is very popular as well. However, adult baseball has not prospered as was expected. The government spent $22.2 million to construct a 40,000-seat baseball stadium near Uganda's capital city of Kampala. Named after South Africa's Nelson Mandela, the stadium is well constructed, but it has attracted so few games that it has fallen into virtual disuse and is a painful embarrassment, not to mention a financial burden, to the government. Even so, thanks to two British nationals who reside in Kampala, Little League baseball, known as KKL for "Kampala Kids League," has seen more than 2,000 boys and girls play baseball, thanks to sponsorship from more than 55 companies. Many parents watch their children play with great interest. Uganda's teams in the Eighth All-Africa Games in Nigeria won four bronze medals and one silver medal, a fine showing considering how little support they received from the government.

Baseball was brought to the Congo Republic in 1959 by U.S. Consul Frank Magliozzi, a long time baseball fan. Lacking access to modern baseball equipment, he fashioned hollow rubber balls with seams that were soft enough to be caught comfortably by players who lacked gloves. Under Magliozzi's direction, bases were sewn together, and bats were lathed from a hard red wood called *ogouwe*. The bare-footed Congolese youngsters in the city of Brazzaville took to the game with a passion, loving the sound of bat on ball and the sight of home runs. The game quickly spread across the border to the nearby city of Leopoldville (now Kinshasa) in Zaire, where Belgian friends of Magliozzi helped to equip and coach a team.[9]   Teams from the two cities have competed many times since then.

Baseball was not played in neighboring Cameroon until 1991, when the U.S. military attaché, Major Rousseau, introduced it. There are no youth teams in Cameroon, although the sport is now taught in schools. There are five adult teams in the two major cities of Donala and Yaoundé. The game is played on converted soccer fields with enough skill that a Cameroonian team took part in the 2003 Eighth All-Africa Games in Abuja, Nigeria. Thanks to equipment donated by Japan and many free clinics conducted by officials from the International Baseball Association and several   U.S. major league teams, baseball has blossomed in Cameroon, and the Cameroonian adult teams have competed well against other African teams.   The game is so popular there that in 2003 an African championship tournament was held in Yaoundé, Cameroon. Teams from Nigeria, South Africa, Lesotho, Ghana, Kenya, Botswana, and Zimbabwe, as well as two teams from Cameroon, competed against one another before large and enthusiastic crowds of men, women, and children.

Baseball was played in nearby Ghana in the 1980s by American Embassy staff at a place called Budweiser Field (now called Brynn Park). It was not played widely by Ghanaians until 1992, however, when a wealthy Ghanaian, Albert K. Frimpong, became involved. Frimpong was a fine player himself, who had learned to play the game in Kinshasa, Zaire, while his father was there on ambassadorial duty. He formed a national baseball association and served as the captain of the Ghanaian national team. In addition to eight senior club teams, there are now 20 Little League teams, and, thanks to Frimpong, who is known as the "father of Ghana baseball," the senior national team boasts highly skilled players trained by Cuban, American, and Japanese coaches, who have made extensive visits to Ghana. However, a shortage of funds for equipment and playing fields has slowed the game's development. Baseball is also played in neighboring Togo, although the lack of equipment has slowed its progress there even more than it has in Ghana. Youngsters in Togo are very interested in playing baseball but cannot locate enough bats, balls, and gloves to meet their needs.

Baseball is also played throughout the Middle East, from Morocco in the west all the way to Afghanistan, Pakistan, and India in the east. In 1937, an Italian professor, Corrado Gini, discovered blond Arabic-speaking Berber tribesmen in the remote high desert plateau of western Libya playing a baseball game similar to the early American game of "one old cat." Using a ball the size of the American baseball, a batter was considered out if a fielder caught his hit on the fly, or if the fielder was able to catch a ground ball then throw, and hit the runner with the ball—in what was called "plugging," "plunking," "soaking," or "burning" him—before he was able to reach the single base used in the game.[10] This game, which he filmed, was strikingly similar to early American baseball, with the pitcher standing very close to the batter. Gini believed that this game had been brought to North Africa by Norsemen in the Old Stone Age. What became of these baseball-playing, blond Berber tribesmen is not known.

However, as early as 1921, an American with a Ph.D. from Johns Hopkins University, former ballplayer, Dr. Caleb Guyer Kelly, formed the Carthage Orioles baseball team in the city of Tunis. Tunis is not far from Western Libya, where Gini saw the blond Berbers. Soon after, Kelly began to coach the game, and it spread across Morocco, Tunisia, and Algeria, from the city of Tunis to Casablanca 1,900 miles to the west. As Kelly pointed out, North Africa is huge.

The French-speaking portion of North Africa alone is comprised of Morocco (as large as Florida, Georgia, South Carolina, and Virginia combined), Algeria (the size of New Jersey, New York, Ohio, Pennsylvania, and Tennessee combined), and Tunisia (as large as Louisiana). This enormous territory is inhabited by more than 20 million people. Kelly introduced the majority of the teams that played in North African high schools and colleges, 51 high school teams in Tunis alone. There are also baseball teams representing numerous French military units, as well, including the French Foreign Legion, made up of men from 47 nations as diverse as Afghanistan, Venezuela, and Yugoslavia, as well as 1,000 men who have no nationality. There is a photograph of young Moroccans playing the game in what was said to be 1918.[11]

By 1939, Kelly had helped to establish 160 baseball teams stocked by thousands of Arab, French, Turkish, Israeli, Greek, Italian, Maltese, and Spanish North African players, as well as White Russian exiles. There were also Kabyle-Berber players, but they were dark-haired Arabs, not the blond Berber tribesmen mentioned above. Remarkably, all of these men played with and against one another without any apparent concern for the ancient barriers of religious or racial prejudice or for the heat, wind, and dust. In 1931, a team from Tunis played against a team of American crew members and passengers from the ocean liner *President Johnson*. This game was followed by dozens of others between Tunisians and the crews of visiting American ships. Baseball is still avidly played in Tunis by school, college, and military teams. Long-established soccer clubs have also adopted baseball.

Thanks to donations by Americans, including Connie Mack, John McGraw, and Clark Griffith, as well as other major league managers and owners, most of these Moroccan, Tunisian, and Algerian players had modern baseball uniforms and equipment, but it was not uncommon to see an Arab running the bases with his *jibba* and *burnous* flying in the wind. Fans were enthusiastic and loved to eat while watching the game, but instead of buying hot dogs and peanuts,

Arabs balanced trays of *merghez* and *makueuths* on their fezzes, while European fans asked for lemonade, *brioches,* and *croissants.* Moslem women wearing veils attended games alongside men. Boys aged 8 to 12 played baseball on the vacant lots of Algiers and Tunis with a tennis ball, broom handle, and homemade gloves of goat skin.[12]

All championship games were played on Sunday because Europeans observed Thursday as a mid-week holiday, Friday was the Muslim Sabbath, and Saturday the Jewish holy day. Ramadan also posed a problem because games had to be played late in the day but halted at sundown. Despite the scheduling problems, many games were played, and Kelly insisted, "Baseball teaches good sportsmanship and give and take – two qualities badly needed in the world today as men meet men in many fields where hostility or friendship is largely a matter of playing together." He also believed that baseball taught resourcefulness, vigilance, and team spirit while it developed the mind and body. The widespread lasting friendships that resulted from playing the game together were Kelly's legacies to North Africa. He died in Casablanca in 1960 at the age of 73.[13]

The first Egyptian baseball team ever to take the field was made up of faculty members of the Department of Commerce at Fuad I University in Cairo. They were led by their dean, Hussein Kamel Selim Bey, who had come back from his year-long tour of the United States completely enthralled by baseball. On March 24, 1951, the Egyptians played a team from the American Embassy in Cairo made up mostly of U.S. marines. The game was rained out after five innings, with the score 11-6 in favor of the Americans.[14] Baseball is played today in Cairo at Victory College, which has its own baseball diamond, and there is an Egyptian baseball league with four teams. Softball is widely played in the Cairo American Softball League (CASL) by players from the United States, Egypt, and various parts of Europe and Asia. And Middle East softball teams from Oman, Saudi Arabia, Bahrain, Kuwait, and the United Arab Emirates have been competing in well-played games for over 40 years.

Since 1986, the Israeli Association of Baseball, a non-profit organization, has created an infrastructure for baseball by teaching youth baseball. This association has built baseball fields and procured equipment. In addition to setting up clinics for coaches, players and umpires, it has created youth teams and leagues that bring together observant and secular Jews, evangelical Christians, U.N. workers, a star pitcher from Ethiopia, and even a few Palestinians. Israeli youth teams have competed well in European championship tournaments, and Israeli fans give these youngsters vociferous support. In 1989, the Israeli Little League team faced Saudi Arabia's youngsters for the European Little League championship. The two nations were officially at war, but the game was played in a gentlemanly fashion, no small achievement considering the score – Saudi Arabia 50, Israel 0. The Saudi coaches were two Americans who praised the efforts of the Israeli boys.[15] In 2002, the Israelis played in the Maccabi Games in Omaha, Nebraska, and although they lost all five games they were warmly greeted by Jewish families in St. Louis and Kansas City. Israeli youth teams have even played against several teams from the Middle East. Adult teams are now being organized. *Ra'anana*, or Israeli baseball, has taken hold so fervently that some Israelis refer to it as "A field of dreams in the Holy Land."

Iran has developed ten adult baseball teams since the Baseball Federation of Iran was founded in 1992. They have modern equipment and often play on excellent fields with comfortable stands for spectators.[16] Iranian baseball is led by Dr. Mohammad Bajher Zolfagharian, president of the Baseball Federation of the Islamic Republic of Iran, a man who discovered baseball while living in the United States in the 1970s. He tried to introduce baseball to Iran in the early 1980s, but Iran's ruling clerics flatly rejected the idea. They said that the game was considered to be "too American." However, as anti-American sentiment in Iran lessened, Zolfagharian kept trying, insisting that "there is nothing unIslamic about baseball." The game was approved a few years later. There are now ten teams that are coached by a number of Americans brought to Iran by

Zolfagharian, among them retired umpires, college coaches, some former major league players including Mike Brumley, and a former college baseball coach, Glenn Johnson. Johnson is also a Christian missionary but does not ply his religious trade in Iran. In addition to hands-on coaching by the Americans, players learn the game by watching videotapes of major league games that are provided for them. Many young Iranian men are captivated by the game. The 21-year-old pitcher Sasan "Easy" Karimpour said, "Baseball has become my life. It's my dream and my love. I can't stop thinking about it."[17]

In 2001, Iran's national Little League team won a 4-3 game over the Dubai Athletics of the Dubai Little League. The elegant, modern city of Dubai in the United Arab Emirates (UAE) has a standardized grass baseball diamond, and several Little League teams, including one from Jordan, have agreed to play games there. In addition to UAE nationals in the Dubai League, there are teams of boys from 20 other nationalities, almost all of them Arab. The Dubai Little League is funded by U.S. corporations, principally Ford, McDonald's, and Coca-Cola. Saudi Arabia also has Little League teams. One team in Dhahran, Saudi Arabia, is stocked with American players, the sons of Arabian American Oil Company employees. In 1996, a bombing in Dhahran killed 19 U.S. servicemen and wounded 64 others. Despite attacks like this, Saudi Arabia has made the Little League World Series four times but has never won the series.[18] Saudi Arabia produces one-fifth of all the crude oil in the world, and its teams are composed largely of the sons of American workers in Saudi oil, but some players are Arabs. Saudi boys play in Little League games every year, including one in 2000 played in Kutno, Poland. The Saudis won the game, 1-0, before a crowd of 3,500, the largest ever at any baseball game in Poland.[19] Middle East countries also compete in both men's and women's softball, with teams from Egypt, Oman, Saudi Arabia, Bahrain, Kuwait, and the United Arab Emirates competing against one another.

There are also national baseball teams in countries as diverse as Malaysia, Pakistan, and Uzbekistan. Peace Corps volunteers introduced the game to Kyrgyzstan, and Little League Baseball in the United States has sent bats, balls, and gloves to players in this remote country. As early as 1917, baseball was played in India, particularly in the Bombay League by Englishmen, Americans and, even more often, by Japanese who were there on business. It was difficult to find an empty cricket pitch to play the game on, but during Sunday mornings when it was still cool and most cricketers were said to be nursing hangovers, baseball was played. Both the Americans and Japanese were said to have played the game skillfully.[20] They often competed against one another, but by 1939 the Japanese had moved out of Bombay and baseball was no longer played there.[21] It was reintroduced to India in 1942 by a group of African-American U.S. Army soldiers who played a game against a team of Indians recruited from the Calcutta police force, winning by a score of 11-3.[22] During the post-war years, teams from the U.S. Army and Air Force played against one another in French Morocco, where they were warmly befriended by the French military.

An American visitor to New Delhi in 1986 watched a game being played by two Indian teams and was shocked to see that the pitchers, who were not on a pitching mound, did not know how to pitch from a stretch or how to make a pickoff move to first. He stopped the game and showed them how to do both.[23] In 1991, the government of India officially recognized India's Amateur Baseball Federation, and the game has continued to spread around the country. Little League baseball is flourishing in India as well. Neighboring Pakistan has also taken up baseball and hosted the Sixth Baseball Asia Cup in 2004 in Islamabad. The competing teams came from India, Indonesia, Iran, Hong Kong, Malaysia, Singapore, Sri Lanka, Thailand, and Uzbekistan. Pakistanis were taught to play baseball by a Japanese coach, Hirotoshi Watanabe, sent there by the Asian Baseball Federation in the hopes of making Pakistani players competitive with other top Asian teams. Pakistani teams soon learned to compete well against these opponents.[24] In 1995, Kazakstan began a Little League with eight teams and 130 youngsters using equipment sent to them by a man in California of Kazakstani descent, Alex Yaworski.[25]

After the end of major combat in Iraq, late in 2003, U.S. soldiers devoted any free time they could find to playing baseball, using old tennis balls wrapped in toilet paper then smothered in duct tape. Bases were paper plates left over from their meals. Their bats were wooden tent stakes. They had no gloves, and they wore combat boots. At first, men of the 101st Airborne played on bubbling hot tarmac 250 miles north of Bagdad. Before long they had built themselves a much better playing field, smoothed by a tractor and provided with outfield fences made of plastic mesh. They even installed maintenance lights and generators so that they could play in the cool of the night. They were so engrossed in the pleasure of their games that they were not concerned about attacks by insurgents, although they usually did take the precaution of posting armed infantry around the field.[26] Before long, both American Major League and Little League baseball sent many bats, balls, and gloves to the soldiers and to Iraqi children as well. These Americans were surprised to learn that for at least ten years Iraqi adults have played the game in a league of ten teams. Warfare and insurgency have at times disrupted play, but the game remains popular.

Thanks to the training provided by Americans, baseball has become very popular in Amman, Jordan, where a Little League is thriving. Every year, the number of Jordanians who want to play the game is increasing, and Jordanian teams have competed in tournaments in Poland and Germany.[27] And, according to the *CBBC Newsround*, baseball is "the latest craze in Afghanistan." Thanks to American soldiers who taught them the game, two teams of Afghan boys play each other every Friday before large and growing crowds. When they first began to play, they used sandbags for bases and a giant tent peg for a bat, but thanks to the American soldiers, they now have regular aluminum bats, leather gloves, and regulation baseballs. An Afghan teenager said, "I am very happy to come here and play. This is my favorite game." Two teams of boys play every Friday. The soldiers hope to organize girls' teams as soon as they are able to obtain more equipment.[28]

Sri Lankans have traditionally played a baseball-like game called *elle*, which features a bamboo bat, a shaved tennis ball, and three bases. In the early 1980s, the U.S. ambassador to Sri Lanka arranged for a large supply of baseball equipment to be sent to Sri Lanka, and the American game quickly became such a hit that by 1982 it had become a cherished sport in the nation's school system. Sri Lankan adult teams have gone on to compete well in international tournaments.

NOTES

[1] New York Times, May 14, 1959.

[2] Ibid., January 29, 1956.

[3] Ibid., June 27, 2000.

[4] Light (1997: 7).

[5] Los Angeles times, August 1, 1990.

[6] World Baseball Magazine, Winter 1993.

[7] Kansas State Collegian News, September 11, 2000.

[8] Akalonu (2002:2).

[9] New York Times, February 28, 1959.

[10] Gini (1939).

[11] Garcia (1979: 71); Kelly (1941).

[12] Kelly (1941:44).

[13] New York Times, May 17, 1944; New York Times, January 31, 1960.

[14] New York Times, March 25, 1951.

[15] Los Angeles Times, July 24, 1989.

[16] Parsbaseball@yahoo.com

[17] Iran Today, www.irantodayonline.com/newspaper/sport/aug01

[18] Gulf News, January 19, 2001; The Associated Press, August 23, 1988.

[19] Associated Press, August 14, 2000.

[20] New York Times, October 18, 1928; Ibid. July 10, 1930; Ibid, November 7, 1942.

[21] Ibid., July 20, 1936.

[22] Ibid., November 3, 1942.

[23] Los Angeles Times, May 15, 1988.

[24] The Pakistan Newswire, September 4, 2003.

[25] International Baseball Rundown, June 1996.

[26] Sports Illustrated, October 27, 2003.

[27] Jordan Times (Amman), July 2, 2002).

[28] CBBC Newsround, 19 August 2002.

Chapter Eight: Why Do They Play Baseball?

We have seen that baseball has had many origins from bat-and-ball games in medieval Europe to blond Berbers in North Africa and all sorts of zealously played ball games in Meso-America. It has become immensely popular in countries as different as Venezuela, France, Iran, and Thailand. We have seen that it has had an appeal for women as well as men, and that, over time, it has become popular in almost every country around the world. Why do so many men, women, and children in so many radically different kinds of countries play baseball? We know that baseball has enchanted many American boys and men, as well as a good many girls and women, since its inception over one hundred and fifty years ago. Many explanations have been put forward about the sources of this attraction—fathers playing catch with sons—the smell of leather, pine tar, and rosin—the sound of a ball slapping into a leather glove or cracking off a bat—the exhilaration of hitting a ball past an outfielder—the thrill of stealing a base—the joy of striking out an opposing batter or making a dazzling fielding play, then receiving shouts of approval or being given a "high-five" by teammates. Team spirit is also cherished and it can be very rewarding. A fan's request for an autograph can be pleasing, too, and so can the sight of a ballpark filled with fans. Their cheers and applause are treasured, too.

All of these pleasures have made the game joyful for generations of Americans as well as people in many other countries. However, the game can also bring frustration, embarrassment, and even physical injury. A critical error in the field, a strikeout with the bases loaded, a wild pitch to lose a game—all can cause lasting emotional pain. Physical injuries are commonplace, too. Players often pull leg muscles, and pitchers frequently injure their arms. Modern batting helmets protect the skull, but the face is still vulnerable to injury by a high and inside pitch. Other parts of the body are at risk, too. A foul tip off one's foot can produce excruciating pain. Today, more advanced players often wear a protective plastic cup over their groin, but most younger players do not, and every boy who ever played the game must have suffered at least one bad hop to his groin, something not easily forgotten. Infielders can be spiked by runners, pitchers hit by vicious line drives back over the mound, and base runners bruised sliding into a catcher's shin guards at home.

From baseball's earliest years, all sorts of spectators have flocked to games. Today, from Little League games to World Series contests, Americans of all ages watch baseball contests, experiencing exhilaration from great fielding plays, key base hits, or splendid pitching. In many countries around the world, fans' cheering can be cathartic, as is the use of various sorts of noisemakers. Spectators scream, shout, jump with joy, hug each other, even sing, drum, and dance. They also enjoy food, drink, and music during games. In some countries, the sight of scantily-clad young female cheerleaders is cherished as well. Many fans love catching foul balls, balls tossed into the stands by players or ball boys and, best of all, home runs. And in many countries they love to boo umpires and opposing players.

Baseball is not only enjoyed by players and spectators who attend games. In many countries, fans also listen to games on the radio and watch them on television. They also avidly read the sports sections of local newspapers or national baseball publications. Fathers not only play catch with their sons, they talk about the game with other men. They follow the home run totals and batting averages of their favorite players, and the won-lost records and earned-run averages of pitchers. They are uplifted when their team wins and can become despondent when it loses. Most of these devoted baseball fans are men, but some women follow the game avidly as well, and some mothers play catch with their daughters. And in several countries today, women play baseball in international competition. Baseball has impressed some observers as "slow" because pitchers often take a great deal of time between pitches or because a score is one-sided. Recall the comments by Louis Graves in *Harper's Weekly*: "To put it briefly, baseball is the dullest of sports.... There is so little about the game to distract one's attention that the grandstand is an ideal place for meditation and prayer."[1]

Baseball is not as action-packed as football, soccer or basketball, but Graves was assuredly not speaking for everyone, as attendance at baseball games has continued to rise in many countries, and boys and girls alike love to play the game. Even the British who initially disdainfully rejected the game as nothing more than a colonial version of their children's game, rounders, have come to embrace baseball. Although baseball has not replaced cricket in the hearts of most Britons, as we have seen, the game is played widely and skillfully in the United Kingdom with the enthusiastic support of thousands of spectators. And as we have also seen, it is played and avidly supported by fans in virtually every corner of the world.

To be sure, many countries have shown a passionate interest in other sports, such as rugby, basketball, tennis, polo, track and field, and boat racing. And the most popular team sport played in virtually every country on earth is soccer or, as it is known almost everywhere except the United States, football. Like baseball, football has an ancient origin, with China being one of the countries where it took its modern form. In Britain, football was played at least 1,000 years ago and was the chosen sport of Oxbridge undergraduates from the sixteenth century on.[2] Known as "the violent British game," football spread across the world, being played by both women's and men's teams almost everywhere. In 2002, the *Fédération Internationale de Football Association (FIFA)* estimated that 242 million people play football.[3]

Football requires little equipment and can be played by children as well as adults. It is a fast, exciting sport that captivates spectators everywhere, including people all across the United States. The World Cup features immensely skilled athletes who dazzle fans with their speed, footwork and energy. Anyone can see why football is so popular, both as a sport to play and to watch. And who can forget the fan violence it stimulates? Ardent British fans, called "hooligans," battle with opponents from all over Europe, and fans from Argentina to Colombia fight each other in support of their teams. In April, 2003, fourteen busloads of fans from two rival teams in Argentina clashed at a toll collection point on a highway. Two people were killed, and scores were injured.[4]

Compared to baseball, however, football is a simple game. To be sure, one must be an athlete to run and kick a ball competitively, and there must be teamwork. In baseball, however, players must not only be able to run, they must slide and know when to try to bowl over a catcher in a close play at the plate. They must also be able to catch a rapidly bouncing ground ball, a sinking line drive, and a high fly ball caught in the glaring sun. They must be able to throw the ball accurately even while off balance, and some must be able to throw the ball past opposing batters. All must learn how to hit a rapidly sinking or curving pitch. Managers and coaches must make decisions about the batting order, when to bunt or attempt to steal a base, when to replace a starting pitcher with a "relief" pitcher, and when to "pinch-hit" for a batter. And because the baseball season is so long, players, coaches, and the team's manager must also master the intangibles of teamwork, camaraderie, and concern for one another. As many have said since baseball's earliest days, the game challenges the body and the mind, and it improves both.

Baseball is complicated, difficult to play, and requires expensive equipment. Playing fields are needed as well. Why, then, has it spread to well over 100 countries in all parts of the world? Why is it cherished by people as different as the Chinese, French, Iranians, Zimbabweans, Guamese, and Dominicans? Poet Donald Hall has tried to explain its popularity in America in his book, *Fathers Playing Catch with Sons*: "Baseball is continuing, like nothing else among American things, an endless game of repeated summers, joining the long generations of all the fathers and all the sons."[5] But as we have seen, it has been played for different reasons in Japan, Cuba, Australia, Brazil, and many other countries. And in many countries that have only recently taken up the game, it is not clear what its appeal is for players or for spectators. There is clearly no long history of fathers playing catch with sons in most of these countries.

Baseball is played for many different reasons around the world. And if it doesn't evoke the same physical passion that football does, it nevertheless captures the interest and captivates the hearts of millions of people in places as different as Cameroon, Croatia, Fiji, India, Morocco, Norway, Peru, Russia, Sri Lanka, Turkey, and Yemen. It is not "only a game," it is a challenge, an opportunity, an obsession. For many people in many places it is more than a game. It is one of life's treasures. Remember the words of the 21-year-old Iranian pitcher, Sasan "Easy" Karimpour: "Baseball has become my life. It's my dream and my love. I can't stop thinking about it."[6]

220

NOTES

[1] Wallop (1969:100-101).

[2] Giulianotti (1999:3).

[3] Bellos (2002).

[4] Los Angeles Times, April 22, 2003, p.D3.

[5] Hall (1985:46).

[6] Iran Today, www.irantodayonline.com/Newspaper/sport/aug01

References

Adelman, M. L. *A Sporting Time: New York City and the Rise of Modern Athletics, 1820-70.* Urbana: University of Illinois Press, 1986.

Adelson, B. *Brushing Back Jim Crow: The Integration of Minor-League Baseball in the American South.* Charlottesville: University Press of Virginia, 1999.

Akalonu, E. "Noc Awards: Baseball Names Williams, Okereke-Onyinke, Boyd." *Vanguard*, December 14, 2002. Pp.1-2.

Alexander, C.C. *Our Game: An American Baseball History.* New York: Henry Holt, 1991.

_____. *Breaking the Slump: Baseball in the Depression Era.* New York: Columbia University Press, 2002.

Allen, L. *100 Years of Baseball.* New York: Bartholomew House, 1950.

Angell, R. *The Summer Game.* New York: Viking, 1962.

_____. *Five Seasons: A Baseball Companion.* New York: Simon and Schuster, 1972.

_____. *Late Innings: A Baseball Companion.* New York: Simon and Schuster, 1982.

Appel, M. *Slide, Kelly, Slide: The Wild Life and Times of Mike "King" Kelly, Baseball's First Superstar.* Lanham, MD: The Scarecrow Press, 1996.

Arbena, J. L. (ed.), *Sport and Society in Latin America: Diffusion, Dependency, and the Rise of Mass Culture.* New York: Greenwood Press, 1988.

Ardell, J. H. "Mamie 'Peanut' Johnson: The Last Female Voice of the Negro Leagues." *Nine: American Journal of Baseball History and Policy Research*, 10: 181-191, 2001.

Astor, G. *The Baseball Hall of Fame 50th Anniversary.* New York: Prentice Hall, 1988.

Baldassaro, L. and R. A. Johnson (eds.). *The American Game: Baseball and Ethnicity.* Carbondale, IL: Southern Illinois University Press, 2002.

Banner, L. *American Beauty.* New York: Alfred A. Knopf, 1983.

Barzun, J. *On Baseball: God's Country and Mine.* Boston: Little Brown, 1954.

Beale, M. *The Softball Story.* Washington, D. C.: Columbia Publishing Co., 1957.

Beals, R. L. *The Acaxee, a Mountain Tribe of Durango and Sinaloa.* Ibero-Americana 6. Berkeley, CA: University of California Press, 1933.

Beezley, W. H. "The Rise of Baseball in Mexico and the First Valenzuela." *Studies in Latin American Popular Culture*, 4: 3-13, 1985.

Belich, J. *Paradise Reforged: A History of the New Zealanders From the 1880s to the Year 2000.* Honolulu: University of Hawaii Press, 2001.

Bellos, A. *Futebol—The Brazilian Way of Life.* London: Palimpsest, 2002.

Berkow, I. (ed.), *Hank Greenberg: The Story of My Life.* New York: Times Books, 1989.

Berlage, G. I. *Women in Baseball: The Forgotten History.* Westport, CT: Praeger, 1994.

_____. "Women, Baseball, and the American Dream." In, R. Elias (ed.), *Baseball and the American Dream: Race, Class, Gender and the National Pastime.* Armonk, NY: M. E. Sharpe, 2001. Pp. 235-247.

Bjarkman, P. C. *Baseball With a Latin Beat: a History of the Latin American Game.* Jefferson, NC: McFarland, 1994.

----------. *Diamonds Around the Globe: The Encyclopedia of International Baseball.* Westport, CT: Greenwood Press, 2005.

Bloyce, D. " 'Just Not Cricket': Baseball in England, 1874-1900." *The International Journal of the History of Sport*, 14: 207-218, 1997.

Borhegyi, S. F. *The Pre-Columbian Ballgames: A Pan-Mesoamerican Tradition.* Contributions in Anthropology and History, No. 1. Milwaukee: Milwaukee Public Museum, 1980.

Bouton, J., and L. Shecter. *Ball Four: My Life and Hard Times Throwing the*

Knuckleball in the Big Leagues. New York: World Publishing Company, 1970.

Bruce, J. *The Kansas City Monarchs: Champions of Black Baseball.* Lawrence: University Press of Kansas, 1985.

Bullock, S. "Playing for their Nation: The American Military and Baseball During World War II." *Journal of Sport History,* 27: 67-89, 2000.

Burk, R. F. *Much More Than a Game: Players, Owners, and American Baseball Since 1921.* Chapel Hill: University of North Carolina Press, 2001.

_____. *Never Just a Game: Players, Owners, and American Baseball to 1920.* Chapel Hill: University of North Carolina Press, 1994.

Butterfield, F. "Taiwan Little Leaguers Stun Japan." *New York Times,* August 3, 1969. P. 4.

Cashman, R. *Paradise of Sport: The Rise of Organised Sport in Australia.* Melbourne: Oxford University Press, 1995.

Chadwick, B. *When the Game Was Black and White: The Illustrated History of the Negro Leagues.* London: Abbeville Press, 1992.

Clark, J. *A History of Australian Baseball: Time and Game.* Lincoln, NB: University of Nebraska Press, 2003.

Clune, F. J. *A Functional and Historical Analysis of the Ballgame of Mesoamerica.* Berkeley, CA: University of California, 1963.

Cohen, G. L. (ed.), *Women in Sport: Issues and Controversies.* Newbury Park, CA: Sage, 1993.

Collins, C. (ed.), *Sport in New Zealand Society.* Palmerston North, New Zealand: Dunmore Press, 2000.

Collis, J., and W. Lingo (eds), *Prospect Handbook.* Durham, NC: Baseball America, 2002.

Cooper, J. M. "Games and Gambling." *Bureau of American Ethnography,* 5:503-524, 1949.

Cottrell, R. C. *The Best Pitcher in Baseball: The Life of Rube Foster, Negro League Giant.* New York: New York University Press, 2001.

Couvin, H. E. "Baseball Gets Serious in South Africa." *New York Times*, June 27, 2000.

Creamer, R. W. *Babe: The Legend Comes to Life.* New York: Simon and Schuster, 1974.

Dabscheck, B. "Australian Baseballers Form a Team of Their Own." *Sporting Traditions*, 12: 61-73, 1995.

Dawidoff, N. *The Catcher was a Spy: The Mysterious Life of Moe Berg.* New York: Pantheon Books, 1994.

_____. "Where Have You Gone Yu Kong Kai?: As They Grow Up, Taiwan's Little League Champions Used to Fade Out of Baseball. But Not Anymore." *Sports Illustrated*, August 19, 1991.

DiClerico, J. M., and B. J. Pavelec. *The Jersey Game: The History of Modern Baseball from its Birth to the Big Leagues in the Garden State.* New Brunswick, NJ: Rutgers University Press, 1991.

Doulens, R. B. "Chinese Grabbing Chance to Learn Game." *The Sporting News*, March 14, 1946. P. 13.

Dreier, P. "Jackie Robinson's Legacy: Baseball, Race, and Politics." In, R. Elias (ed.), *Baseball and the American Dream: Race, Class, Gender and the National Pastime.* Armonk, NY: M.E. Sharpe, 2001. Pp. 43-63.

Durant, J. *The Story of Baseball in Words and Pictures.* New York: Hastings, 1973.

Durocher, L. with E. Linn. *Nice Guys Finish Last.* New York: Simon and Schuster, 1975.

Eagle, S. J. *Work and Play Among the Basques of Southern California.* Ph.D. Dissertation, Purdue University, 1979.

Elfers, J. E. *The Tour to End All Tours: The Story of Major League Baseball's 1913-1914 World Tour.* Omaha: University of Nebraska Press, 2003.

Fainaru, S., and R. Sánchez. *The Duke of Havana: Baseball, Cuba, and the Search for the American Dream.* New York: Villard, 2001.

Fairburn, M. *The Ideal Society and Its Enemies: The Foundations of Modern New Zealand Society 1850-1900.* Auckland: Auckland University Press,

1989.

Fischer, D. H. *Albion's Seed: Four British Folkways in America*. Oxford: Oxford University Press, 1989.

Fleitz, D. L. *Louis Sockalexis: The First Cleveland Indian*. Jefferson, NC: McFarland, 2002.

Forbes, W. C. *The Philippine Islands*. Vol. 1. Boston: Houghton Mifflin, 1928.

Fox, J. R. "Pueblo Baseball: A New Use for Old Witchcraft." *Journal of American Folklore*, 74: 1961. Pp. 9-16.

Franks, J. S. *Whose Baseball? The National Pastime and Cultural Diversity in California, 1859-1991*. London: The Scarecrow Press, 2001.

Garcia, C. J. *Baseball Forever!* Mexico: [s.n.], 1979.

Gendin, S. "Moses Fleetwood Walker: Jackie Robinson's Accidental Predecessor." In, J. Dorinson and J. Warmund (eds.), *Jackie Robinson: Race, Sports, and the American Dream*. Armonk, NY: M. E. Sharpe, 1998. Pp.22-29.

Gerlach, L.R. "Baseball's Other 'Great Experiment': Eddie Klep and the Integration of the Negro Leagues." *Journal of Sport History*, 25: 1998. Pp. 453-481.

Gini, C. "Rural Ritual Games in Libya (Berber Baseball and Shinny)." *Rural Sociology*, 4: 283-299, 1939.

Gildner, G. *The Warsaw Sparks*. Iowa City: University of Iowa Press, 1990.

Giulianotti, R. *Football: A Sociology of the Global Game*. Cambridge: Polity Press, 1999.

Gmelch, G. "Baseball Magic." In, R. R. Sands (ed.), *Anthropology, Sport, and Culture*. Westport, CT: Bergin & Garvey, 1999. Pp.191-200.

Goldstein, R. *Spartan Seasons: How Baseball Survived the Second World War*. New York: Macmillan, 1980.

Goldstein, W. J.. *Playing for Keeps: A History of Early Baseball*. Ithaca: Cornell University Press, 1989.

Golenbock, P. "Men of Conscience." In, J. Dorinson and J. Warmund, (eds.),

Jackie Robinson: Race: Sports and the American Dream. Armonk, NY: M. E. Sharpe, 1998. Pp.13-21.

González Echevarría, R. *The Pride of Havana: A History of Cuban Baseball.* New York: Oxford University Press, 1999.

Gordon, D. "An Invitation to See the Hanshin Tigers: Japanese Baseball as Seen Through the Eyes of a Female Fan." *Nine: American Journal of Baseball History and Social Policy Research*, 9(2). 2001. Pp. 249-252.

Gregorich, B. "Stranded." *North American Review.* May/August 1998. Pp. 4-9.

_____. *Women at Play: The Story of Women in Baseball.* New York: Harcourt Brace & Co., 1993.

Guttmann, A. *Games and Empires: Modern Sports and Cultural Imperialism.* New York: Columbia University Press, 1994.

_____. *Women's Sports: A History.* New York: Columbia University Press, 1991.

Hall, D. *Fathers Playing Catch with Sons.* San Francisco: North Point Press, 1985.

Hall, D. (with D. Ellis). *Dock Ellis: In the Country of Baseball.* New York: Coward, McCann & Geoghegan, 1976.

Hargreaves, J. *Critical Issues in the History and Sociology of Women's Sports.* London: Routledge, 1994.

Henderson, R. W. *Ball, Bat and Bishop: The Origin of Ball Games.* New York: Rockport Press, 1947.

Hibbert, C. *The English: A Social History, 1066-1945.* New York: W. W. Norton, 1987.

Hicks, B. "The Legendary Babe Didrikson Zaharias." In, G. L. Cohen (ed.) *Women and Sport: Issues and Controversies.* Newbury Park, CA: Sage, 1993. Pp. 38-48.

Holway, J. B. *Blackball Stars: Negro League Pioneers.* Westport, CT: Meckler Books, 1988.

Holway, W. (ed.), *Black Diamonds: Life in the Negro Leagues From the Men*

Who Lived It. New York: Stadium Books, 1991.

Hughes, S. F. (ed.), *Letters and Recollections of John Murray Forbes.* Boston: Houghton-Mifflin, 1891.

Ichioka, Y. *The Issei: The World of the First Generation Japanese Immigrants, 1885-1924.* New York: The Free Press, 1988.

Ivanov, M. "Russia's Boys of Summer." *Russian Life*, 43: 1-18, 2000.

Jamail, M H. *Full Count: Inside Cuban Baseball.* Carbondale: Southern Illinois University Press, 2000.

Johnes, M. " 'Poor Man's Cricket': Baseball, Class and Community in South Wales c. 1880-1950." *The International Journal of the History of Sport*, 17: 2000. Pp. 153-166.

Joseph, G. M. "Forging the National Pastime: Baseball and Class in Yucatán." In, J. L. Arbena (ed.), *Sport and Society in Latin America: Diffusion, Dependency, and the Rise of Mass Culture.* New York: Greenwood, 1988. Pp. 29-61.

Kahn, R. *The Boys of Summer.* New York: Harper & Row, 1972.

_____. "The Greatest Season: From Jackie Robinson to Sammy Sosa." In, R. Elias (ed.), *Baseball and the American Dream.* Armonk, NY: M. E. Sharpe, 2001. Pp. 37-42.

Karlen, N. "Diamonds Are a Girl's Best Friend." *New York Times*, September 6, 1998.

Kelley, B. *The Negro Leagues Revisited: Conversations with 66 More Heroes.* London: McFarland, 2000.

Kelly, C. G. "Baseball in the Garden of Allah." *The Moslem World: A Christian Quarterly Review of Current Events, Literature, and Thought Among Mohammedans*, 31: 1941. Pp. 39-47.

Kirsch, G. B. *The Creation of American Team Sports: Baseball and Cricket, 1838-72.* Urbana: University of Illinois Press, 1989.

Klein, A. M. *Baseball on the Border: A Tale of Two Laredos.* Princeton: Princeton University Press, 1997.

_____. *Sugarball: The American Game, The Dominican Dream.* New Haven: Yale University Press, 1991.

Kolatch, J. *Is the Moon in China Just as Round? Sporting Life and Sundry Scenes.* Middle Village, NY: Jonathan David Publishers, 1992.

LaFargue, T. E. *China's First Hundred.* Pullman: State College of Washington Press, 1942.

Leavy, J. *Sandy Koufax: A Lefty's Legacy.* New York: Harper Collins, 2002.

Levine, P. *To Ebbetts Field: Sport and the American Jewish Experience.* Oxford: Oxford University Press, 1992.

Levy, A. H. *Rube Waddell: The Zany, Brilliant Life of a Strikeout Artist.* Jefferson, NC: McFarland, 2000.

Light, J. F. *The Cultural Encyclopedia of Baseball.* London: McFarland, 1997.

n.a. "Little League Baseball Grows in Poland." *Polish-American Journal.* 90: 1-6, 2001.

Maitland, B. *Japanese Baseball: A Fan's Guide.* Rutland, VT: Charles E. Tuttle, 1991.

Mann, A. *Branch Rickey: American in Action.* Boston: Houghton Mifflin, 1957.

Marcano, A. J. and Fidler, D. P. *Stealing Lives: The Globalization of Baseball and the Tragic Story of Alexis Quiroz.* Bloomington: Indiana University Press, 2002.

Marshall, L. *The !Kung of Nyae Nyae.* Cambridge: Harvard University Press, 1976.

Marshall, M. *Weekend Warriors: Alcohol in a Micronesian Culture.* Palo Alto, CA: Mayfield, 1979.

Mays, W. (as told to Charles Einstein). *Willie Mays: My Life In and Out of Baseball.* New York: E.P. Dutton, 1972.

McKay, J. *No Pain, No Gain? Sport and Australian Culture.* New York: Prentice Hall, 1991.

McNeil, W. F. *Baseball's Other All-Stars.* Jefferson, NC: McFarland, 2000.

Modrizuki, K. *Baseball Saved Us*. New York: Lee & Low Books, 1993.

Mooney, J. "The Cherokee Ball Play." *American Anthropologist*, 3: 105-132, 1890.

Mossop, B. "C'mon, Aussie, C'mon." *The Bulletin*, October 24, 1989.

Mott, M. "The British Protestant Pioneers and the Establishment of Manly Sports in Manitoba, 1870-1886." *Journal of Sport History*, 7: 25-36, 1980.

Mullan, M.L. "Ethnicity and Sport: The Wapato Nippons and Pre-World War II Japanese American Baseball." *Journal of Sport History*, 26: 82-114, 1999.

Murdock, G. P. "Waging Baseball in Truk." *Newsweek*, 32: 69-70, 1948.

Nagata, Y., and J. B. Holway. "Japanese Baseball." In, J. Thorn, P. Palmer, and M. Gershman (eds.), *Total Baseball*. New York: Viking, 1995. Pp. 547-559.

Nakagawa, K. Y. "The Road to Cooperstown: Japanese American Baseball, 1899-1999." In, R. Elias (ed.), *Baseball and the American Dream: Race, Class, Gender, and the National Pastime*. Armonk, N. Y.: M. E. Sharpe, 2001. Pp. 123-134.

Norwood, S. H., and H. Brackman. "Going to Bat for Jackie Robinson: The Jewish Role in Breaking Baseball's Color Line." *Journal of Sport History*, 26: 115-141, 1999.

Obojski, R. *All-Star Baseball Since 1933*. New York: Stein and Day, 1980.

_____. *The Rise of Japanese Baseball Power*. Radnor, PA: Chilton Book Co., 1975.

Oh, S., and D. Falkner. *Sadaharu Oh: A Zen Way of Baseball*. New York, N. Y.: Times Books, 1984.

Ortiz, A. *The Tewa World: Space, Time, Being, and Becoming in a Pueblo Society*. Chicago, University of Chicago Press, 1969.

Palmer, H.C., *et. al*. *Athletic Sports in America, England and Australia*. Philadelphia: Hubbard Brothers, 1889.

Park, R. J. "Sport and Recreation Among Chinese American Communitites of the

Pacific Coast from the Time of Arrival to the 'Quiet Decade' of the 1950s." *Journal of Sport History*, 27: 445-480, 2000.

Peary, D..(ed.), *We Played the Game: 65 Players Remember Baseball's Greatest Era, 1947-1964*. New York: Hyperion, 1994.

Perez Medina, R. G. *Historia Del Baseball Panameño*. Tomo I, II. Dutigrafia, Panama, 1992.

Peterson, H. *The Man Who Invented Baseball*. New York, Scribner, 1973.

Peterson, R. *Only the Ball Was White*. New York: McGraw-Hill, 1984.

Pettavino, P. J. and G. Pye. *Sport in Cuba: The Diamond in the Rough*. Pittsburgh: University of Pittsburgh Press, 1994.

Pomfret, J. "Gambling Scandal Throws a Curve Ball to Taiwanese Baseball League." *Washington Post*, March 3, 1997.

Postal, B., J. Silver, and R. Silver (eds.), *Encyclopedia of Jews in Sports*. New York: Bloch, 1965.

Powers-Beck, J. "'Chief': The American Indian Integration of Baseball, 1897-1945." *American Indian Quarterly*, 25: 508-530, 2001.

Pratt, M. "The All-American Girls' Professional Baseball League." In, G. L. Cohen (ed.), *Women in Sport: Issues and Controversies*. Newbury Park, CA: Sage, 1993. Pp. 49-58.

Prentice, B.L., and M. Clifton. "Baseball in Canada." In, J. Thorn, P. Palmer, and M. Gershman, (eds.), *Total Baseball*. New York: Viking, 1995. Pp. 569-572.

Press, I. *Tradition and Adaptation: Life in a Modern Yucatan Maya Village*. Westport, CT: Greenwood Press, 1975.

Rader, B. G. *Baseball: A History of America's Game*. Urbana: University of Illinois Press, 1992.

Rampersad, A. *Jackie Robinson: A Biography*. New York: Alfred A. Knopf, 1997.

Reaves, J. A. *Taking in a Game: A History of Baseball in Asia*. Lincoln: University of Nebraska Press, 2002.

Redfield, R. *A Village that Chose Progress.* Chicago: University of Chicago Press, 1950.

Regalado, S. O. *Viva Baseball: Latin Major Leaguers and Their Special Hunger.* Urbana: University of Illinois Press, 1998.

Reichler, J., and B. Olan. *Baseball's Unforgettable Games.* New York: The Ronald Press, 1960.

Ribowsky, M. *Don't Look Back: Satchel Paige in the Shadows of Baseball.* New York: Simon & Schuster, 1994.

Rielly, E. J., *Baseball: An Encyclopedia of Popular Culture.* Santa Barbara, CA: ABC-CLIP, 2000.

Riess, S. A. *Touching Base: Professional Baseball and American Culture in the Progressive Era Sport and Society.* Urbana: University of Illinois Press, 1999.

Ritter, L. S. *The Glory of Their Times: The Story of the Early Days of Baseball Told by the Men Who Played It.* New York: Macmillan, 1966.

Robinson, J. (as told to Alfred Duckett). *Never Had It Made.* New York: G.P. Putnam Sons, 1972.

Robinson, R. *Iron Horse: Lou Gehrig in His Time.* New York: Harper Perennial, 1991.

Roden, D. "Baseball and the Quest for National Dignity in Meiji Japan." *American Historical Review*, 85: 511-534, 1980a.

_____. *Schooldays in Imperial Japan.* Berkeley: University of California Press, 1980b.

Rogosin, D. *Invisible Men: Life in Baseball's Negro Leagues.* New York: Atheneum, 1983.

Roosevelt, T.R. *The Strenuous Life.* New York: 1900.

Rowse, T. *Australian Liberalism and National Character.* Melbourne: Kibble, 1978.

Ruck, R. *The Tropic of Baseball: Baseball in the Dominican Republic.* Westport, CT: Meckler, 1991.

_____. "Baseball in the Caribbean." In, J. Thorn, P. Palmer, and M. Gershman (eds.), *Total Baseball*. New York: Viking, 1995. Pp.560-568.

Sands, R. R. (ed.), *Anthropology, Sport, and Culture*. Westport, CT: Bergin & Garrey, 1999.

Scarborough, V. L., and D. R. Wilcox (eds.), *The Mesoamerican Ballgame*. Tucson: University of Arizona Press, 1991.

Seymour, H. *Baseball: The Early Years*. New York: Oxford University Press, 1989.

Spalding, A. G. *America's National Game: Historic Facts Concerning the Beginning, Evolution, Development and Popularity of Baseball*. New York: American Sports Publishing Co., 1911.

Springwood, C. F. *Cooperstown to Dyersville: A Geography of Baseball Nostalgia*. Boulder, Colorado: Westview Press, 1996.

Stoddart, B. *Saturday Afternoon Fever: Sport in Australian Culture*. London: Angus & Robertson, 1986.

Sutton, D. "In Brief: Baseball in Germany." *German Life*, 9: 1-8, 2002.

Sutton-Smith, B., and Rosenberg, B.G. "Sixty Years of Historical Change in the Game Preferences of American Children." *The Journal of American Folklore*, 74: 17-46, 1961.

Takaki, R. *Strangers From a Different Shore: A History of Asian Americans*. Boston: Little, Brown, 1989.

Tarasco, B. P. "Baseball in Ukraine: A Periodic Progress Report." *Ukrainian Weekly*, 114: 1-8, 1996.

_____ "Baseball Journal 1998: An Inside Look at Ukraine in the International Competitions." *Ukrainian Weekly*, 116: 1-13, 1998.

Thorn, J. *A Century of Baseball Lore*. New York: Hart, 1974.

Twopenny, R. *Town Life in Australia*. London: Penguin, 1973.

Tygiel, J. *Past Time: Baseball as History*. Oxford: Oxford University Press, 2000.

Tyrrell, I. "The Emergence of Modern American Baseball c. 1850-1880." In, R.

Cashman and M. McKernan (eds.), *Sport in History: The Making of Modern Sporting History.* St. Lucia, Queensland: University of Queensland Press, 1979. Pp.205-226.

Underhill, R. M. *Red Man's America.* Chicago: University of Chicago Press, 1953.

Vamplew, W. et al. (eds.), *The Oxford Companion to Australian Sport.* Melbourne: Oxford University Press, 1992.

Vamplew, W., and B. Stoddart (eds), *Sport in Australia: A Social History.* Cambridge: Cambridge University Press, 1994.

Van Bottenburg, N. *Global Games.* (translated from the Dutch by Beverly Jackson). Urbana: University of Illinois Press, 2001.

Vanstone, J. W. *The Snowdrift Chipewyan.* Ottawa: Northern Co-ordination and Research Centre, Department of Northern Affairs and National Resources, 1963.

Veeck, B. *Veeck as in Wreck.* New York: G. P. Putnam's Sons, 1962.

Veeck, B. with E. Linn. *The Hustler's Handbook.* New York: G. P. Putnam's Sons, 1965.

Voigt, D. Q. *American Baseball.* 2 vols. University Park, PA: The Pennsylvania State University Press, 1983.

Wagner, E.A. "Sport in Revolutionary Societies: Cuba and Nicaragua." In, J. L. Arbena (ed.), *Sport and Society in Latin America: Diffusion, Dependency, and the Rise of Mass Culture.* New York: Greenwood Press, 1988. Pp.113-136.

Wallop, D. *Baseball: An Informal History.* New York: W. W. Norton, 1969.

Waterhouse, R. *Private Pleasures, Public Leisure: A History of Australian Popular Culture Since 1788.* Melbourne: Longman, 1995.

Wecter, D. *The Saga of American Society: A Record of Social Aspiration, 1607-1937.* New York, Charles Scribner's Sons, 1937.

Wells, K. M. *New God, New Nation: Protestants and Self-reconstruction Nationalism in Korea, 1896, 1937.* Honolulu: University of Hawaii Press, 1990.

White, G. E. *Creating the National Pastime: Baseball Transforms Itself, 1903-1953*. Princeton, NJ: Princeton University Press, 1996.

Whiting, R. *The Chrysanthemum and the Bat: Baseball Samurai Style*. New York: Dodd, Mead, & Co., 1977.

_____. *You Gotta Have Wa*. New York: Vintage Books, 1990.

_____. *The Meaning of Ichiro: The New Wave from Japan and the Transformation of Our National Pastime*. New York: Warner Books, 2004.

Williams, P. "Every Religion Needs a Martyr: The Role of Matty, Gehrig and Clemente in the National Faith." In, J. L. Price (ed.), *From Season to Season: Sports as American Religion*. Macon, GA: Mercer University Press, 2001. Pp.99-112.

Youngen, L. J. "A League of Their Own." In, R. Elias (ed.), *Baseball and the American Dream: Race, Class, Gender and the National Pastime*. Armonk, NY: M.E. Sharpe, 2001. Pp. 247-254.

Yung Wing (Rong Hong). *My Life in China and America*. New York: Henry Holt, 1909.

Zang, D. W. *Fleet Walker's Divided Heart: The Life of Baseball's First Black Major Leaguer*. Lincoln: University of Nebraska Press, 1995.

Zoss, J., and J. Bowman. *Diamonds in the Rough: The Untold Story of Baseball*. New York: Macmillan, 1989.

Index